The Scientific Basis

of

Vegetarianism

William Harris, M.D.

H-P

**HAWAII
HEALTH
PUBLISHERS**

Harris, William

The Scientific Basis of Vegetarianism

Library of Congress Catalogue Card Number   95-094448
ISBN   0-9646538-0-X
Copyright © 1995 William Harris, M.D.
Includes graphs by the author, index,
and illustrations.
Edited by Ruth Heidrich, Ph.D.

1. Vegetarianism. 2. Nutrition. 3. Economics.

Printed in the United States of America
Second printing 1996

Hawaii Health Publishers
1415 Victoria St.
Suite 1106
Honolulu, HI 96822-3663

WHAT OTHERS ARE SAYING:

- "This is not just a re-hash of McDougall, Ornish, and others. It is an original and provocative look at the wider web of a meat-centered diet. Bill Harris has done the vegetarian movement and thinking people everywhere a service by boldly addressing the social as well as the health aspects of vegetarianism."
-Keith Akers, author of A *Vegetarian Sourcebook.*

"Anyone interested in the science of healthy eating will find a gold mine in Dr. Harris's work. It delivers the underpinnings of a vegetarian diet in the detail that doctors will appreciate, but so understandably that lay readers will be enriched with practical new knowledge."
-Neal Barnard, M.D., President, Physician's Committee for Responsible Medicine (PCRM).

"I consider Dr. Harris one of the greatest health educators in America today. His insightful viewpoints are enlightening and even thrilling as he uncovers and gets right to the heart of the health problems facing us. His book *The Scientific Basis of Vegetarianism* is must reading for every health seeker and health professional in America."
-Joel Fuhrman, M.D., Internist, Belle Meade, New Jersey.

TABLE OF CONTENTS.

I. THE ORIGIN OF NUTRIENTS

> *"If the Great Zuzu hadn't wanted people to eat people, he wouldn't have made them out of meat!"*
>
> -Old cannibal's answer

A related *question*: Why do humans continue to eat animal source food? Is there some essential nutrient for humans synthesized only by animals?

The current list of nutrients for which human RDAs (Recommended Dietary Allowances) have been set includes essential amino acids, essential fatty acids, minerals and vitamins.

The minerals can be dismissed readily; they're all nuclear fusion products cooked in stars, and made neither by plants nor animals. In this abbreviated periodic table of the elements carbon (C), hydrogen (H), nitrogen (N), and oxygen (O) are the chief players in the game of life. On the next page are the other shaded players, their chemical symbols, chief metabolic functions and RDA ranges from infancy to adulthood, with most of the high numbers given for pregnancy.[1]

Periodic Table of the Elements

H																H	He
Li	Be											B	C	N	O	F	Ne
Na	Mg											Al	Si	P	S	Cl	Ar
K	Ca	Sc	Ti	V	Cr	Mn	Fe	Co	Ni	Cu	Zn	Ga	Ge	As	Se	Br	Kr
Rb	Cr	Y	Zr	Nb	Mo	Tc	Ru	Rh	Pd	Ag	Cd	In	Sn	Sb	Te	I	Xe
Cs	Ba	La	Hf	Ta	W	Re	Os	Ir	Pt	Au	Hg	Ti	Pb	Bi	Po	At	Rn
Fr	Ra	Ac															

Ce	Pr	Nd	Pm	Sm	Eu	Gd	Tb	Dy	Ho	Er	Tm	Yb	Lu
Th	Pa	U	Np	Pu	Am	Cm	Bk	Cf	Es	Fm	Md	No	Lw

Twenty Essential Inorganic Nutrients[2]

Name	Symbol	Function	RDA Range
Calcium	Ca	Bone, nerve regulation, cell membrane gates.	400-1200 mg
Chloride	Cl	Chief negative ion in blood, hydrochloric acid in stomach.	275-5100 mg
Chromium	Cr	Present in "Glucose tolerance factor."	.01-.2 mg
Cobalt	Co	Component of Vitamin B_{12}.	?
Copper	Cu	Constituent of oxidase enzymes.	.4-3 mg
Fluoride	F	Increases hardness of bones, teeth.	.1-4 mg
Iodine	I	Component of thyroid hormones.	40-200 μg
Iron	Fe	Component of hemoglobin, cytochromes. Electron donor.	6-15 mg
Magnesium	Mg	Bones. Enzyme co-factor.	40-400 mg
Manganese	Mn	Enzyme cofactor. Glycoprotein synthesis.	.3-5 mg
Molybdenum	Mo	Constituent of oxidase enzymes.	15-250 μg
Phosphorus	P	Bone, ATP, nucleic acids, phosphate buffer in blood.	300-1200 mg
Potassium	K	Chief positive intracellular ion. Nerve and muscle function.	350-5625 mg
Selenium	Se	Acts with vitamin E as anti-oxidant.	10-75 μg
Silicon	Si	Bone development in some species[3].	?
Sodium	Na	Chief positive extracellular ion. Nerve and muscle function.	115-3300 mg
Sulfur	S	Component of sulfur amino acids. Cartilage repair.	?
Tin	Sn	Traces essential in rats. Function unknown[4].	?
Vanadium	V	Traces essential in lower plants, rats, some marine species.	?
Zinc	Zn	Cofactor of many enzymes. Prostatic fluid component.	5-19 mg

The remaining nutrients are organically synthesized in chemical pathways which have developed during the 3-1/2 billion years of biological evolution on Earth[5].

On page 4 are organic nutrients with functions, origins, RDA ranges, and abbreviated structural formulas which omit hydrogen atoms and bonding angles for clarity. Unless so stated carbon atoms occupy the corners of the ring structures and the ends of lines. Most of the nutrients are coenzymes (the active part of an enzyme that the body cannot make) involved in energy transactions. The three with asterisks require exposition in light of the following definition:

"Vitamins are organic molecules in food that are required for normal metabolism but cannot be synthesized in adequate amounts by the human body."[6]

*Ascorbic Acid (Vitamin C) is an antioxidant also involved in amino acid metabolism, maintenance of blood vessel integrity, and the synthesis of collagen and adrenal hormones. Plants and most animals can synthesize vitamin C, but prehumans and other primates probably lost the ability 25 million years ago as a result of a mutation which was non-lethal and in fact adaptive since ascorbic acid was a plentiful component of the arboreal diet[7].

*β-Carotene is usually called pro-vitamin A and retinol is called "Vitamin A". I believe this is an error on the part of the nutritional establishment. Two molecules of retinol, an essential hormone-like metabolite required for skin, vision, and reproduction[8], are formed in the body by enzymatically splitting one molecule of β-Carotene, a photosynthetic[9] plant pigment[10] interacting with chlorophyll and found in green leafy vegetables.

This being so retinol fails the definition of vitamin. β-carotene should be called the true Vitamin A. It is synthesized only by plants. Retinol is synthesized only by animals[11], but there can be no retinol in the animal kingdom unless somewhere in the food chain there is an animal eating plant β-Carotene.

3

Essential Organic Nutrients

Name	Alternate	Structure*	Major Functions	Original Synthesis by:	RDA Range
Ascorbic Acid*	Vitamin C		Antioxidant, collagen	Plants, most animals	35-60 mg
Biotin			A carboxylase coenzyme	Intestinal Bacteria	.15-.5 mg
β- Carotene*	Vitamin A		Skin, vision	Chloroplasts (in leaves)	1500-8000 IU
Folic Acid			Nucleoprotein synthesis	Plants, bacteria	.1-.8 mg
Menadione	Vitamin K		Blood clotting	Plants, intestinal bacteria	5-65 µg
Niacin*	Vitamin B₃		Redox protein carrier	Plants, animals	5-20 mg
Pantothenic Acid			Forms coenzyme A	Yeast, bacteria, plants	3-10 mg
Pyridoxine	Vitamin B₆		Amino acid metabolism	Microorganisms, plants	.2-.7 mg
Riboflavin	Vitamin B₂		Redox coenzyme	Microorganisms, plants	.6-2 mg
Thiamine	Vitamin B₁		Carbohydrate coenzyme	Microorganisms, plants	.5-1.7 mg
α-Tocopherol	Vitamin E		Antioxidant (with Selenium)	Plants	5-30 IU

4

Analogously, consider riboflavin, vitamin B_2, metabolized after absorption to a flavoprotein, an important enzyme in oxidation-reduction reactions.[12] Correctly, riboflavin is identified as a vitamin, the flavoprotein made from it is not.

Strangely, the US Hospital Formulary refers to β-carotene as a drug and retinol as a vitamin[13], an exact inversion of the reality. β-Carotene is also an anti-oxidant and protective against several forms of cancer. Except for yellowing of the skin, it is non-toxic.

By contrast retinol is toxic when taken in excess and retinol supplements alone may increase the risk of esophageal cancer.[14] About 10 cases of "vitamin A" toxicity are reported yearly, usually in people who have taken an excess of retinol[15], in what they believe to be harmless vitamin pills.

*Niacin (formerly vitamin B_3) is a proton carrier in oxidation/reduction reactions.[16] Niacin is synthesized by both animals and plants. It also fails the definition of vitamin since in humans, 60 mg of left-over dietary tryptophan, an essential amino acid, can be used to synthesize 1 mg of niacin.[17]

All the rest of the nutrients in the table are synthesized by microorganisms and plants, not animals.[18]

Calciferol ("Vitamin D") was intentionally omitted from the table. It is now 16 years since W.F Loomis, writing in the *Scientific American*[19] explained the series of historical errors that led to the term "vitamin D." The substance in question does not look like a vitamin nor act like a vitamin, does look like a hormone and acts like a hormone, and, like a hormone, is made in the body. Thus by definition it is *not* a vitamin and its continued misclassification as a vitamin is an indictment of the nutritional establishment's inertia and inability to correct its basic errors.

Loomis in brief: rickets, a deforming childhood bone disease reached epidemic proportions in 19th century England. It was found that a substance in cod liver oil could treat and prevent rickets and this was isolated and christened "vitamin D." Meanwhile, the British Medical Association had mapped out the distribution of rickets and found it peaked in cities like Birmingham, London, and Manchester, all shrouded by a thick pall of coal smoke from the industrial revolution. When they put the kids out in the country sunlight, they got over their rickets.

SYNTHESIS OF CALCIFEROL

By enzymatic means a hydrogen atom is removed from the #7 position in the B ring of cholesterol which is thus destabilized. When it is moved to the skin and struck by a photon of ultra-violet light, the B ring opens up to form cholecalciferol:

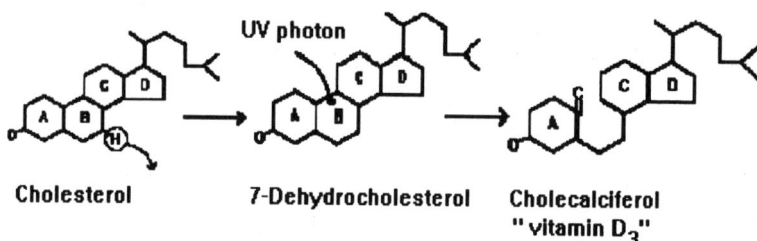

| Cholesterol | 7-Dehydrocholesterol | Cholecalciferol "vitamin D$_3$" |

This is further modified enzymatically in the liver and kidney to become calcitriol, one of a triad of potent calcium-regulating hormones (calcitonin and parathyroid hormone are the other two) synthesized in the body and expressly designed to "bypass the vagaries of dietary calcium."

Ergosterol, a molecule similar to cholecalciferol, is synthesized by yeast and added to cow's milk, which in its fresh-from-the-teat condition contains only 5-45 IU calciferol/quart. (Human milk has about 60 IU/quart and colostrum 150 IU/quart.[20]) Macrobiotic and black vegan children living in northern climates, whose skin pigment protects them from *excess* ultra violet radiation, are at risk for rickets[21] without calciferol supplements. Hence there are legitimate grounds for recommending this hormone to selected population groups.

However, 400 IU calciferol/quart is added to milk even in Hawaii, although a search of the Hawaii Medical Journal back to the inaugural issue in 1856 failed to disclose a single reported case of rickets. Under ordinary exposure to sunlight (estimated at 30 minutes per week during the month of June, longer in winter months) humans synthesize adequate calciferol.

The RDA for "vitamin D" (calciferol) is 400 IU/day. Toxicity in infants has been reported at 2000 IU/day and in adults at 50,000 IU/day.[22] Abnormal (ectopic) tissue calcifications form in rabbits fed 2 mg/day[23] (no other vitamin is toxic in a dosage of 2 mg) and in rats fed 10,000 IU/day.[24] Since the cause of ectopic calcification (phleboliths, Mönckeberg's medial sclerosis, calcific tendinitis) in humans is not known, it might be a good idea to stop giving calciferol to *everybody* until we find out.

An analogy here would be to cortisol, a necessary sterol hormone replacement for patients with Addison's disease who are unable to synthesize their own. We do not call cortisol "Vitamin C" because a small minority require it. Neither should we call calciferol a vitamin on the same grounds. Both are toxic when taken in excess or by people who don't need them.

There is no question that "Vitamin D" cow's milk put an end to rickets in the U.S. Irradiated ergosterol added to any common food would have done the same, but the chief selling point of cow's milk is its calcium content, so the addition of calciferol to milk was not only logical but financially rewarding to the dairy industry. I am old enough to recall the advertising blitz that hit my elementary school in St. Paul, Minnesota in the 1930's when "Vitamin D" milk came in.

About 10 cases of "vitamin D" toxicity are also reported yearly in the U.S. The most recent investigators[25] traced their cases to a dairy that not only used the wrong form of "vitamin D" but used it in doses ranging from zero to 500 times too much.

"Vitamin D" fails the definition of vitamin whether from plant or animal sources. And science fails when language is distorted by special interest.

7

Vitamin B_{12}:

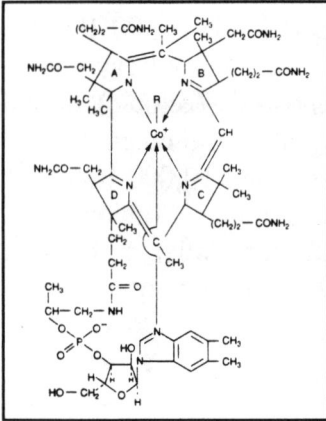

This large complex molecule acts with folic acid in the production of genetic nucleoproteins.[26] It is synthesized only by bacteria, including intestinal bacteria. The absorption and transport of vitamin B_{12} requires several binding proteins, including "intrinsic factor" secreted by the stomach.

Studies of British unsupplemented vegans in the 1960's showed that while they had lower mean B_{12} levels than omnivores, only one out of seven had a true deficit (30 pg/ml).[27] Were they eating dirt, or had their bacteria recolonized high enough into their small intestines so the B_{12} could be absorbed? B_{12} bacteria live in the colon but supposedly B_{12} cannot be absorbed there. B_{12} analogues in tempeh and spirulina are thought to be inactive.[28] Some brands of yeast have B_{12} added but B_{12} ("cobalamin") supplementation should be considered by all strict vegetarians (vegans), at least until the scientific dust settles.

ESSENTIAL FATTY ACIDS:

There are two essential fatty acids in the human diet:

Linoleic acid, found in plant cell membranes[29] and seeds:

$$C-C-C-C-C-C=C-C-C=C-C-C-C-C-C-C-C-COO-$$

And α-linolenic acid synthesized only in the chloroplasts of green plants and microorganisms:[30]

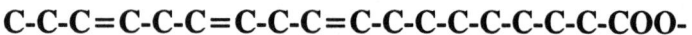

$$C-C-C=C-C-C=C-C-C=C-C-C-C-C-C-C-C-COO-$$

8

ESSENTIAL AMINO ACIDS

Amino acids were among the earliest organic molecules on earth. Given a primitive environment four billion years ago that included hydrogen, water vapor, ammonia, and methane, a random lightning bolt could assemble amino acids in a hurry.[31] Such high energy transactions aren't appreciated by biological systems however, so they synthesize amino acids in low energy reactions that are catalyzed by enzymes and that don't knock over the furniture.

Hundreds of amino acids exist in nature,[32] more can be synthesized in the laboratory, but only about 36 are used in higher animals and only 20 of those are involved in protein metabolism.[33] Way back in the beginning the amino isomers that rotated polarized light to the left rather than the right got the Darwinian nod and were permanently locked into evolution so they're called levorotatory (L)-aminos. They also have an amine group (NH2) and a carboxylic acid group (COOH) hooked to the same (alpha) carbon atom so they're called L-α-(alpha)-aminos. A polymer is a string of identical molecules daisy-chained together by chemical bonds. A copolymer is a string of similar but not identical molecules. Proteins are copolymers of the 20 L-α-amino acids.

An (alpha) amino acid

$$R-\overset{\displaystyle |}{\underset{\displaystyle NH_3^+}{C}}-C=O \quad O-$$

(R=any attached molecule)

Abbreviated:

$$R-\overset{\displaystyle |}{\underset{\displaystyle N+}{C}}OO-$$

A variety of side chains hang off the alpha carbon so protein is a long string of similar but not identical α-amino acids linked by NH2-COOH bonds. Proteins form a wide variety of enzymes and cellular structures, and act in the transfer of molecular information.

Shown below is a short length of protein, a tri-peptide copolymer composed of alanine, cysteine, and valine.

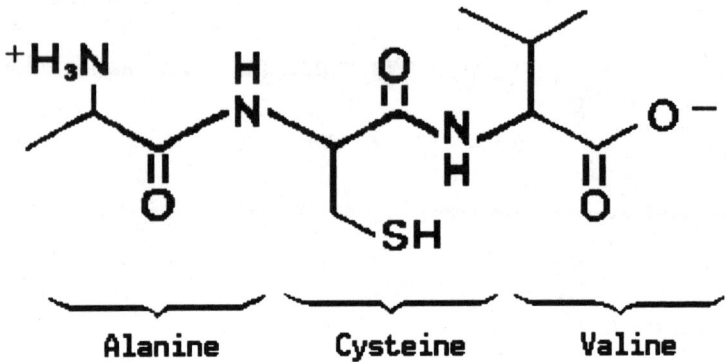

$^{+}H_3N$ H   O   H   O^{-} ... Alanine   Cysteine   Valine

Some life forms (plants, many bacteria) can form all 20 protein amino acids from carbon, hydrogen, nitrogen, oxygen, and sulfur. Essential amino acids are those that can't be synthesized by animals and humans. They require an average of 6 enzymes for synthesis while the non-essential aminos only require one or two. The plants have enough enzymes to make the essential aminos so those animals that continue to make their own are using up matter and energy to make something they can more easily eat. The survival value is negative rather than nil so these animals are selected out, leaving only animals that depend on plant-synthesized amino acids.[34]

On the next page are the twenty protein amino acids with their abbreviated structural formulas and the number of enzymes needed for synthesis. The COO- of any one can be linked to the N+ of any other so the possible combinations are extensive.

Protein Amino Acids

Essential: (Synthesized only by plants)

	Symbol	[S]	Enzymes*	Structure
Arginine	Arg	R	7	N-C-C-C-C-COO- / C=N N+ / N+
Histidine	His	H	6	-C-COO- N+ (ring with N)
Isoleucine	Ile	I	8(6)	C-C-C-C-COO- N+
Leucine	Leu	L	3(7)	C-C-C-COO- C N+
Lysine	Lys	K	8	C-C-C-C-C-COO- N+ N+
Methionine	Met	M	5(4)	C-C-C-COO- S-C S N+
Phenylalanine	Phe	F	10	C-C-COO- N+ (benzene ring)
Threonine	Thr	T	6	C-C-COO- O N+
Tryptophan	Trp	W	5(8)	C-C-COO- N+ (indole ring)
Valine	Val	V	1(7)	C-C-COO- C N+

*Enzymes for synthesis (mean) = 5.9   ( ) = Shared

Non-Essential: (Synthesized by plants and animals)

	Symbol	[S]	Enzymes*	Structure
Alanine	Ala	A	1	C-C-COO- N+
Asparagine	Asn	N	1	N-C-C-C-COO- O N+
Aspartic Acid	Asp	D	1	-OOC-C-C-COO- N+
Cysteine	Cys	C	2	-OOC-C-C-S N+ S
Glutamic Acid	Glu	E	1	-OOC-C-C-C-COO- N+
Glutamine	Gln	Q	1	N-C-C-C-C-COO- O N+
Glycine	Gly	G	1	C-COO- N+
Proline	Pro	P	3	-C-COO- N (ring)
Serine	Ser	S	3	C-C-COO- O N+
Tyrosine	Tyr	Y	1	C-C-COO- N+ (phenol ring)

*Enzymes for synthesis (mean) = 1.5

11

From the above it can be concluded that none of the nutrients essential to humans are synthesized by animals. Short cuts would have arrived at the same point: essential amino and fatty acids are essential simply because animals cannot synthesize them, hence, must obtain them from the plants that do. Vitamins are organic molecules necessary in the diet of humans, but most of the same molecules are necessary in the diet of other animals too, so those animals cannot synthesize them either and must also obtain them from plants. It thus follows that essential nutrients obtained from animal foods all originated in the plant kingdom. Hence, animal source food amounts to second hand nutrition, and the only unique ingredients in animal source food are cholesterol and saturated fat, both harmful to human health.

If we were cats, it would be different. Cats have been on a carnivorous track for as long as there have been cats, so they've lost the ability to synthesize arachidonic acid, carnitine, niacin, retinol, and taurine, which they get by eating other animals. But we're not cats.

There is no teleology implied here; no benevolent nature is creating plant foods to suit the dietary requirements of man. Rather, primitive animals adapted their metabolism to the only game in town, the plants, and humans evolved from them. Animals are plant predators, appropriating nutrients the plants made for their own use. Animals thus free themselves of the need to maintain primordial biosynthetic pathways. That some humans prey on other animals as well reflects feeding strategy, not biochemistry.

II. DIET AND EVOLUTION

"Then God said, 'I give you every seed-bearing plant on the face of the whole earth and every tree that has seed in it. They will be yours for food...I give every green plant for food.' And it was so."

-Genesis 1:29[35]

This biblical quote is an obvious injunction to vegetarianism. It's therefore amusing to witness the theological rationalizations applied to it by devouts who wish to continue eating meat. Not infrequently, they also reject the Darwinian theory of evolution as well on the grounds that it violates their biblical teachings. Perhaps religion itself is subject to natural selection; the selection of those passages that are convenient.

The first 3-1/2 billion years of organic evolution on Earth led to the emergence of self-replicating DNA molecules, their biochemical support systems, and finally a membranous envelope that surrounded the system and transformed it into the cell.

Cells could then remain solitary in the environment (bacteria and protozoa) or they could colonize and distribute various adaptive functions among the colony's member cells (metazoa, higher plants and animals).

Additional options related to feeding strategy. Some cells synthesized their own nutrients from carbon, hydrogen, oxygen, nitrogen and other elements using sunlight to drive chemical reactions. This option was employed by photosynthetic bacteria and higher plants.

A second option was to eat organisms which employed the first option, thus sparing a good deal of biochemical baggage. This was the option employed by members of the animal kingdom. A third option arose, the subgroup of animals that also eat other animals and this was the option of omnivorism, carnivorism, and cannibalism.

After the first cells appeared, it was a relatively short 500 million years before the colonization strategy led to the present host of organisms that exploit every ecological niche.

The stages of evolution that led to man are pictured below beginning with the single-celled amoeba and early colony forms, filter feeders, fish, amphibians, and transitional mammals. There is little information on the diet of these early creatures, but it's reasonable to assume that whatever could be eaten was eaten. For instance, the shrew-like creature(*) who preceded the first primates was a small insectivore.

EVOLUTION

During 56 million years of primate evolution the predecessors of man became bigger, smarter, and increasingly vegetarian, exploiting the fruits and leaves of their arboreal habitat.[36] Why?

Kinetic energy is proportional to weight which increases as the cube of linear dimensions. While small primates (e.g., mouse lemur) can recover the Caloric energy they expend in hunting insects, a gorilla would waste more energy catching an insect than it would recover by eating it.

Early primates who speciated into large ones moved into that part of the tree where the food did not run away from them, but this put them out in the upper branches where the leaves and fruit are. Large animals must deal with the mortal

14

consequences of falling out of trees.   There is a scaling effect in operation here.   The strength of a bone or muscle is a function of its cross sectional area which is proportional to the square of the animal's linear dimensions.   The kinetic energy dissipated at impact with the ground is again a function of the cube of the linear dimensions.   A .06 Kg. mouse lemur falling from a tree might bounce and run back up the tree but a 160 Kg. gorilla falling out of a tree will have to dial 911 even though it is much stronger than the lemur.

Hence, selection pressures favored the emergence of stereoscopic vision,   opposable thumbs, and large brains capable of accurate judgement calls.   The gorilla, a genetically close human relative, is intelligent enough to learn the American sign language.   Perhaps its dumber sibling ancestors fell out of the trees before they could reproduce.

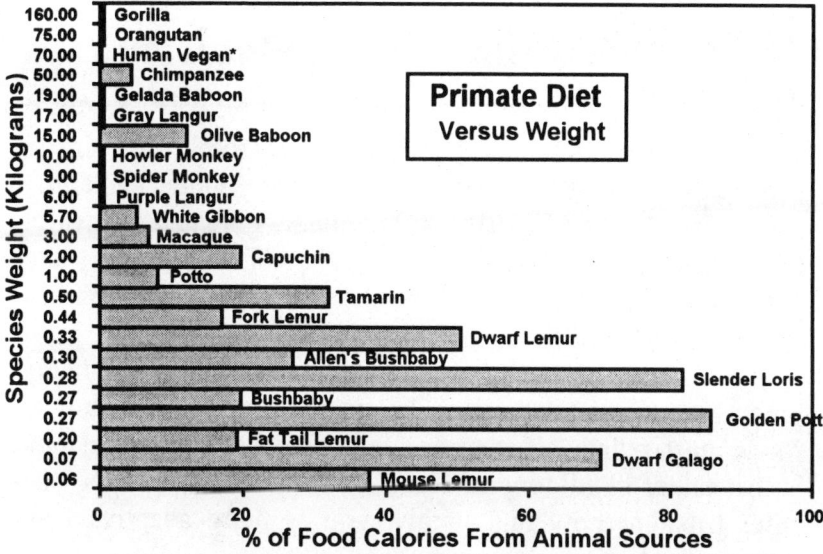

Primate Diet Versus Weight

Species Weight (Kilograms) vs % of Food Calories From Animal Sources

Weight	Species
160.00	Gorilla
75.00	Orangutan
70.00	Human Vegan*
50.00	Chimpanzee
19.00	Gelada Baboon
17.00	Gray Langur
15.00	Olive Baboon
10.00	Howler Monkey
9.00	Spider Monkey
6.00	Purple Langur
5.70	White Gibbon
3.00	Macaque
2.00	Capuchin
1.00	Potto
0.50	Tamarin
0.44	Fork Lemur
0.33	Dwarf Lemur
0.30	Allen's Bushbaby
0.28	Slender Loris
0.27	Bushbaby
0.27	Golden Pott
0.20	Fat Tail Lemur
0.07	Dwarf Galago
0.06	Mouse Lemur

The graph above shows the rough correlation between body weight and animal source food intake in some contemporary primates.[37,38,39]   At length some of the larger primates descended from the trees,   possibly as the result of a drought that caused their forests to recede.   Down on the savannah food was harder to find,   so as the hominids emerged several million years ago,   they evidently broke off with their predecessors and made many revolutionary adaptations, one of which was the scavenging, hunting, and eating of other animals, a strategy made possible by their cunning.

A near-vegetarian hominid, Australopithecus robustus, apparently died out 500,000 years ago, perhaps with a cannibalistic assist from the more successful omnivore Australopithecus africanus (left).

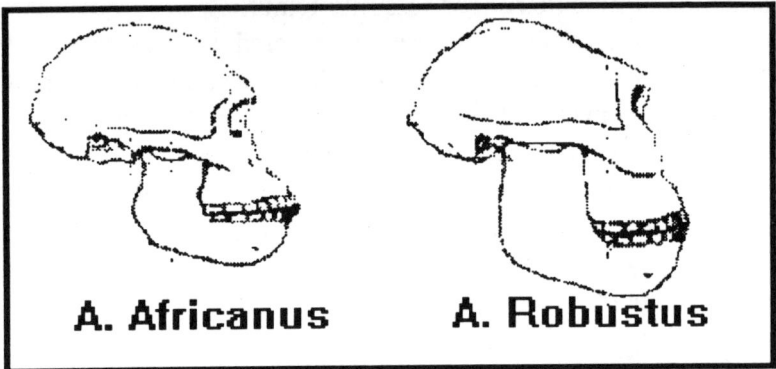

A. Africanus   A. Robustus

Dietary data on hominids is scarce, but of 76 subsistence tribes[40] in 1978 all were hunter/gatherers, consuming 33% of Calories from animals (!Kung bushmen of the Kalahari) through 80% (the Ache' of Paraguay),[41] and 100% (Copper Eskimos).[42] Similar dietary ranges probably applied to hominids.

Since no nutrients essential to man or any of his likely predecessors are synthesized by animals, the use of animal foods must reflect other priorities. The simplest explanation is that under conditions of scarcity, Calorie acquisition is the chief tribal activity and omnivorism is more adaptive than limiting food choices to plants.

Meat is high in fat and each gram of fat carries nine Calories. Protein and carbohydrate only carry four Calories per gram. High fat food protects against starvation since fat can be stored under the skin. The high Calorie/weight ratio of meat must be an important factor in primitive food transportation and that, in turn, is important to the development of centralized camps, social cohesion, and primitive culture.

Consider a lucky hominid hunter who kills a 1900 pound bison by himself. (It's rare but a lone pygmy has been known to down an elephant.) The bison is 65% edible and 1500 Calories/lb so the hunter has collected 1900x.65x1500=1,852,500 Calories. If in the same interval the hunter's mate gathers 10,000 Calories of plant food, a reasonable estimate for a day's gathering in the off season,[43] hunting was 1,852,500/10,000=185 times more Calorie efficient than gathering. Perhaps this astounding figure explains some of the mystical machismo of hunting.

Calories, of course, are not the only nutritional factors but a wide variety of unprocessed diets, vegan included, if adequate in Calories will also be adequate in protein, vitamins, essential fatty acids, and minerals.

Hunting also promoted cunning and social cooperation since, in the general case, it was not a lone hunter but a team of hunters who cornered and killed the prey.

A remarkable change began 10,000 years ago in the Mediterranean basin: the agricultural revolution. Where before time and energy considerations favored hunting, the domestication of plants and animals led to a new set of rules.

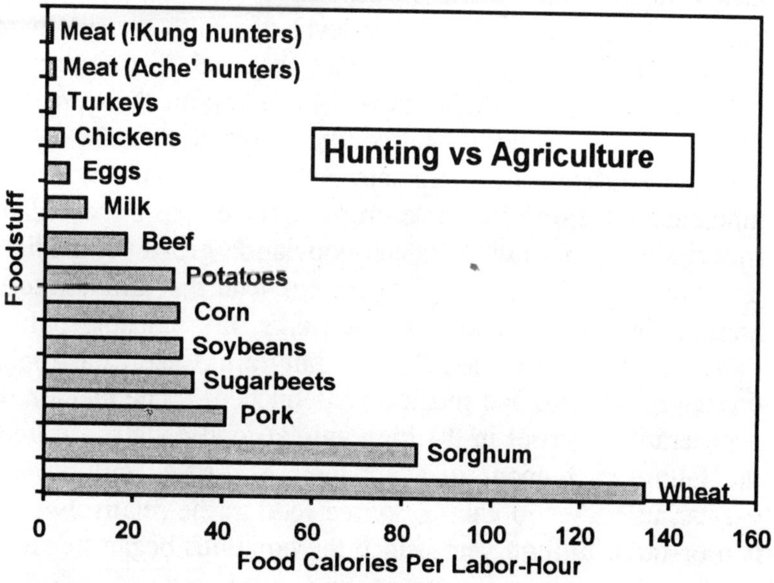
Hunting vs Agriculture
Meat (!Kung hunters)
Meat (Ache' hunters)
Turkeys
Chickens
Eggs
Milk
Beef
Potatoes
Corn
Soybeans
Sugarbeets
Pork
Sorghum
Wheat
Foodstuff
0
20
40
60
80
100
120
140
160
Food Calories Per Labor-Hour

The graph above suggests that in a given period of time one can collect between 1.1 and 35 times more Calories from turkeys and pigs kept on a known area of land, rather than stalking meat as an Ache' hunter. One can then extract 5.5-50 times more Calories still if the land has been planted in crops for direct human consumption rather than used to graze animals that are subsequently eaten.[44] The efficiency ratio of a modern wheat farmer over a !Kung hunter is roughly 135,000 (Cals/hr)/793(Cals/hr) which comes out to 170.

In any event animal agriculture (circa 1935) was more efficient than aboriginal hunting (circa 1978) and, except for pork, plant agriculture generally more efficient than either.[45,46,47] Such figures should have driven the agricultural revolution in the direction of vegetarianism. Unfortunately, the new rules favored the acquisition of more land and the start of organized warfare for that purpose.

The new agriculture also fueled a sixteen-fold population increase by 6000 B.C. that promptly devoured what would otherwise have been a luxuriant food supply. Nutrient-dense vegetables and fruits spoil easily so instead, humans ate grazing animals and the cheaper, less nutritious, but more easily stored grains. The result was overcrowding, warfare, epidemic disease, and a lower level of health than even the hunter-gatherer predecessors had enjoyed.[48] Repressive religions and governments moved in to exploit the existential anxiety of the unhealthy and conflicted people.

Thousands of years later modern nations, even with ample distribution of diverse crops agonize over the avoidable miseries inherent in unrestrained population growth and animal agriculture even as they fail to comprehend that animal foods, containing only second hand nutrients, are valuable only if there is not enough food.[49] This failure has had catastrophic ecological, ethical, and medical consequences. The plethora of degenerative diseases in the high animal food countries reflects the failure of humans to adapt their fifty-seven million year vegetarian bodies to animal source food in the relatively short two or three million years since the hominids began to eat it.

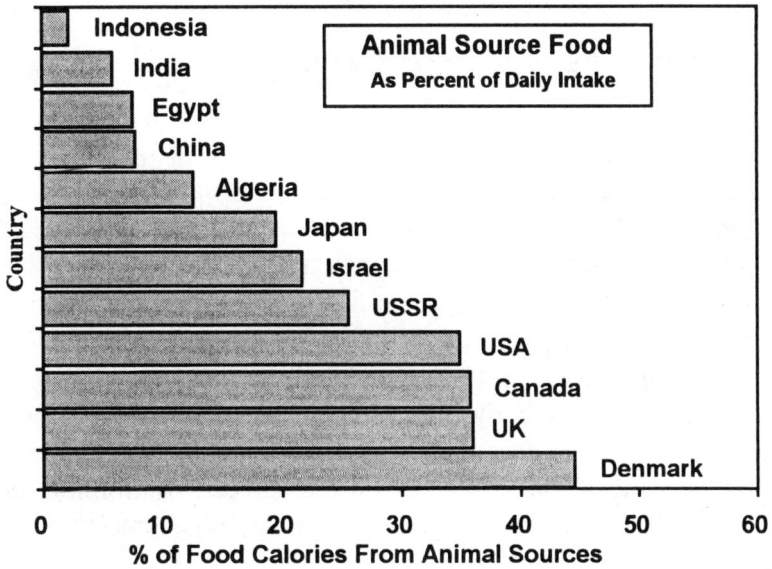

Animal Source Food
As Percent of Daily Intake

% of Food Calories From Animal Sources

Country

- Indonesia
- India
- Egypt
- China
- Algeria
- Japan
- Israel
- USSR
- USA
- Canada
- UK
- Denmark

III. THE FAT FOLLIES

"The United States is the only nation where even the poor people are pudgy."

-Anon.

Linoleic acid and linolenic acid are apparently the only fats required in the human diet.[50] They are synthesized only by plants and are needed in the amount 1-2% of Calories/day (about 3-6 grams).[51] From them dozens of other fatty acids can be synthesized by adding or removing two carbons at a time and adding or removing double bonds, all by enzymatic processes within the body. It's difficult to design a whole food vegan diet that has less than 6 grams of linoleic and linolenic acid/day or which has less than the recommended minimum of 10-14% total Calories from fat.[52] The average American fat intake is 40%.[53]

The structure of neutral fat (triglyceride) is straightforward. It consists of a molecule of glycerol, synthesized in the body from carbohydrate, and enzymatically linked to various fatty acids. Three of the commonest are shown:

A TRIGLYCERIDE

CH2 CH2 CH=CH CH=CH CH2 CH2 CH2 C-OH HO-CH2   G
CH3 CH2 CH2   CH2   CH2 CH2 CH2 CH2   l
Linoleic Acid   y

CH3 CH=CH CH=CH CH=CH CH2 CH2 CH2 C-OH HO-CH   c
CH2   CH2   CH2   CH2   CH2 CH2 CH2   e
Linolenic Acid   r

CH2 CH2 CH=CH CH=CH CH=CH CH=CH CH2 C-OH HO-CH2 o
CH3 CH2 CH2   CH2   CH2   CH2   CH2 CH2   l
                                           3 H2O
Arachidonic Acid

We'll abbreviate
triglyceride thus:

Neutral fats are characterized by the number of carbons and the number of double bonds in their fatty acids. Unsaturated fatty acids (mostly vegetable) have up to five double bonds[54] and tend to be short. Saturated (mostly animal) fats have few double bonds, longer carbon chains and they're heavier, have higher melting points and are more likely to be solid at body temperature.

The fatty acids synthesized in an animal reflect the animal species but the type of fatty acid stored in the animal's adipose tissue in part reflects the dietary fat.[55] The fat you eat is the fat you wear.[56]

Now, water molecules have been around four billion years and they're a very exclusive bunch. If water molecules get together they look like Mickey Mouse:

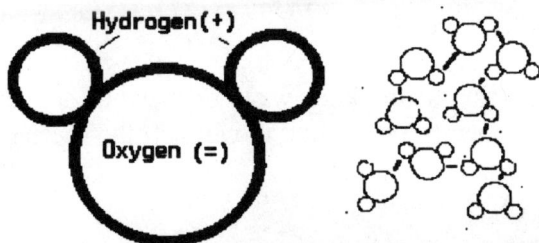

The positively charged hydrogen atoms link transiently to the negatively charged oxygen atoms of adjacent water molecules. Because of this "hydrogen bonding" water is liquid at room temperature whereas most other such small molecules are gases.[57]

Water molecules are so in love with each other that most other molecules just get squeezed out, but if one of the fatty acids in a triglyceride is replaced by a phosphoryl group, the new molecule looks like this:

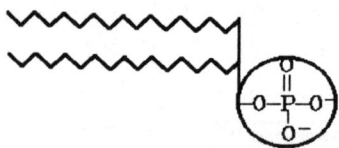

which we'll graphically abbreviate with this:

The phosphoryl end of the phospholipid has a negative charge that interests the fickle positive charges on the oxygen atoms in the water. When the first phospholipids turned up 3-1/2 billion years ago, they got a grudging acceptance from the water molecules that covered most of the Earth. The phosphoryl end gets to play with water which at the same time rejects the fatty acid tails:

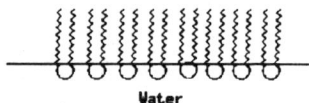

Water

The fatty ends of the phospholipid the water doesn't like get along okay with each other so a natural arrangement is the lipid bilayer which looks like this:

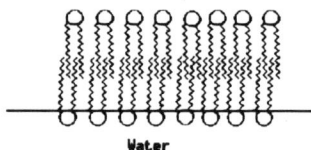

Water

If something (say, a breaking wave or a wind) shakes up the bilayer floating on the water, we get the perfect segregation scheme, a little bilayer bubble of phospholipids with water on the outside and inside and everybody happy because none of the molecules have to associate with molecules they don't like.

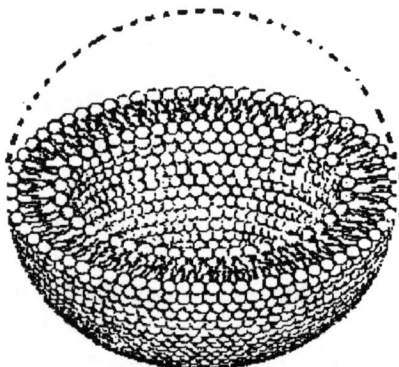

22

Evolution then threw in a few molecules of that great new invention, cholesterol, to stabilize the bubble membrane and the first animal cells were born. On the outside were predatory molecules looking for customers, on the inside were well behaved molecules of DNA, enzymes, protein, etc., who'd learned to conduct civilized transactions with each other.

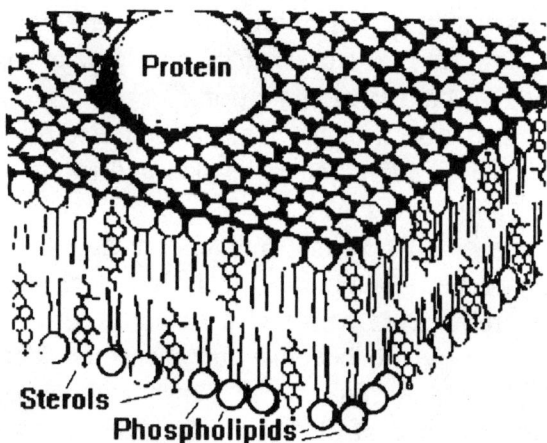

Plants use a similar gimmick. Their cell membranes are also made of phospholipids and plant sterols[58] but the fatty acids have more double bonds and there is no cholesterol.

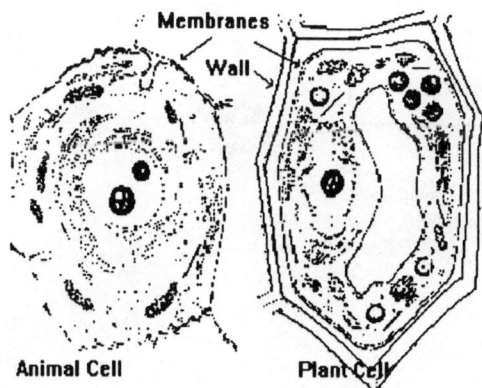

On the outside of the plant membrane, there's a cell wall made of cellulose, a tough and rigid polymer of glucose. Animal cell membranes are like tough flexible inner tubes. Plant cell membranes are like flimsy inner tubes with tough tires on the outside.

That's the first reason why animal source food is full of fat and cholesterol and plant food isn't. The second reason is that those civilized "inside" molecules learned how to extract nine Calories of biochemical energy from each gram of fat while they could get only four Calories from a gram of carbohydrate or protein. Calories were hard to come by so animals learned to hoard fat in special adipose cells in case of famine. Under those conditions it was still a useful evolutionary strategy for animals to eat other animals, since as we can now see, fat stores easily and it stays around forever, so there's no danger of starvation.

Fat is also a dandy thermal and electrical insulator so it's found in quantity under the skin and in the Schwann cells that surround nerves.

It seems likely that humans are now a genetically fat-addicted species. Eating fat in lean times was such a life-saver that the pre-humans who had a strong taste for it were most likely to survive to become our ancestors. They graciously passed along their fat-craving genes without knowing there would come a time of plenty in which those genes would be a disaster.

It's fairly intuitive that consumption of animal food increases the intake of fat. The data points are so dense that only a few labels are given for clarity.[59,60]

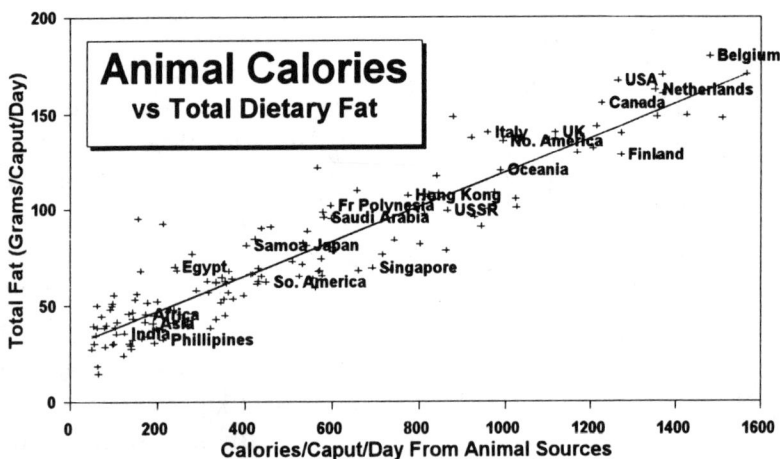

24

Similar linear graphs (not shown) make it clear that in dietary analysis we can interchange the terms "Animal Calories," "Total Calories," "Animal Fat," and "Total Fat."

Unfortunately there's not much epidemiological data on obesity. The following is from six Asian countries which keep median weight and height figures for their children.[61] Body Mass Index (BMI) is defined as weight (kgs) divided by the square of the height (meters). A BMI of 30 or more signifies "a high degree of fatness." Since these six countries are not big time fat eaters to begin with the graph does not suggest obesity but perhaps a tendency in that direction in the countries using the most animal fat.

Animal Fat
vs Body-Mass Index, Age 11, Both Sexes

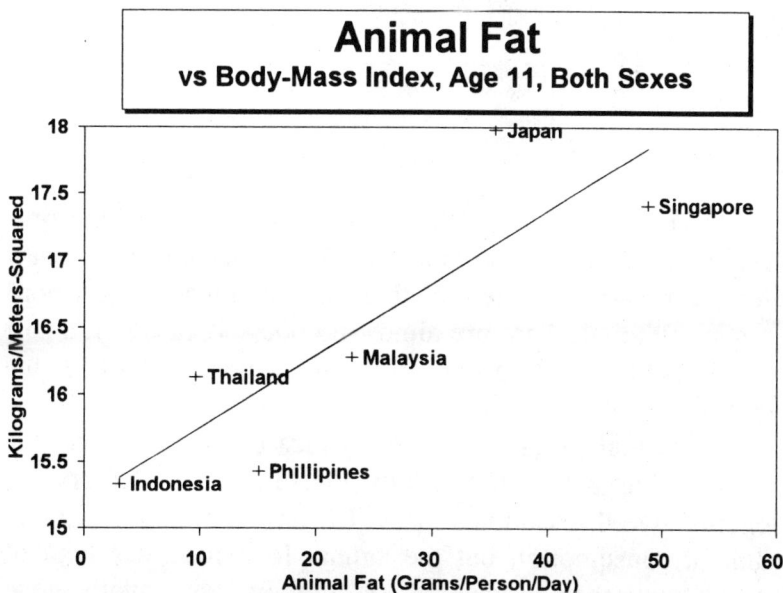

Recent work indicates that increased fat intake is the only distinct difference in eating behavior between obese and lean adults.[62] On the next page is evidence from the World Health Organization on the correlation between animal fat consumption and obesity.[63] Children under five and adults over forty who have had longer exposure to high fat diets seem to be primarily affected.

Animal Fat vs Obesity
(Ages 0-59 months and over 40 Years)

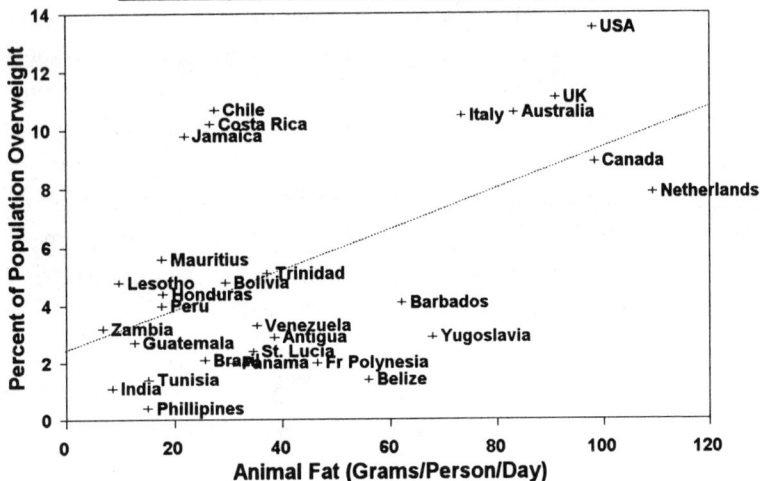

Chart: Percent of Population Overweight (y-axis, 0 to 14) vs Animal Fat (Grams/Person/Day) (x-axis, 0 to 120). Data points labeled: USA, UK, Italy, Australia, Chile, Costa Rica, Jamaica, Canada, Netherlands, Mauritius, Lesotho, Bolivia, Trinidad, Honduras, Peru, Barbados, Zambia, Venezuela, Antigua, Guatemala, St. Lucia, Yugoslavia, Brazil, Panama, Fr Polynesia, India, Tunisia, Belize, Phillipines.

There are at least 1800 weight-loss diet books in print. The checkout stand tabloids and the ladies mags feature a new diet every month but few of them say the dreaded "V" word (vegan) although there are almost no obese vegans. It's part of addictive behavior to look for answers in every spot but the right one.

Animal fat is a bad dietary idea but refined vegetable fat is no bargain, either. Since the turn of the century the degenerative disease rates in the US have gone up in parallel with fat consumption but the animal food folks are fond of pointing out that animal fat consumption has actually gone down which means that our use of vegetable oils has gone up.

Aside from using the stuff in the first place, there are a few other marginal things you can do to vegetable oil *before* you eat it.

First off, you can hydrogenate it by heating it in the presence of nickel and hydrogen,[64] thus removing some of the double bonds and making it thicker. This technique is favored by commercial peanut butter and chip/dip manufacturers, but the problem is that in this non-enzymatic hydrogenation process as some of the double bonds are being converted to single bonds, others are isomerized from *cis* to *trans*.

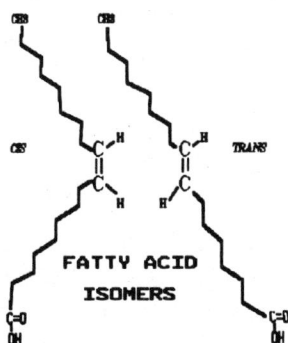

Some bacteria synthesize *trans* fatty acids but higher animals only synthesize *cis* fatty acids. Not all the returns are in yet in but it appears that unsaturated *trans* fatty acids behave like saturated fatty acids. They can be used for fuel but they raise cholesterol and LDL (Low Density Lipoprotein) levels,[65] while lowering HDL (High Density Lipoproteins). That may only be the tip of the iceberg since they accumulate in the phospholipids of cell membranes[66] with unknown results.

A normal cell membrane bilayer is made up mostly of kinky and folded *cis* fatty acids. Add *trans* fatty acids and the kinks start to disappear. Membrane permeability is almost certainly affected, so it may not be a coincidence that as the food industry has increasingly bombarded the market with hydrogenated fat, the incidence of viral diseases like Herpes simplex[67] has gone up. Unlike bacterial infections, viruses have to get inside the host cell; it's not likely that *trans* fats do much to keep them out.

Prehistoric humans did not have refined oils. The Egyptians by 2500 BC appear to have used vegetable oils for food and for painting materials.[68] The Mediterranean peoples found out about pressing olives, an apparently benign discovery since as yet no one has pinned the rap on mono-unsaturated olive oil. There does seem to be a problem with poly-unsaturated vegetable oils which lower the risk of Coronary Heart Disease (CHD) but raise the risk of bowel and breast cancers.

One of the true culinary catastrophes, the frying of food in hot oil first appears in English references around 1290 AD.[69] Whose bad idea it was in the first place is difficult to determine.

Raw fooders object to baking, boiling, and steaming. Possibly they're right but these processes simply predigest food by hydrolyzing it (breaking chemical bonds with hot water). Proteins, fats, and carbohydrates are broken down in the GI tract by the same process using enzymes instead of heat.[70]

Frying is a whole different ballgame. One hundred grams of raw potato in the skin carries 76 Calories of food energy. Boiled, it still has 76 Calories. Baked, it has 93 Calories since it dehydrates slightly. Stripped and deep fried, it's now French fries and 274 Calories. Thin sliced and fried, it becomes 568 Calories of potato chips.[71] In addition to a lowered nutrient/Calorie ratio, it also has an outer layer of fat that has been subjected to oxygen and heat. Conventional wisdom holds that frying temperatures are not high enough to degrade fat, but there is evidence that if fat is reboiled and recycled often enough, it will contain peroxides, epoxides, aldehydes, ketones, cyclic monomers, dimers, and polycyclic hydrocarbons.[72] These substances interfere with normal metabolism, and some are carcinogenic.

On balance it appears that vegetable fat in any amount above that found in unprocessed vegetables is a poor idea. Animal fat is worse since it's more likely to be saturated and accompanied by cholesterol. As for cooking with oil, an anonymous author observed: "God sends the food, the devil sends the cook." The cook usually brings his frying pan.

IV. THE CHOLESTEROL CAPER

"An ounce of prevention gathers no bucks. "

-Willy Sutton's brother.

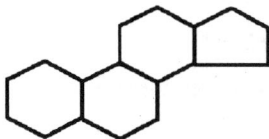

Sterol Nucleus

Ah, the jetés, the arabesques, the fandangos make
Baryshnikov look like a rank amateur!   Americans *dance*
around the cholesterol issue, and the pop media carries almost
as much cholesterol in its pages as the readers carry in their
arteries.   Full-on front cover bleats about the cholesterol
problem (Oops! Make that "crisis") list all the band-aid
remedies (cut the eggs, hold the bacon), but seldom is
vegetarianism mentioned.   The dreaded "V" word remains on
the editorial hit list although it would seem sensible for people
who want their serum cholesterol to drop to just stop eating the
stuff.
    So what is cholesterol and why is everyone saying such
bad things about it?
    Cholesterol is a sterol molecule and a survivor in the
three billion year molecular evolution that led to the first cells.
It's synthesized by most animal cells from Coenzyme A (a
molecule made of pantothenic acid and a complicated carbon
chain) that links to acetate, a two carbon molecule related to
vinegar.   After repeated enzymatic transfers, the acetate
molecules form into a long carbon chain which, because of its
bonding angles, looks
like this:

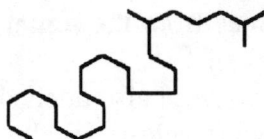

Squalene

29

From here, even if one is not a biochemist, it's pretty obvious what happens next:

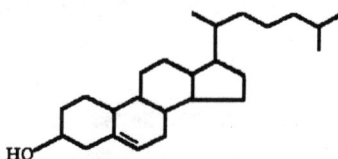

Cholesterol

Straight chain carbon compounds assemble easily, but once they form rings, the energy needed to disassemble them goes up drastically. Several species of bacteria which have time to split molecules nobody else wants can break down the sterol nucleus into carbon dioxide and water,[73] but for animals it's not worth the trouble. Animals can get rid of cholesterol only by dumping it, modified slightly, as a bile acid in the stool.

Cholesterol is rugged stuff. The inflexible nucleus gets along well with fat, so incorporated into the fatty membrane that acts as the animal cell wall, it becomes a strengthening material.

Humans synthesize 500 mg cholesterol/day,[74] further evidence the molecule is essential to normal function. Most omnivores *eat* an additional 500 mg/day,[75] which may raise the serum cholesterol above the liver's ability to modify and dump it. It then simply winds up in cells, a serious problem if the cell is on the inside of an artery. It may be that the cell's lysosome (its "stomach") is unable to digest the nucleus[76] which accumulates until the lysosome ruptures and kills the cell which is replaced by an irregular plaque that disturbs the smooth flow of blood. The result is coronary heart disease (CHD), peripheral vascular disease, stroke, and a few oddities so rare as to require *proper* names. All the cholesterol in the plaque comes from the serum cholesterol, not from synthesis within the cell.[77]

Cholesterol also applied to the Bureau of Evolution for the hormone franchise. Both plants and animals do a virtuoso performance modifying its carbon side chains to produce a string of related sterols, only a few of which are shown below:

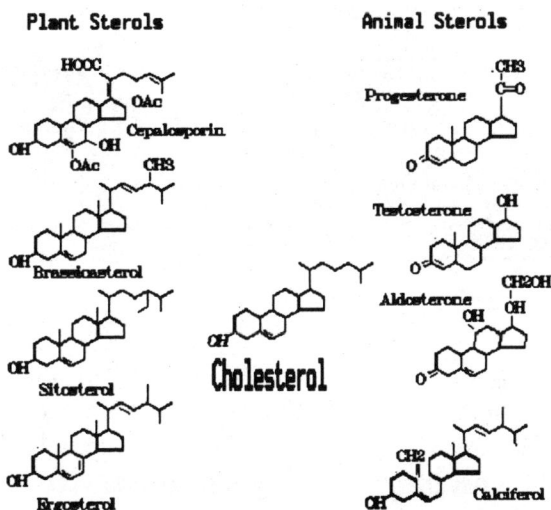

Plant Sterols

Animal Sterols

Cepalosporin

Brassicasterol

Sitosterol

Cholesterol

Ergosterol

Progesterone

Testosterone

Aldosterone

Calciferol

Plants synthesize small amounts of cholesterol on the pathway that leads to the other plant sterols[78] which are structural components in plant cell membranes and probably serve also as plant reproductive hormones.

However, the cholesterol content of plants is very much less than that of animals. In fact, the cholesterol in plants is generally much less than 1 mg/100 gms. This is below the level of detection by USDA assay methods,[79] so the cholesterol content of plant foods is always reported as zero. However, by compiling information from several obscure sources[80,81,82,83,84] the following graph was constructed (next page):

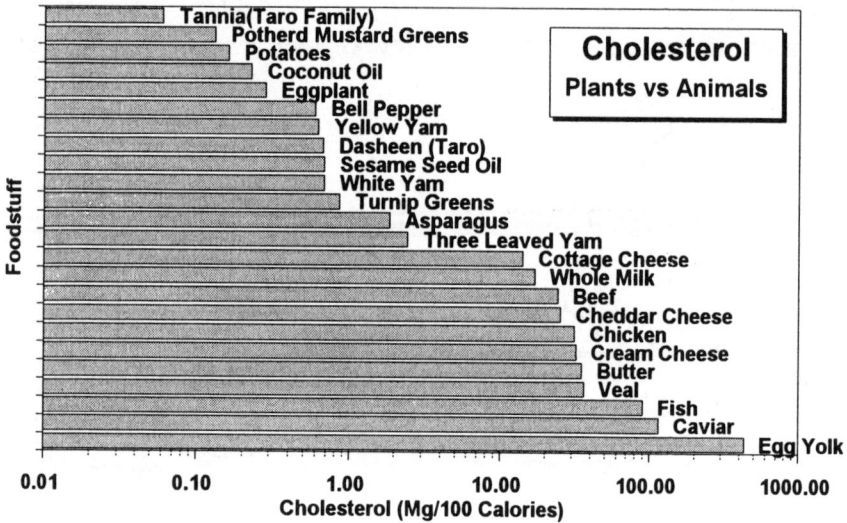

Cholesterol

Plants vs Animals

Foodstuff (Y-axis), Cholesterol (Mg/100 Calories) (X-axis)

The cholesterol content of some plants appears formidable until we note the above graph has a logarithmic X-axis. When we redraw it with a normal X-axis the cholesterol content of most plants virtually disappears:

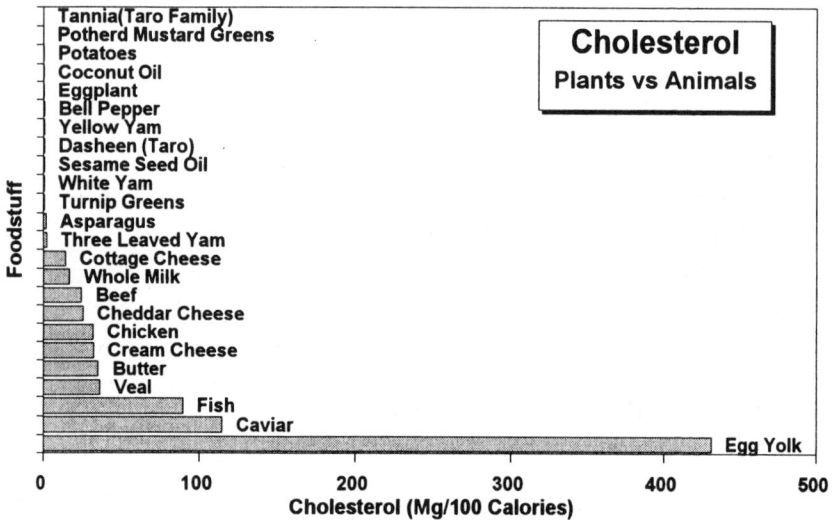

Cholesterol

Plants vs Animals

Foodstuff (Y-axis), Cholesterol (Mg/100 Calories) (X-axis)

If one consumed nothing but 2400 calories/day of three-leaved yams, the cholesterol intake would be about 48 mgs. This is no reason to forswear yams although it is notable that yams are such a good sterol source that pharmaceutical companies use them as a starting point in the synthesis of steroid drugs such as cortisone[85] and natural progesterone (which if we're all really lucky may turn out to be the best solution yet for post-menopausal hormone replacement.)[86]

Taking the average of all the known plant sources of cholesterol, it's unlikely a 2400 Calorie vegan diet would exceed 10 mg cholesterol per day.[87] By contrast, omnivores are trying to cut their intake to 300 mgs/day. The highest reported edible plant cholesterol/Calorie ratio (three-leaved yam) is 5.8 times less than the lowest reported animal cholesterol/Calorie ratio (cottage cheese) with the exception of egg white which is very questionably listed as a zero cholesterol food. The vegan diet for practical purposes remains a no cholesterol diet, and there is no RDA for cholesterol.

There are 3683 references in Medline to the effects of hypercholesterolemia. The 79 studies on *hypo*cholesterolemia are primarily concerned with strategies to produce the condition; apparently there are no reports of clinical illness resulting solely from inadequate cholesterol intake although problems can surface if cholesterol-lowering drugs are continued after a vegan diet has lowered serum cholesterol below 150 mg%.

A favorite establishment dietary remedy is the substitution of fish and poultry for meat on the theory these foods have less of the bad stuff.

Meat looks bad when it's sorted by cholesterol/weight ratio because it's high in fat which is light, so the meat denominators are small and the ratios large. Meat looks better when it's sorted by cholesterol/Calorie ratio because the fat carries nine Calories per gram so the meat denominators get larger and the ratios get smaller. Vice versa for fish. Animal food aficionados have no easy out; there's 300 mg of cholesterol in 10 ozs (680 Cal) of beef and in 577 Calories (18 ozs) of codfish. Neither sorting method supports much value in eating poultry rather than meat. Eggs and shrimp are no contest. The solution is to quit eating animals, fish included.

There is a genetic condition called familial hypercholesterolemia (FH) characterized by serum cholesterol levels in the 1000 mg/dL range and early death from Coronary Heart Disease (CHD). It's said to be unresponsive to diet[88] but this reasoning is flawed. There have been few studies of familial hypercholesterolemia treated with a vegan diet because the researchers can't conceive of such a diet and hence seldom try it.[89] The diets that have proven inadequate in controlling this condition may drop to 200 mg cholesterol/day, but this is still a toxic cholesterol load for a species that evolved most of its genes in a sixty million year arboreal primate phase eating only leaves and fruit. The more recent hominids and modern humans have had a relatively short four million year exposure to the dietary cholesterol introduced by their omnivorous diet.

Whatever cultural adaptations the hominids made in response to the survival value of Calorie-rich animal food, it's unlikely that the hypercholesterolemia genes were ever subjected to Darwinian selection. The burden of high dietary fat and cholesterol does not become lethal until the fourth or fifth decade of life, well beyond reproductive age and beyond the life expectancy of the hominids, estimated at 30 years.[90] Thus, no selection process can be expected to weed out the "high-cholesterol genes."

FH is cited by Medline in 472 articles. Many of them deal with the reduction of serum cholesterol using drugs. None of them mention the words "vegan" or even "vegetarian." There have been some recent shots fired in the right direction, however. Connor achieved serum cholesterol reductions of 18-21% in FH patients limited to 100 mg cholesterol/day.[91] More recently a cholesterol *free* diet reduced cholesterol levels in heterozygous (dissimilar pairs of genes) FH patients from 323 $\pm$ 67 mg/dL to ~ 277 mg/dL.[92] The authors achieved this in a time period "for as long as eleven days," a phrase that suggests either they or their patients could not conceive of a vegan diet on a permanent basis.

The current preoccupation with random genetic predisposition may be unfruitful. A whole food vegan diet *is* the treatment for high serum cholesterol. In addition to an undetectable cholesterol intake, it's also low in fat. Vegan population studies confirm low serum cholesterol and LDL levels, high HDL/LDL ratios, infrequent coronary events, almost non-existent obesity and a ten-year increase in longevity.[93]

The familial hypercholesterolemics may be sitting under the far end of a bell-shaped distribution curve that includes in its middle the CHD patients of Ornish[94] who, when put on no more than a lacto-vegetarian, *near*-vegan diet rapidly lowered their serum cholesterol. Like humans,[95] rabbits, and laboratory primates everywhere,[96] they also reabsorbed their cholesterol plaques and improved their coronary circulation.

The Ornish study has been ignored by some cardiologists who object that the one-year vegetarian regime only increased coronary artery inside diameter by 3%. Curiously, they continue to prescribe cholesterol-lowering drugs to their patients which accomplishes in an expensive manner what diet does for free. However, the flow of any fluid through a pipe is a fourth power function of pipe diameter (Poiseulle's Law).[97]

$$F \text{ (Flow)} = \Delta V / \Delta t = (P_1 - P_2)(\pi R^4)/8L\eta$$

where:

Δ = change
V = volume
t = time
$(P_1 - P_2)$ = pressure differential across the length (L) of the pipe
R = radius of the pipe = D(diameter)/2
η = coefficient of viscosity of the fluid

If we hold all variables constant except the diameter, and take for a start a coronary lumen diameter of 3 mm we can compare the initial flow (F_1) with flow (F_2) after a year on the vegetarian diet:

$$F_2/F_1 = kR_2^4/kR_1^4 = (3+.03 \times 3)^4/3^4 = (3.09)^4/81 =$$
$$91.17/81 = 1.13 = 113\%$$

35

So, coronary perfusion has been improved 13% although coronary diameter has only increased 3%. This probably explains why the Ornish patients experienced a 91% reduction in the frequency of heart pain. Nor is there any reason to think the resorption of cholesterol plaque would not continue indefinitely on a vegan diet.

In recent years there has been much talk of lipoproteins, the little bubbles of cholesterol, cholesterol esters, phospholipids and neutral fat that carry the insoluble fats through the bloodstream. The bigger the lipoprotein bubble, the more fat and cholesterol it has and the lower its density relative to water. In a centrifuge the big bubbles wind up on top. Chylomicrons are very large lipoproteins formed during intestinal absorption.[98]

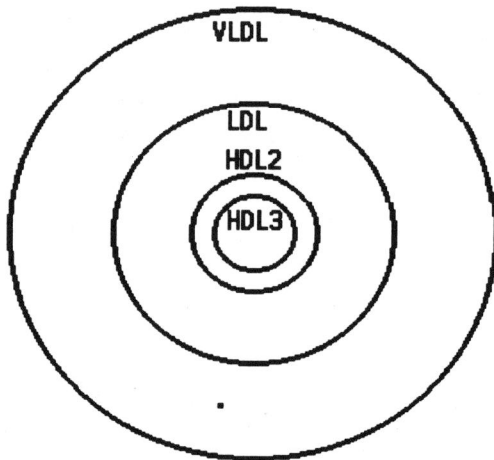

| 55 Millionths of a millimeter |
(A chylomicron is ten times larger)

Low density lipoprotein (LDL) is "bad cholesterol"; it dumps cholesterol in cells. High density lipoprotein (HDL) is "good cholesterol"; it can absorb more cholesterol, so it carries cholesterol away for eventual disposal in the bile.

The usage is erroneous. Cholesterol is cholesterol and has exactly the same structural formula whether it's taking a ride in HDL or in LDL.

A Lipoprotein Particle
(Segment)

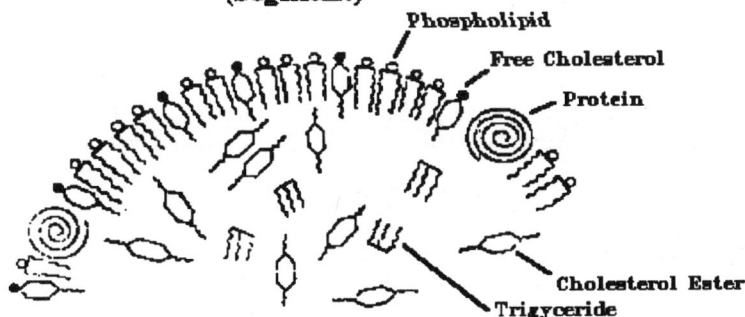

Phospholipid
Free Cholesterol
Protein
Cholesterol Ester
Triglyceride

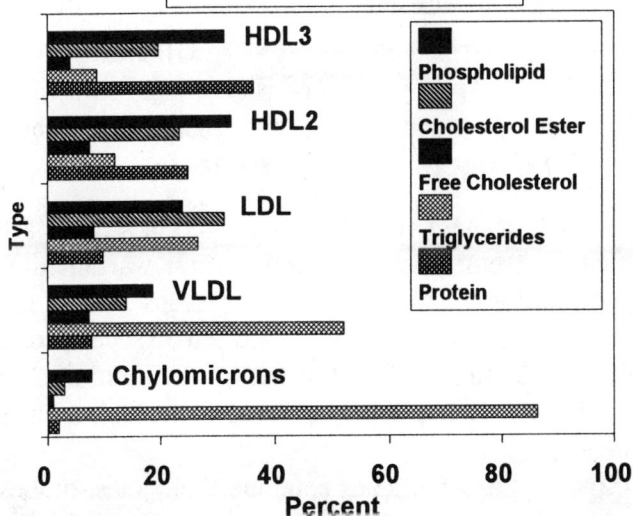

Lipoproteins
Percent Composition

HDL3

HDL2

LDL

VLDL

Chylomicrons

Phospholipid

Cholesterol Ester

Free Cholesterol

Triglycerides

Protein

Type

0   20   40   60   80   100

Percent

   Protein synthesis is under genetic control. One can be stuck with genes that code for lots of LDL and with this piece of bad luck in mind, overlook that one has complete control over dietary cholesterol, regardless of genes.

   On a vegan diet the lipoproteins are irrelevant. Vegans average serum total cholesterol levels of 150.8 mg/dL.[99] In the Framingham Heart Study, CHD vanished at cholesterol levels below 150 mg/dL.[100]

Reference labs currently report any value below 200 mg/dL as "normal" but it should be noted this is only normal in a population dying of CHD at the rate of 978,500 in 1986.[101]

Lipoprotein Contents
Logarithmic Plot

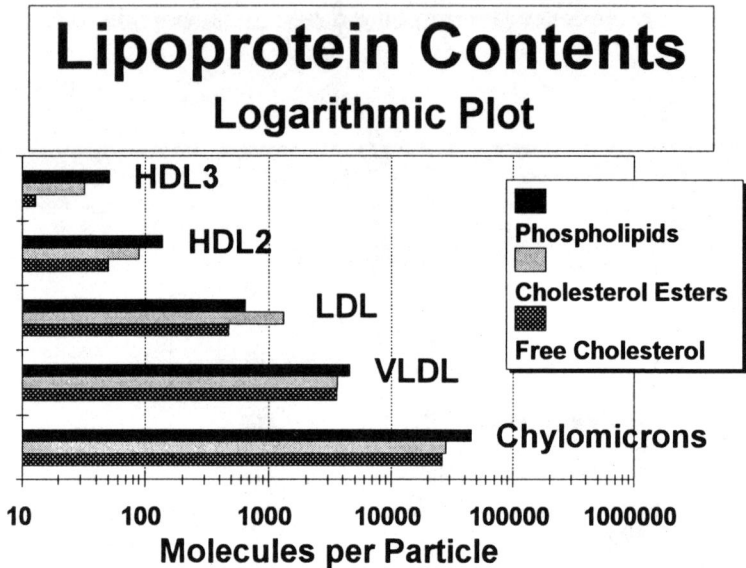

HDL3

HDL2

LDL

VLDL

Chylomicrons

Phospholipids

Cholesterol Esters

Free Cholesterol

10   100   1000   10000   100000   1000000

Molecules per Particle

In spite of these considerations a recent science article[102] stated that "extreme dietary change is not warranted for the entire population." Among the reasons cited for this conclusion was that such change would have "severe social and economic consequences." Apparently the authors did not regard 978,500 preventable coronary deaths as a severe consequence.

Meanwhile, Americans continue their jetés, arabesques, and fandangos based on the cholesterol two-step. It's a *danse macabre*.

V. THE PROTEIN PERPLEX

The big question encountered by vegans: "How do you get enough protein?" The answer should be: "How much do you think you need?"

Over the years dietary protein recommendations have gone up and down like a yo-yo. In 1881 Carl Voit M.D. surveyed German laborers and found they consumed 118 grams of protein/day.[103] Voit had a deserved reputation in nutritional physiology[104] so when he said, "That's how much you need!" it stuck.

In 1904 Chittendon lowered the figure after extensive research,[105] but then the USDA brought it back up to 125 grams.[106] In 1920 after extensive nitrogen balance studies, Sherman[107] cut the figure to 1 gram/kg body weight/day which translated to $\approx$ 70 gram/day for a 154-pound person. In 1946 Hegsted[108] cut the figures to 30-40 grams/day, but by 1958 the Minimum Daily Requirement (MDR) was back up to 1 gram/kg/day.

Alas, that was about the time the MDRs went down the Orwellian memory hole. The Food and Nutrition Board (FNB) of the National Research Council (NRC), of the National Academy of Sciences (NAS), had switched to Recommended Dietary Allowances (RDAs). RDAs are set 2 standard deviations above the mean nutrient requirement to insure that only 2.5% of the population will fall below nutrient needs, but this insures that 97.4999...% of the population meeting the RDAs will exceed its nutrient *and* Calorie requirements.[109]

The Canadians, in an independent turn of thought, set their protein RDA at 50 grams/day in 1967,[110] and the US responded with a counter bid of .8 grams/kg/day which comes out to about 56 grams a day for that 154-pound person. To keep things jumping, in the '70s the Food and Drug Administration (FDA) came out with the U.S. RDAs which are different from the RDAs of the (FNB) of the (NRC) of the (NAS)[111] which, parenthetically, is *not* a branch of the U.S. government.[112]

Now, an adult male on a fast only puts out 4.32 grams of urinary nitrogen per day.[113]   Each gram represents 6.25 grams of broken down protein, so under conditions in which some protein is actually being catabolized and used for fuel, only about 4.32x6.25 = 27 grams/day are actually needed. Furthermore, 75-80% of the amino acids from used protein are pooled and used over again for new protein synthesis.[114] Therefore, it's not clear why a non-fasting subject should even need 56 grams/day, since carbohydrate will be burned before protein under ordinary conditions.

Confused? Fortunately, there's an easy way out. We can take the RDA of 56 grams protein/day, be generous and raise it to 60, then match it to a Calorie RDA of 2400.   Each gram of protein carries 4 Calories, so the percent of Calories/day   needed   from   protein   comes   to 60x4/2400 = 240/2400 = .10 = 10%.   It's interesting to note that human milk, which seems to support adequate growth in human infants, has only 5.9% Calories from protein.[115] Most plant food is well above the 10% figure, watercress (78%) and spinach (53%) being good examples, so most vegan diets exceed even the good ol' MDR of 70 grams protein/day. The average American consumes about 103 gm protein/day, of which 70 gm is animal protein.[116]

Some day a computer will doubtless find a way to display all the foods in the USDA database at one time, but for now it can only be done piecemeal. Excluding junk foods, processed foods, and recipes, 100 gram portions of various foods in 10 categories of the Nutritionist III database[117] were averaged for protein. The large number of fruits (59) and vegetables (93) reflects only the abundance of species available. By contrast, eggs (6) and poultry (11) had a relative paucity of species.

With the exception of fruit, all the categories exceed the 10% protein requirements. If one consumed nothing but averaged foods from the vegetable category, one would get about 25% of the day's Calories from protein (next page).

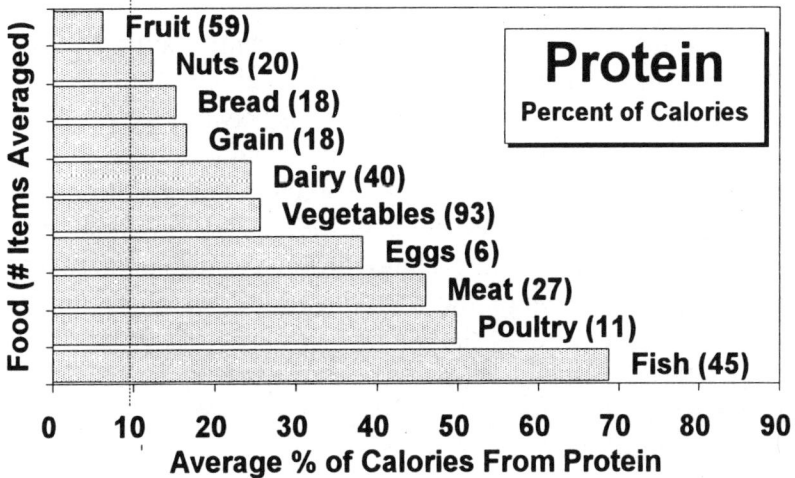

Protein
Percent of Calories

Food (# Items Averaged)

- Fruit (59)
- Nuts (20)
- Bread (18)
- Grain (18)
- Dairy (40)
- Vegetables (93)
- Eggs (6)
- Meat (27)
- Poultry (11)
- Fish (45)

0 10 20 30 40 50 60 70 80 90
Average % of Calories From Protein

Therefore, unless fruit is the only food, if the day's Calorie requirements are met, so is the 10% protein requirement.

"Well, then," asks the questioner, "you may be getting enough protein but is it *quality* protein; does it have the right proportion of amino acids?" The question originates from studies[118,119] that showed that weanling rats grow fastest on an amino mix which resembles rat's milk, which has about 26% of its Calories from protein.

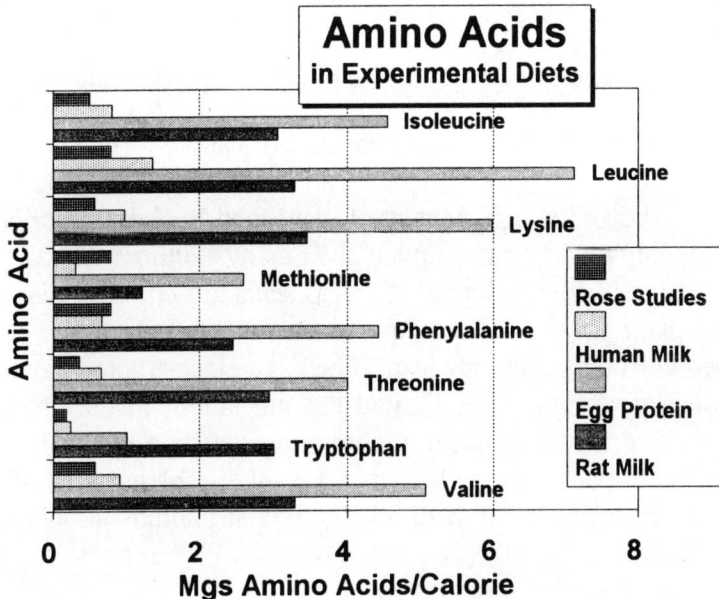

Amino Acids
in Experimental Diets

Amino Acid

- Isoleucine
- Leucine
- Lysine
- Methionine
- Phenylalanine
- Threonine
- Tryptophan
- Valine

Rose Studies
Human Milk
Egg Protein
Rat Milk

0 2 4 6 8
Mgs Amino Acids/Calorie

41

William Rose studied minimum amino acid requirements in adult males and then doubled his figures.[120] The preceding graph shows the similarity between Rose's adult human requirements and the amino composition of human milk. It also shows the disparity between human requirements and the foods that make weanling rats grow fast.[121] Whole eggs (32% of Calories from protein) grow rats just fine, so for many years eggs were the amino gold standard and infant health was measured by the pound.

Next came a zoo full of amino acid efficiency formulas[122]:

Protein Efficiency Ratio:

(PER) = (Weight gain of a growing animal)/(protein intake).

Mitchell's Biological Value:

(BV) = The ratio of nitrogen retained to nitrogen absorbed.

Net Protein Utilization:

NPU = the proportion of food nitrogen retained.

Coefficient of utilization of test products:

P_r(The coefficient) = P_{tp}(test protein)/P_{em}(evaporated milk protein).

After all this, Arnould concluded that the formulas were inadequate.[123]

The amino acid content of plant food has been described as incomplete or inadequate by many authors, and the impression is often gained that amino acids are entirely missing from plant foods. In general, that's not correct; however a milled corn-only diet may lead to pellagra since tryptophan and its derivative niacin are limited but not absent in the protein (zein) of corn. The niacin in corn is present in a bound form, niacytin;[124] Mexican cooks deal with this problem by treating their corn tortilla flour with alkali, which unbinds the niacin.

In Africa there's a disease called kwashiorkor, "the disease the first child gets when the second child is born,"[125] that results from early weaning onto cassava root (from which Westerners make tapioca). Cassava leaf is a good protein source[126] but unfortunately it contains cyanide.[127] The root is low in methionine and has only 2% of Calories from protein.[128]

Using the same 10 categories of foods, the following two graphs show their amino acid patterns. The X axis gives the percent of the RDA required from each Calorie of food "the percent of (RDA per Calorie)."

Some conclusions can be drawn:
1. Once again, fruit is shown to be the only non-junk category consistently short in protein constituents (amino acids).
2. The vegetable category averages at least 500% of (RDA per Calorie) for its limiting amino, methionine.
3. Animal foods are higher in amino acids to the point of overkill. The well documented allergic reactions to fish are due to its high content of histidine, which undergoes bacterial decomposition to histamine.

Amino Acids
Percent of (RDA per Calorie)

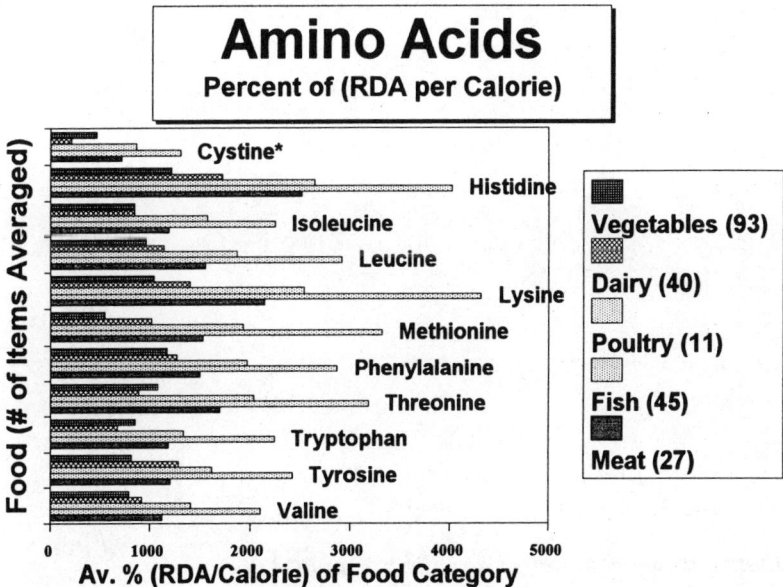

Food (# of Items Averaged)

Cystine*
Histidine
Isoleucine
Leucine
Lysine
Methionine
Phenylalanine
Threonine
Tryptophan
Tyrosine
Valine

Vegetables (93)
Dairy (40)
Poultry (11)
Fish (45)
Meat (27)

Av. % (RDA/Calorie) of Food Category

43

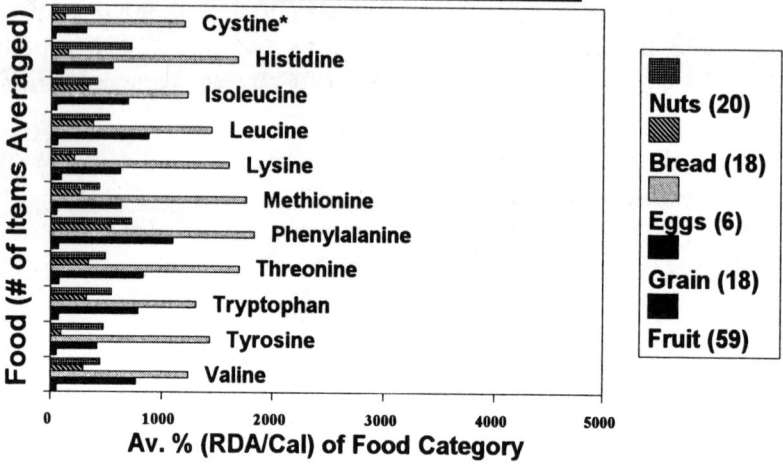

Amino Acids
Percent of (RDA per Calorie)

Food (# of Items Averaged)

Cystine*
Histidine
Isoleucine
Leucine
Lysine
Methionine
Phenylalanine
Threonine
Tryptophan
Tyrosine
Valine

0   1000   2000   3000   4000   5000

Av. % (RDA/Cal) of Food Category

Nuts (20)
Bread (18)
Eggs (6)
Grain (18)
Fruit (59)

Cystine is non-essential so actually has no RDA.

VI. THE PROTEIN PROFUSION

Proteins are well recognized for structural and enzymatic properties, but they have another important function: they're the "words" nature employs to communicate information between and within living organisms.

Protein is a sequence of the 20 biological amino acids, which are the "alphabet" in the protein "language."

THE ENGLISH ALPHABET

A	H	O	V
B	I	P	W
C	J	Q	X
D	K	R	Y
E	L	S	Z
F	M	T	
G	N	U	

THE PROTEIN ALPHABET

[A]-Alanine	[K]-Lysine	[S]-Serine
[C]-Cysteine	[L]-Leucine	[T]-Threonine
[D]-Aspartic acid	[M]-Methionine	[V]-Valine
[E]-Glutamic acid	[N]-Asparagine	[W]-Tryptophan
[F]-Phenylalanine	[P]-Proline	[Y]-Tyrosine
[G]-Glycine	[Q]-Glutamine	[1]-Isoleucine
[H]-Histidine	[R]-Arginine	

Given a protein with a chain length of 100 amino acids, there are $20^{100}=10^{130}$ possible sequences[129] in which those twenty aminos can be linked. By comparison Webster's New World Dictionary, with an alphabet of 26 letters, has only 1.42×10^5 (142,000) words. The human genome only codes for 100,000 proteins,[130] although the immune system maintains a "library" that can discriminate about a billion foreign proteins.[131]

Thus, only a tiny fraction of those possible 10^{130} protein "words" are expressed in nature so the tree of life is made of amino acid sequences, and the empty space around the tree represents the myriad sequences that were never used.

Pro-insulin is a protein, a long spiral sequence of amino acids[132] linked together. After synthesis in the pancreas, it is cleaved to active insulin (shown below the arrows):

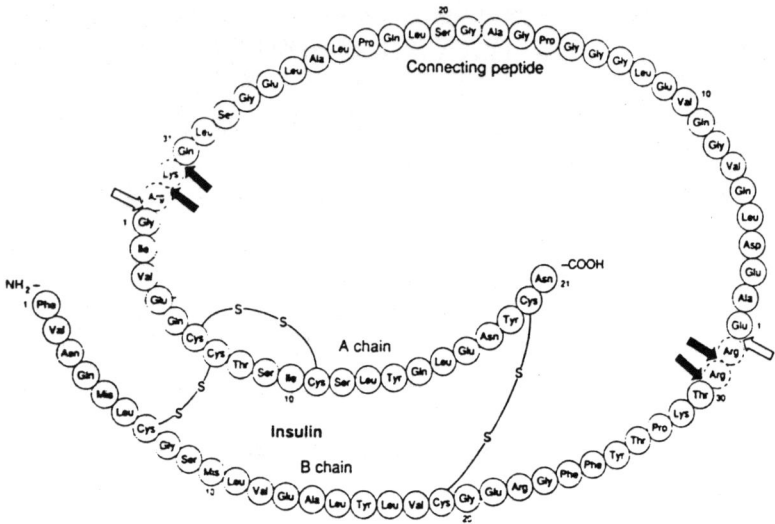

This sequence has variations from species to species:[133]

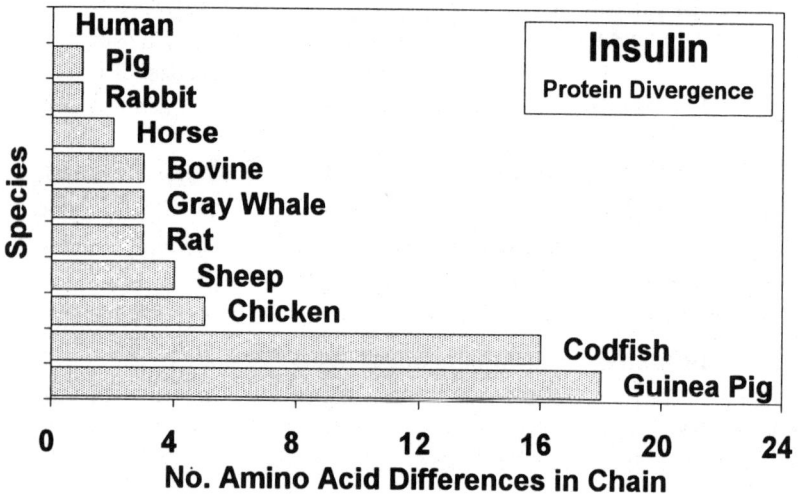

46

Before human insulin became available, diabetics who developed antibodies to beef insulin were commonly switched to pork insulin, closer to the structure of human insulin, and less likely to be detected as a foreign protein by the immune system.[134]

As another example of protein divergence, here is cytochrome C, an electron transfer enzyme in the mitochondria of plant and animals cells.[135] Clearly the sequence diverges in proportion to the evolutionary distance from humans:

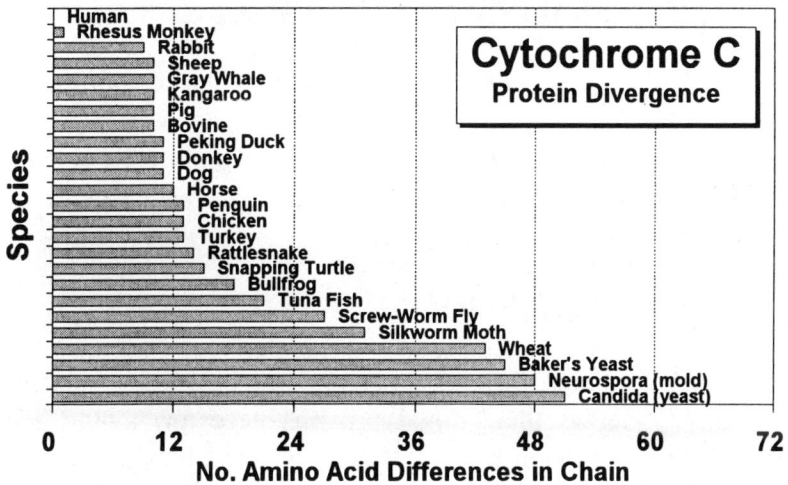

Cytochrome C
Protein Divergence

Species:
Human
Rhesus Monkey
Rabbit
Sheep
Gray Whale
Kangaroo
Pig
Bovine
Peking Duck
Donkey
Dog
Horse
Penguin
Chicken
Turkey
Rattlesnake
Snapping Turtle
Bullfrog
Tuna Fish
Screw-Worm Fly
Silkworm Moth
Wheat
Baker's Yeast
Neurospora (mold)
Candida (yeast)

No. Amino Acid Differences in Chain
0   12   24   36   48   60   72

Protein is identified by its amino acid sequence; the sequence is reflected by the antibodies that the immune system forms against it. Proteins need only be about 36 amino acids long to be strong antigens.[136] In the above graphic abbreviation, the lines represent sequences of amino acids folded into geometric shapes.

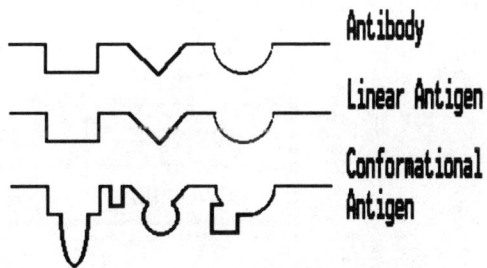

Antibody

Linear Antigen

Conformational Antigen

47

Ordinarily, about 98% of dietary proteins are digested and absorbed as harmless amino acids.[137] However, fragments of whole protein may be absorbed by pinocytosis, a sort of "swallowing" by intestinal lining cells.[138]   Once in the circulation the protein fragments can provoke the formation of antibodies.

For the sake of analogy, let us invent the amino acids [I], [O], and [U]. Suppose then that the immune system encounters this protein fragment:

[I]-[A]-[M]-[N]-[O]-[T]-[Y]-[O]-[U]

This is a message that the immune system seeks diligently since such information is usually associated with a microbiological invader. It will generate antibodies and the question is whether the antibodies will cross-react against the body's own protein fragment:

[I[-[A]-[M]-[Y]-[O]-[U]

A browse through a computer sequence analysis database[139] shows that animal proteins have few amino acid sequences in common with plant proteins while they are similar to each other.   Myoglobins, collagens, immunoglobulins, hemoglobins, and their genes from various animal species resemble those from humans. Many of these proteins are not even present in plant species.

T = thymine	G = guanine
C = cytosine	A = adenine

These four nucleic acid bases are the business end of DNA.[140]   Three bases in sequence form a "codon" which specifies one amino acid.   Hence, a long sequence of bases specifies a protein about a third the length of its gene.

Shown below is a typical print-out comparing a short

length of the genes coding for human and bovine lactalbumin (milk protein). The vertical lines show the identity of bases generating the two proteins, which for this short segment is 91.6%. The printout went on for 1460 base pairs (bp) with an *overall* identity of 79.9%.

```
DEFINITION  Human alpha-lactalbumin gene, complete cds.
DEFINITION  Bovine gene for alpha-lactalbumin.

        1560      1570      1580      1590      1600      1610
Humlac  TCACACCAGTGGTTATGACACACAAGCCATAGTTGAAAACAATGAAAGCACGGAATATGG
        |||  |||||||||||||||||||||||||||||||  |||||||||| ||||| ||||||||
Bovlac  TCATACCAGTGGTTATGACACACAAGCCATAGTACAAAACAATGACAGCACAGAATATGG
        1240      1250      1260      1270      1280      1290
```

It's not surprising that cow's milk is associated with a glossary of pediatric illness.[141]   If the genes were 100% identical, human and cow milks would be immunologically indistinguishable and these problems would not arise.   The trouble lies in *similar* but not *identical* proteins.

A 62.5% identity was found between corn albumin mRNA and Pea albumin mRNA in this 48 bp segment:

```
DEFINITION  Maize albumin b-32 mRNA, complete cds.
DEFINITION  Pea (P.sativum) albumin 2 (PA2) mRNA, complete cds.

         900       910       920       930       940       950
Mzealb  TTCACGTCCTCCACGGGGAAGATTTCAGTGAACTTTGGTACTATTTTTTTGTTTGTTTGC
        | |||   | || || ||| ||   |   | |||||||||| ||| |
Peaabn  TGCACTATATGCAGGGTGAATATAATAAAAACCTTTGGTACTTTTTAT
        910       920       930       940       950
```

By contrast, the identity for this 60 bp "best fit" segment of human serum albumin mRNA and corn albumin mRNA is about 18.3%, and there were no other matching segments:

```
DEFINITION  Human serum albumin mRNA, complete cds.
DEFINITION  Maize albumin b-32 mRNA, complete cds.

         40        50        60        70        80        90
Humalb  CAGCTTGACTTGCAGCAACAAGTTTTTTACCCTCCTCGGCAAAGCAGGTCTCCTTATCGT
                                     ||||||||||| |
Mzealb  GGTGGGAGTTGGCAAGGCCGGCGACACCCACCTCCTCGGCGACAACCCCAGGTGGCTCGG
          360       370       380       390       400       410
```

49

Matching human albumin against pea and sunflower albumins produced *no* identical segments and the computer locked up attempting to find them. It's likely that an exhaustive search would only disclose that animal proteins are similar to each other and plant proteins are similar to each other, but there is little similarity between plant and animal protein sequences other than their common use of the same 20 amino acids.

Therefore, while plant protein may induce allergy (e.g. hayfever from airborne pollen and hives from wheat), the antibodies do not cross-react with body proteins. Antibodies formed against animal protein *do*.

But scientific textbooks continue to stonewall diet and disease. Legitimate references to genetic and microbial causes are made, but in autoimmunity nary a reference can be found to the similarity of human protein and dietary animal protein. Diseases are called "idiopathic" and not diet-related, without performing vegan diet studies first.

A scanty literature suggests that a diet free of animal protein may be therapeutic in antigen-antibody (ag-ab) disease. Lindahl[142] improved asthmatics with a vegan diet. Kjeldsen-Kragh [143] improved both subjective and laboratory findings in rheumatoid arthritis patients using a lacto-vegetarian regime and the benefits in the diet group were still present after a year.

HYPOTHESIS:

"Clonal deletion" ordinarily eliminates clones of white cells that manufacture antibodies against one's own body proteins,[144] but if dietary protein is similar, though not identical, to the body's own protein, this mechanism may fail. Antibodies formed against dietary animal protein then cross-react with body proteins.[145] The result is autoimmune disease.

Autoimmune disease will surely continue as long as more antigen is being ingested daily. However, it seems likely that if the daily intake of animal protein stops, so also does the daily ag-ab shower into the affected tissues. Normal healing processes are then given a chance.

50

VII. THE HIGH COST OF MEAT

The U.S. medical budget was about $760 billion in 1991. It's projected to go to $2 trillion by AD 2000. About $577 billion of the initial figure went for patient care[146] and $270 billion of that went to the treatment of diseases now known to be partly the result of animal source food consumption.

The US Public Health Service keeps track of major killers. Not all these problems have an obvious relationship to diet and others that do are not shown.[147]

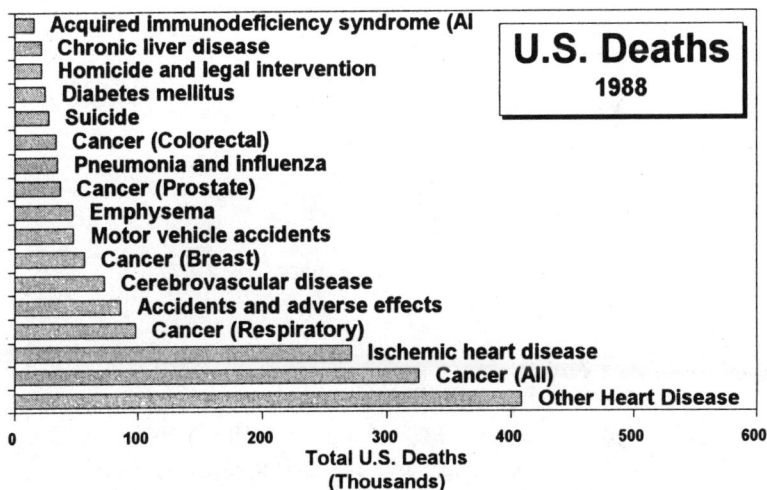

There are multiple factors in the cause of most disease. World Health Organization[148] and Food and Agriculture Organization data[149] show that the following diseases correlate with animal food consumption.

In the graphs below, the Y axis contains the disease, the X axis contains the animal source dietary risk factor. R is the correlation coefficient which reflects the "goodness of fit" of the data points to the sloping regression line. The p-value is the probability the apparent relationship is merely a mathematical coincidence.[150] An R of 1 would indicate a direct linear relationship, while an R of zero would indicate no relationship. A p-value of .05 indicates a 5% chance of mathematical coincidence but numbers less than .05 are traditionally taken to suggest a non-coincidental relationship.[151]

Animal fats are heavier and stickier than vegetable fats and have higher melting points. Lard, for example, is solid at room temperature while olive oil still flows. The heavier the fat, the more it agglutinates blood cells.[152] Photomicrographs taken after a high fat meal show clumping red cells. After a fatty meal the viscosity of the blood increases, a centrifuged blood sample shows a layer of white fat on top, and the circulation in the capillaries slows to a crawl. If it stops completely, it clots. That may explain this:[153]

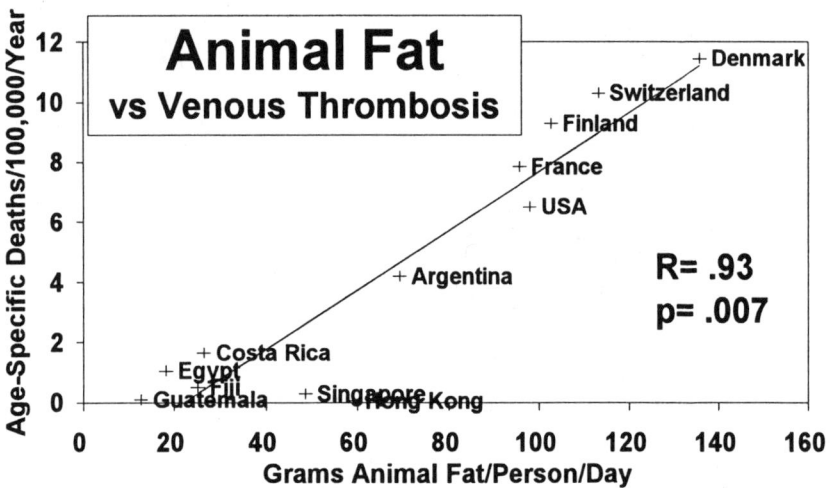

Animal Fat
vs Venous Thrombosis

+ Denmark
+ Switzerland
+ Finland
+ France
+ USA
+ Argentina
+ Costa Rica
+ Egypt
+ Guatemala
+ Fiji
+ Singapore
+ Hong Kong

R= .93
p= .007

Age-Specific Deaths/100,000/Year

0   20   40   60   80   100   120   140   160
Grams Animal Fat/Person/Day

If one purposely set out to plug the circulation, short of inserting corks, it would be hard to find a better combination than cholesterol, which deposits in artery walls, and animal fat, which slows red blood cells in capillaries.[154]

Graphing thrombosis against the percent of Calories from foods of plant origin produces an inverse correlation of -.86 and a p-value of .0004% (next page).

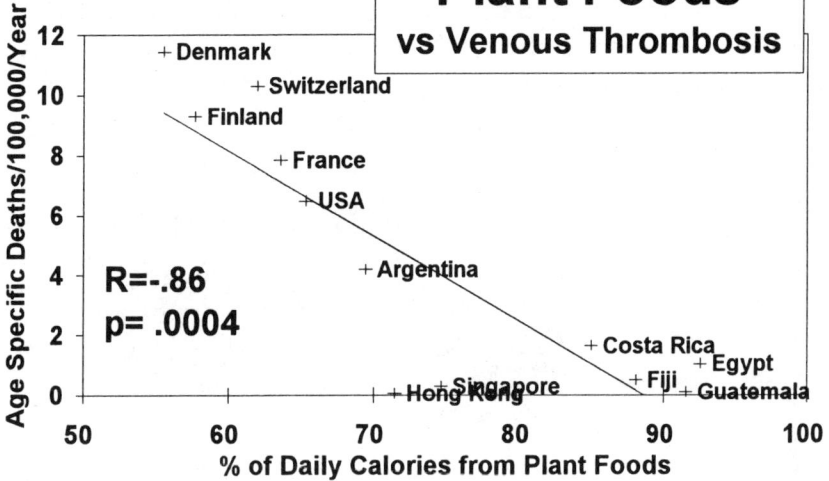

Plant Foods vs Venous Thrombosis

Age Specific Deaths/100,000/Year vs % of Daily Calories from Plant Foods

R=-.86
p= .0004

Denmark, Switzerland, Finland, France, USA, Argentina, Costa Rica, Egypt, Hong Kong, Singapore, Fiji, Guatemala

Animal fat comes with its own supply of cholesterol which deposits in vascular linings and causes coronary heart disease (CHD). Other authors[155] have observed a linear relationship between animal food consumption and CHD. The following database did not discriminate CHD from other forms of heart disease but the results are similar.[156] The computed R value is .76 and the p-value in this graph indicates only a .0004% chance that this apparent linear relationship reflects only a mathematical coincidence.

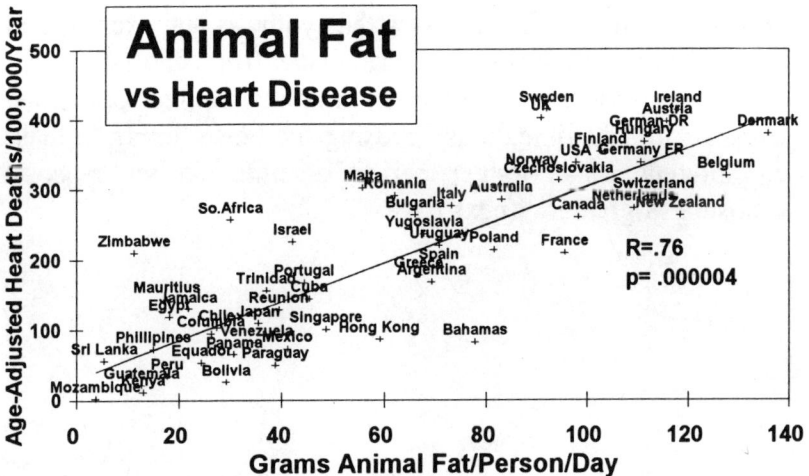

Animal Fat vs Heart Disease

Age-Adjusted Heart Deaths/100,000/Year vs Grams Animal Fat/Person/Day

R=.76
p= .000004

Sweden, UK, Ireland, Austria, Hungary, German-DR, Denmark, Finland, USA, Germany FR, Norway, Czechoslovakia, Switzerland, Belgium, Malta, Romania, Italy, Australia, Canada, Netherlands, New Zealand, So.Africa, Bulgaria, Yugoslavia, Israel, Uruguay, Poland, France, Zimbabwe, Portugal, Cuba, Greece, Spain, Argentina, Trinidad, Mauritius, Reunion, Jamaica, Egypt, Chile, Japan, Colombia, Singapore, Hong Kong, Bahamas, Phillipines, Venezuela, Mexico, Sri Lanka, Ecuador, Panama, Paraguay, Guatemala, Peru, Bolivia, Mozambique, Kenya

Another inverse correlation with plant food consumption appears. It is most obvious for percent of Calories from plant food rather than grams of vegetable fat per person per day. Vegetable fat is not a health promoter, either.

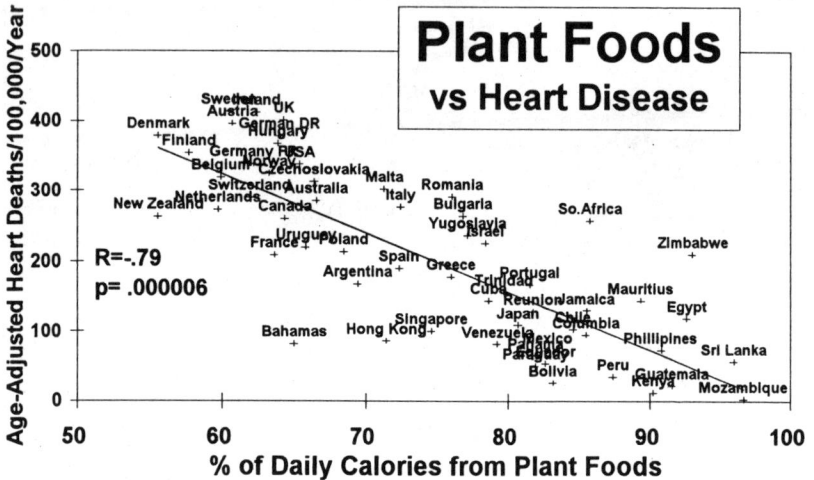

Plant Foods vs Heart Disease

R=-.79
p= .000006

(Y-axis: Age-Adjusted Heart Deaths/100,000/Year, 0 to 500)
(X-axis: % of Daily Calories from Plant Foods, 50 to 100)

Countries plotted: Sweden, Iceland, Austria, UK, Denmark, Germany DR, Finland, Hungary, Germany RFSA, Belgium, Norway, Czechoslovakia, Malta, Switzerland, Australia, Italy, Romania, New Zealand, Netherlands, Canada, Bulgaria, So.Africa, France, Uruguay, Poland, Yugoslavia, Israel, Zimbabwe, Spain, Greece, Argentina, Trinidad, Portugal, Cuba, Reunion, Jamaica, Mauritius, Japan, Chile, Egypt, Singapore, Columbia, Bahamas, Hong Kong, Venezuela, Mexico, Phillipines, Panama, Sri Lanka, Paraguay, Bolivia, Peru, Guatemala, Kenya, Mozambique

Not surprisingly, similar inverse correlations were found for most of the following graphs, but this is somewhat trivial since the more Calories from plant food, the fewer the grams of animal fat in the diet.

Many types of cancer are related to carcinogen exposure. Animal fat increases the synthesis and excretion of carcinogenic bile acids that are made from cholesterol.[157] Simultaneously the lack of fiber in animal source food slows intestinal transit time, thus exposing the bowel lining to these carcinogens for a longer period of time, so the mucosal exposure is greater[158](next page):

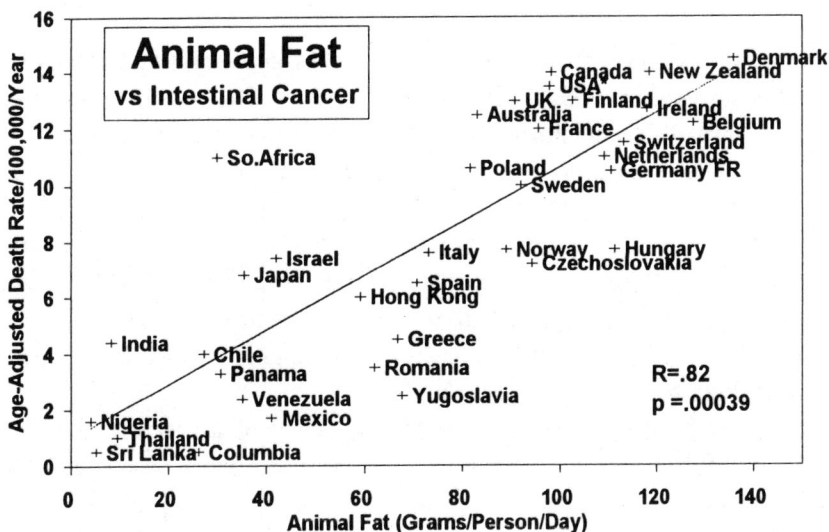

Animal Fat vs Intestinal Cancer

R=.82
p =.00039

(X-axis: Animal Fat (Grams/Person/Day); Y-axis: Age-Adjusted Death Rate/100,000/Year)

Animal fat also induces excessive and fluctuating levels of sex hormones[159] that are synthesized from fat's good buddy, the cholesterol molecule.   Most types of breast cancer are hormone dependent.[160]

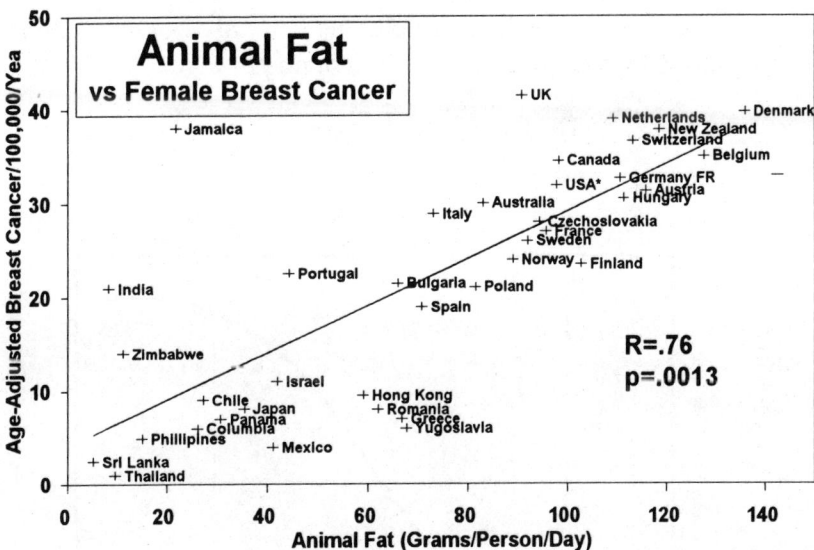

Animal Fat vs Female Breast Cancer

R=.76
p=.0013

(X-axis: Animal Fat (Grams/Person/Day); Y-axis: Age-Adjusted Breast Cancer/100,000/Yea)

Although a recent mail survey of 90,000 American nurses found no relationship between fat consumption and breast cancer, none of the women in the study were vegan (the minimum daily cholesterol intake[161] was 247 mg.) and none of them were on the 10-15% fat intake of the countries in the lower left of the above graph.[162] In effect, a study done to test the international evidence that low-fat diets protect against breast cancer omitted the key population group.

The survey has since received appropriate criticism from breast cancer specialist, Robert Kradjian, M.D.[163] A later study[164] suggests that low fat intake even reduces mortality in women who already have undergone treatment for the disease.

Furthermore, the risk vs incidence of a specific disease often follows a sigmoid curve. At low levels of individual risk nothing happens. Then as the threshold is reached disease rates rapidly increase, levelling off when risk has maximized and random chance takes over. The sigmoid curve is found throughout nature and applies to cardiovascular risk, hemoglobin dissociation, and the hysteresis curve of electromagnetism. The breast cancer researchers may have been measuring incidence rates past the maximum risk level of a sigmoid curve while linearity only appears after a summation of sigmoid curves, one from each country.

The Sigmoid Risk Curve

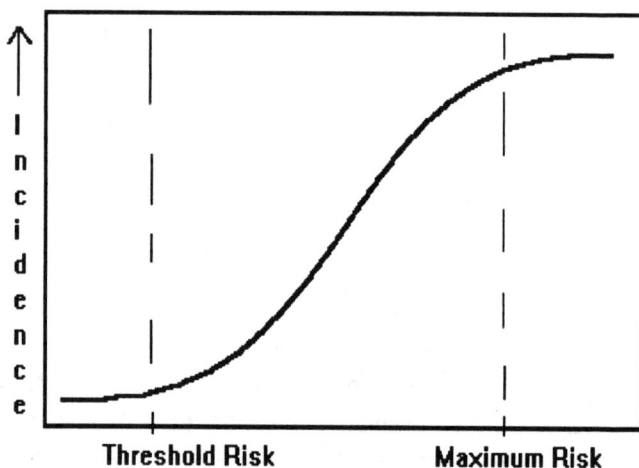

Threshold Risk   Maximum Risk

Most types of prostate cancer are also hormone dependent:[165]

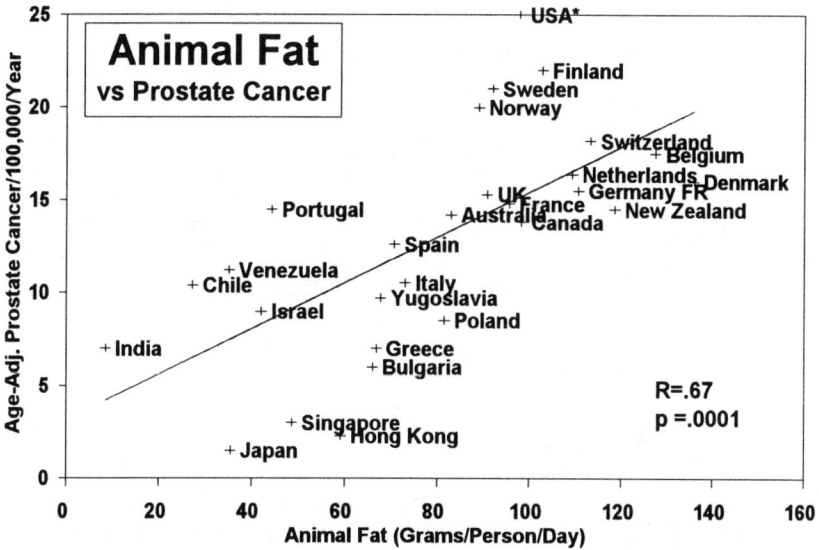

Animal Fat
vs Prostate Cancer

R=.67
p =.0001

Cancer of the womb is hormone dependent and appears to follow the same pattern:[166]

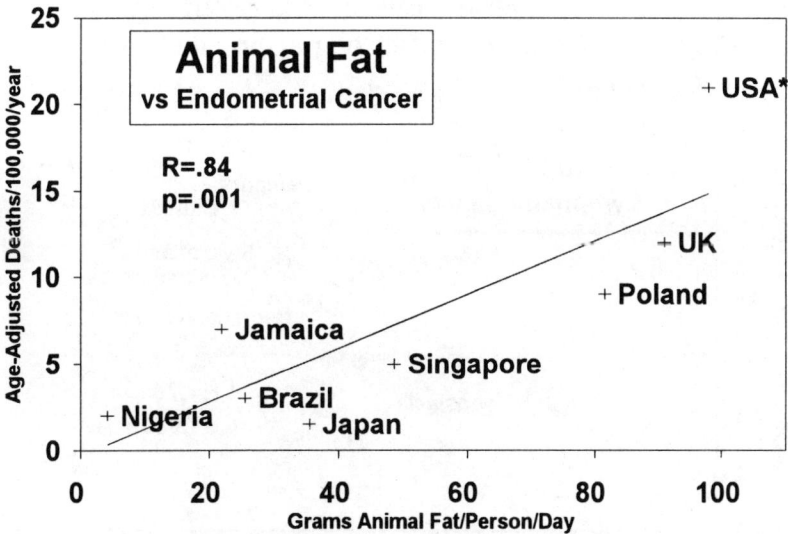

Animal Fat
vs Endometrial Cancer

R=.84
p=.001

57

A recent German study of age-matched males showed the vegetarians to have about twice the natural killer-cell activity of their omnivore controls,[167] an important factor in preventing loose tumor cells from migrating through the circulatory system looking for a new home. There is a higher aggregate death rate from cancer in populations consuming animal foods.[168,169]

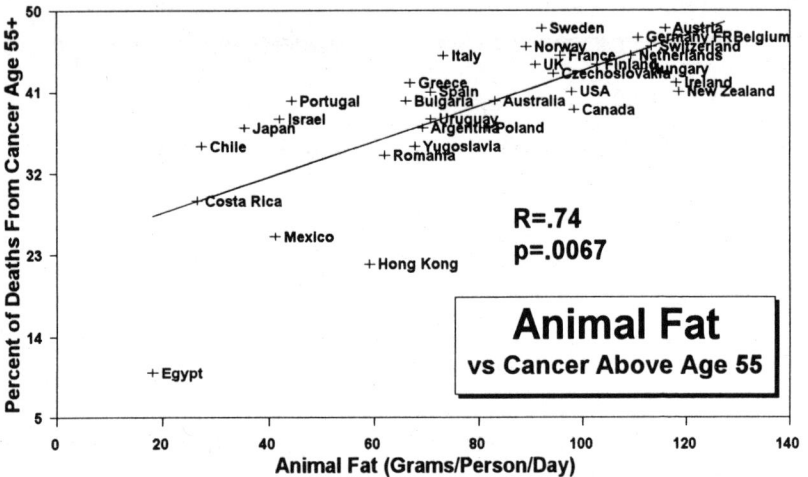

Animal Fat vs Cancer Above Age 55

R=.74
p=.0067

Beef and dairy proteins have been identified as a trigger for lymphoma (lymphatic cancer) and Hodgkins Disease, probably the "confusion" effect of protein similarity on the immune system.[170]

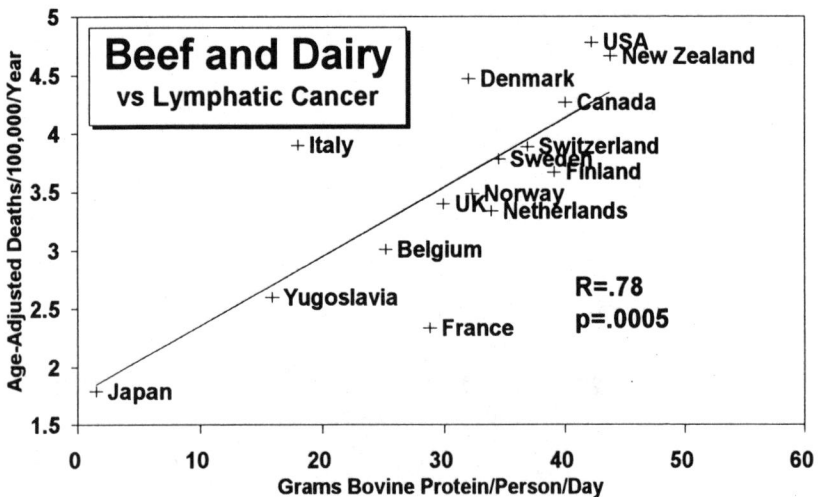

Beef and Dairy vs Lymphatic Cancer

R=.78
p=.0005

Ninety percent of insulin-dependent diabetes mellitus (IDDM) patients have antibodies to their own pancreatic islet cells.[171] A recent study reported antibodies to bovine serum albumin in 142 out of 142 newly-diagnosed IDDM patients.[172] Do fragments of animal protein induce cross-reactive antibodies? Another investigator noted a direct correlation between IDDM incidence and consumption of unfermented cow milk proteins as well as an inverse correlation with the prevalence of breast feeding.[173]

The following graph does not distinguish IDDM from adult onset (Type II) diabetes.[174]

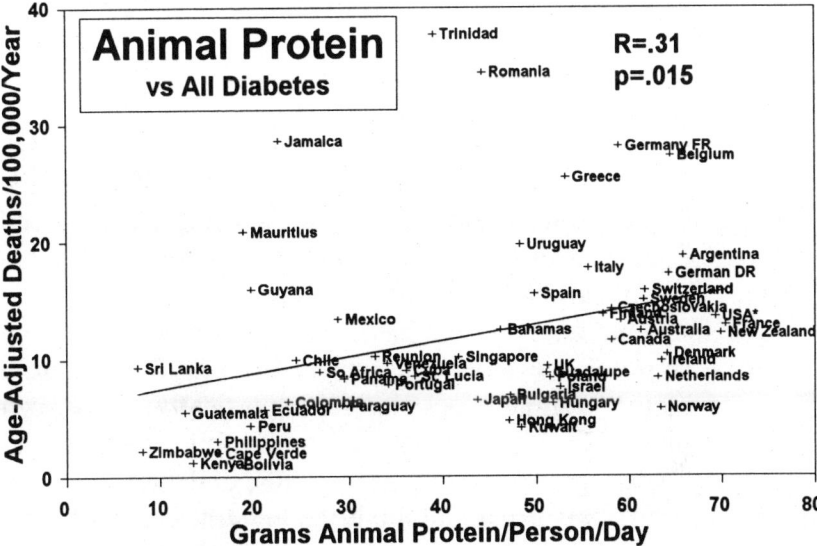

Adult onset diabetics tend to be overweight. They may have normal circulating levels of insulin but the insulin can't find its receptor site on cells. With no insulin on its receptors, the cell has no way of absorbing glucose which stays outside in the serum or spills over in the urine.

Other reported data[175] suggest a correlation of IDDM and animal fat consumption (next page).

Animal Fat
vs Insulin Dependent Diabetes Mellitus

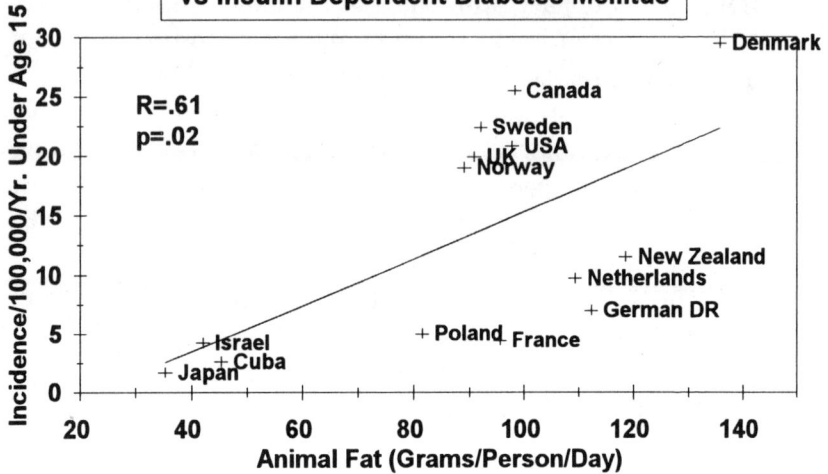

In 1954 Swank[176] reported "sludged blood" in fat-fed subjects. Photomicrographs showed a coating on red blood cells following high fat meals. Since that time at least three other investigators[177,178,179] have incidentally reported similar phenomena but an extensive literature search failed to turn up definitive proof one way or the other. If a fat (or perhaps a glycoprotein) coating does in fact transiently cover cell membranes after high fat meals, it probably hides insulin receptor sites, glucose transport proteins, and tumor antigen sites as well, thus explaining both the high incidence of Type II diabetes and metastatic cancer in obese patients.

Multiple studies[180,181] have demonstrated increased urine calcium loss on high protein diets, or diets supplemented with sulfur containing amino acids,[182] which release sulfate into the urine. Animal food is high in protein and the protein is high in sulfur amino acids (next page):[183]

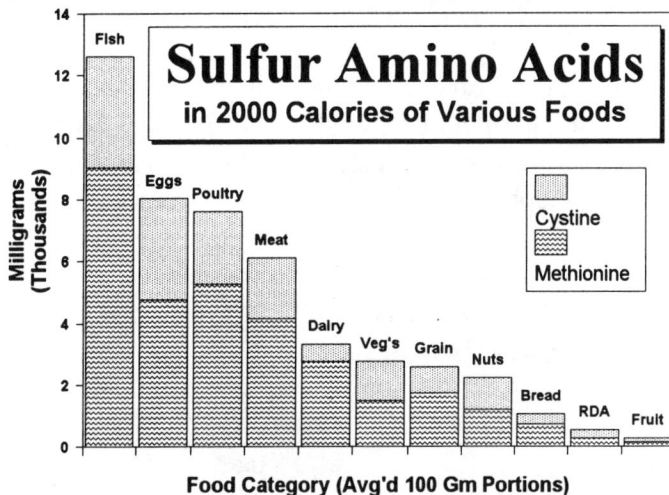

Sulfur Amino Acids
in 2000 Calories of Various Foods

Food Category (Avg'd 100 Gm Portions)

Methionine is the limiting essential amino acid in the vegan diet. Cysteine and cystine (a double cysteine), both derived from methionine,[184] are the source of urinary sulfate.[185] Inorganic sulfates (sodium, potassium, magnesium, ammonium and calcium) comprise 85-95% of urinary sulfate. High dietary sulfur aminos are associated with high losses of calcium in the urine,[186] probably because urinary sulfate must be neutralized by calcium filtered from the blood,[187] which in turn must be replaced by calcium from bone. This may contribute to osteoporosis, a condition that is reflected in the incidence of hip fracture in the elderly:[188]

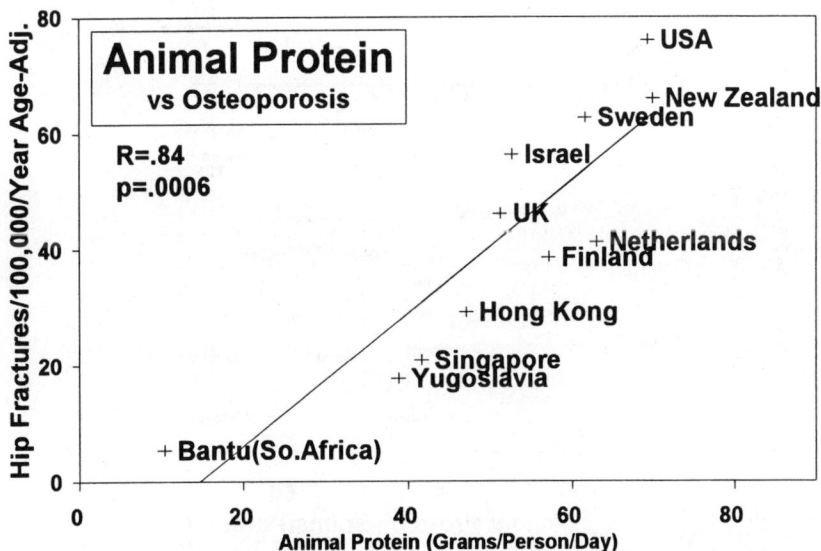

Animal Protein
vs Osteoporosis

R=.84
p=.0006

+ USA
+ New Zealand
+ Sweden
+ Israel
+ UK
+ Netherlands
+ Finland
+ Hong Kong
+ Singapore
+ Yugoslavia
+ Bantu(So.Africa)

Hip Fractures/100,000/Year Age-Adj.

Animal Protein (Grams/Person/Day)

The dairy industry states that milk calcium builds strong bones. "Animal calcium" translates to dairy products since they are the major source of calcium in the omnivorous diet.[189] The following graph fails to confirm a protective value in dairy products:

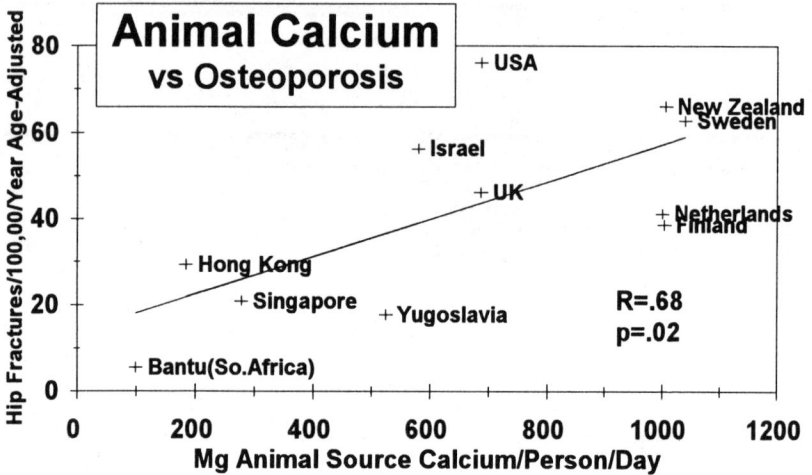

Animal Calcium vs Osteoporosis

y-axis: Hip Fractures/100,00/Year Age-Adjusted
x-axis: Mg Animal Source Calcium/Person/Day

+ USA
+ New Zealand
+ Sweden
+ Israel
+ UK
+ Netherlands
+ Finland
+ Hong Kong
+ Singapore
+ Yugoslavia
+ Bantu(So.Africa)

R=.68
p=.02

World Health Organization[190] data suggest that animal protein may not be helpful in musculo-skeletal problems either:

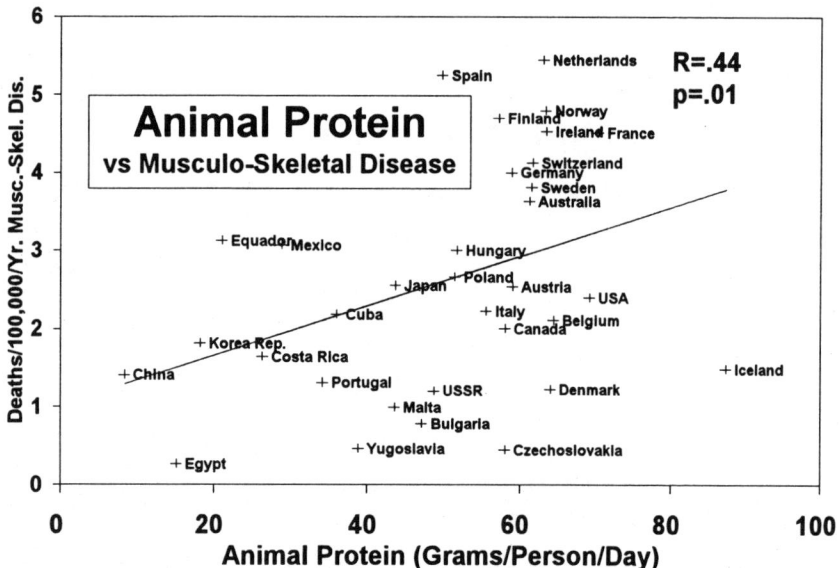

Animal Protein vs Musculo-Skeletal Disease

y-axis: Deaths/100,000/Yr. Musc.-Skel. Dis.
x-axis: Animal Protein (Grams/Person/Day)

+ Spain
+ Netherlands
+ Finland
+ Norway
+ Ireland
+ France
+ Switzerland
+ Germany
+ Sweden
+ Australia
+ Equador
+ Mexico
+ Hungary
+ Japan
+ Poland
+ Austria
+ USA
+ Cuba
+ Italy
+ Canada
+ Belgium
+ Korea Rep.
+ Costa Rica
+ China
+ Portugal
+ USSR
+ Denmark
+ Iceland
+ Malta
+ Bulgaria
+ Yugoslavia
+ Czechoslovakia
+ Egypt

R=.44
p=.01

The statistics reflect the "disease or injury that initiated the train of morbid events leading directly to death." Included in the category of musculoskeletal disease are many autoimmune diseases. Some of them, along with the affected tissues, are: rheumatoid arthritis (joints), lupus erythematosus (virtually all DNA), and scleroderma (collagen).[191] These syndromes can be fatal and therefore likely to appear on the death certificates collected by the WHO. Once again there is a negative correlation with plant food consumption:

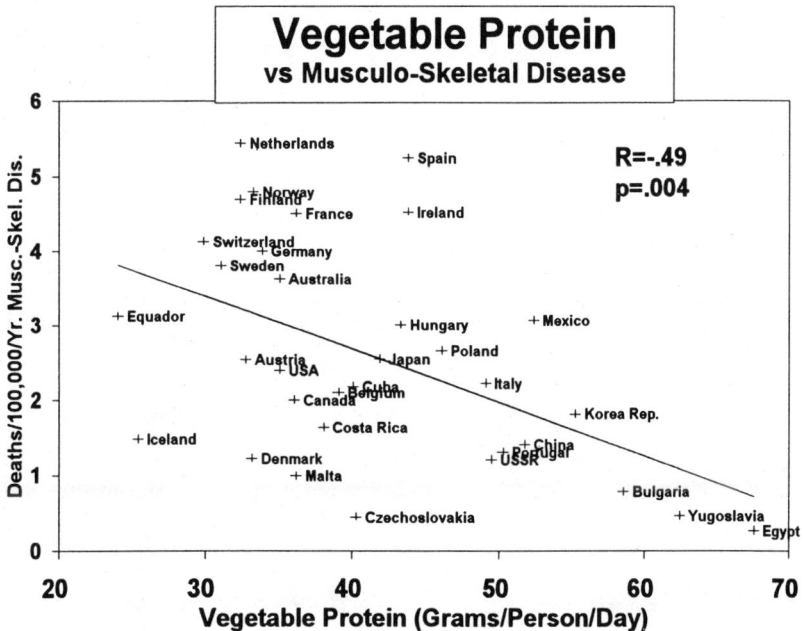

Vegetable Protein
vs Musculo-Skeletal Disease

R=-.49
p=.004

Y-axis: Deaths/100,000/Yr. Musc.-Skel. Dis.
X-axis: Vegetable Protein (Grams/Person/Day)

Data points: Netherlands, Spain, Norway, Finland, France, Ireland, Switzerland, Germany, Sweden, Australia, Equador, Hungary, Mexico, Austria, USA, Japan, Poland, Cuba, Belgium, Italy, Canada, Costa Rica, Korea Rep., Iceland, Denmark, Portugal, China, USSR, Malta, Bulgaria, Czechoslovakia, Yugoslavia, Egypt

The WHO keeps tabs on mortality from nephritis, kidney infection and "other genitourinary diseases," that occur downstream from the glomerulus, the likely site of the initial insult.

Nephritis is generally due to an antigen-antibody (ag-ab) reaction in the filtering membrane of the kidney glomerulus.[192] The membrane becomes thickened and less permeable. As the microscopic filtering "pores" (about 4-8 nm dia.) become fewer, they lose the negative electrical charge that previously prevented the leakage of negatively charged proteins such as albumin.[193] The result is protein loss, edema, a change in

63

urine output, chemical imbalances, and uremia.

One type of nephritis, due to IgA immuno-globulins, is aggravated by cow's milk[194] but classically, glomerulonephritis follows about ten days after streptococcal infection.[195] In this case the ag-ab reaction is a response to the strep antigens. Strep cultures best in lab media containing blood agar[196] so the graph may reflect in part that omnivores are feeding not only themselves but some of their major pathogens.   However, only a fraction of reported nephritis can be traced to strep infection.

Egypt has the highest incidence of genitourinary (GU) disease recorded by the WHO[197] but its "outlier" position reflects schistosomiasis, a parasitic blood fluke transmitted by fresh water snails and associated with bladder cancer.   The Nile formerly flooded annually and wiped out the snails but the Aswan High Dam was completed in 1970 and the snail is now common in irrigation ditches.[198] This is not diet-related so we can remove Egypt from the data and get the graph below:

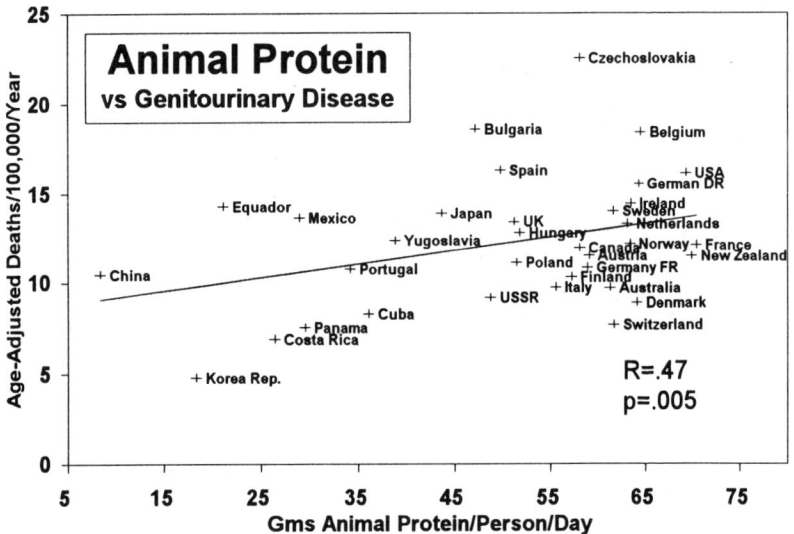

Animal Protein vs Genitourinary Disease

R=.47
p=.005

64

The cause of renal failure is often not established but the current dietary regime for this condition is a low protein diet. Since protein is being lost in the urine, whatever protein is allowed is supposed to of "high biological value."[199]   But if renal failure is the end stage of an autoimmune reaction triggered by the amino acid sequence of animal protein, this is the equivalent of trying to put out a fire by throwing gasoline on it. Barsotti has shown that in at least one type of renal disease (nephrosis), a vegan diet maintains serum proteins adequately and improves kidney function.[200]   The gold standard for protein is egg protein[201]   but WHO data suggest that eggs have an even more adverse effect on nephritis and pyelonephritis (kidney infection)[202] than does animal protein in general:

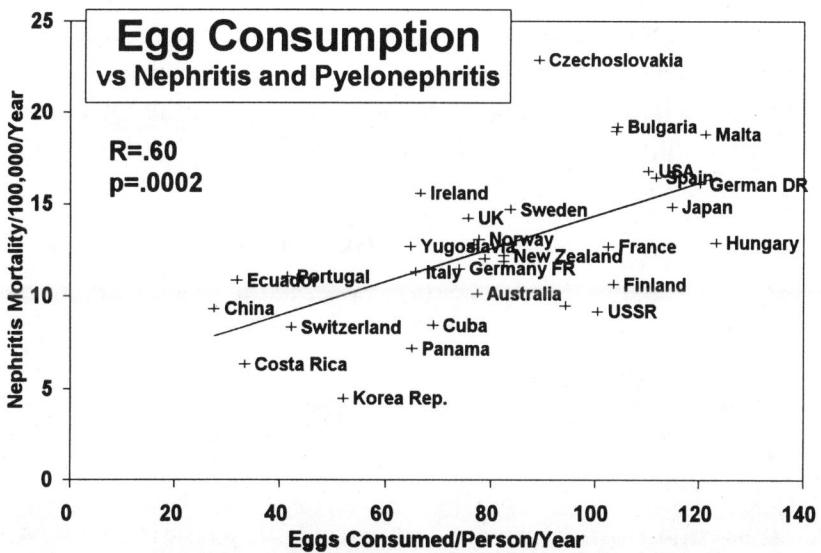

**Egg Consumption
vs Nephritis and Pyelonephritis**

R=.60
p=.0002

Nephritis Mortality/100,000/Year (y-axis)
Eggs Consumed/Person/Year (x-axis)

+ Czechoslovakia
+ Bulgaria + Malta
+ Spain + German DR
+ Ireland
+ UK + Sweden + Japan
+ Yugoslavia + Norway + France + Hungary
+ New Zealand
+ Ecuador + Portugal + Italy + Germany FR
+ China + Australia + Finland
+ Switzerland + Cuba + USSR
+ Costa Rica + Panama
+ Korea Rep.

Egg white is number three on the list of pediatric food allergies, below cow milk and wheat,[203] so its amino acid sequence is sensitizing.

The American Heart Association reported $88 billion for heart disease[204] in 1988 which was price indexed for a 1991

65

figure of $94.79 billion.

Cancer costs run about $103 billion/yr.[205]   Costs for each type of cancer shown in the graphs were estimated by the formula: Cost= type/total x $103 billion using American Cancer Society figures.[206]

Musculo-skeletal disease costs were approximated from figures of the Arthritis Foundation,[207] which includes gout as a common type of arthritis.   Gout is related to consumption of high-purine organ meats.

Genito-urinary disease costs are based on figures from the Public Health Service.[208]

The American Diabetes Association quoted $85 billion for their disease.[209]

Medical costs of osteoporosis are put between $7-10 billion/year.[210]

Multiple regression analysis would include other risk factors such as inactivity, smoking, and genetic risk, but the necessary data could not be found.   Therefore, the total costs were multiplied by R^2 which is roughly that part of each disease figure that can be attributed to the dietary risk.[211]

DISEASE vs ANIMAL SOURCE FOOD

Y (Disease)	X (Specific Animal Ingredient)	p	R	R-Sq'	Cost ($Bil/yr)	Cost x R-Sq' ($Bil/y)
Cardiovascular Dis.	Fat (+Cholesterol)	0.000004	0.76	0.58	94.79	54.75
Intestinal Cancer	Fat	0.00039	0.82	0.67	19.66	13.22
Genito-Urinary Disease	Protein	0.005	0.47	0.22	50.00	11.05
Breast Cancer	Fat	0.0013	0.76	0.58	18.09	10.45
Diabetes Mellitus	Fat, Protein	0.015	0.31	0.10	85.00	8.17
Musculo-Skeletal Disease	Protein	0.01	0.44	0.19	35.00	6.78
Osteoporotic Fractures	Protein	0.0006	0.84	0.71	8.50	6.00
Prostate Cancer	Fat	0.0001	0.67	0.45	11.91	5.34
Lymphatic Cancer	Bovine Protein	0.0005	0.78	0.61	6.31	3.84
Endometrial Cancer	Fat	0.001	0.84	0.71	3.19	2.25
Venous Thrombosis	Fat	0.007	0.93	0.86	1.37	1.19
Totals					$334	$123

This figure, $123 billion (21% of the medical budget actually going for patient care and about 2% of the GNP), is probably a very conservative estimate since the U.S. Surgeon

General's Report on Nutrition and Health[212] indicates that about 69% of U.S. mortality is diet-related.

Estimated U.S Medical Costs
Resulting from Animal Source Food

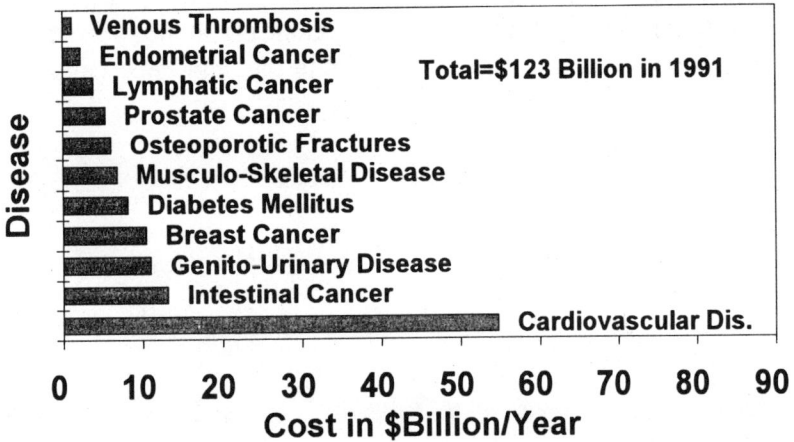

Venous Thrombosis
Endometrial Cancer   Total=$123 Billion in 1991
Lymphatic Cancer
Prostate Cancer
Osteoporotic Fractures
Musculo-Skeletal Disease
Diabetes Mellitus
Breast Cancer
Genito-Urinary Disease
Intestinal Cancer
                            Cardiovascular Dis.

Disease

0   10   20   30   40   50   60   70   80   90
Cost in $Billion/Year

The figure of $123 billion for animal food consumption can be compared with the American Lung Association's estimate for the cost of tobacco use[213] ($65 billion) and the Center for Science in the Public Interest's estimates for the cost of alcohol consumption[214] ($100 billion).

The $123 billion estimate does not include several other food-related problems. For instance, obesity correlates with animal fat consumption but is not included in the estimate. Although it may account for 20% of annual mortality[215] it does so by predisposing to many diseases, including the ones already shown. Ovarian cancer has been linked to galactose (milk sugar) consumption[216] but the WHO does not keep statistics on incidence rates so it is omitted from the estimate. Childhood otitis media is linked to cow milk allergy[217] and although it affects ten million children with an estimated $2 billion/year cost, it also is omitted for lack of WHO incidence data.

This analysis will be attacked on the grounds of

spurious correlation, *e.g.* the cause of all these diseases is not animal source food but the sedentary lifestyles, longer life expectancies, or perhaps some unexpected factor such as television access of the populations in the developed countries. Critics will also argue that medical diagnoses are less accurate in the under-developed countries. However, the figures were already age-adjusted by the reporting authors, and while correlation does not prove causality, each graph was referenced to sources that confirm and illuminate the suggested causality.

VIII. HORSES AND ZEBRAS

"Common diseases commonly occur most commonly. Uncommon diseases commonly occur most uncommonly. If you hear hoofbeats on the lawn, it's probably a horse, not a zebra. "

-old diagnostic adage.

Chapter VII. focussed on the horses.

The zebras are infectious diseases seldom seen in Western countries. Most of them are tied to major lapses in common-sense hygiene: fecal contamination of the water supply (amebic dysentery), an indifference to the presence of biting insects (malaria, sleeping sickness) and human overcrowding (rat-borne typhus). The medical treatment of the zebras is often cheap and effective, but the zebras seldom occur in the U.S.

There are at least 122 *zoonoses*, zebra-type diseases transmitted from animals to man.[218] Omitting the ones not transmitted by food and adding a few super-zebras transmitted by plant foods, we get the list below.[219]

ORGANISMS SPREAD BY ANIMAL SOURCE FOOD.

<u>Parasites:</u> (life cycles abbreviated →)

Anisakis simplex.[220] Sashimi.
Gastrointestinal worm. Epigastric pain, bleeding.
(crustaceans → fish → human gut → eggs in feces → crustacean)

Capillaria philippinensis. Raw fish.
An intestinal worm. Rarely fatal liver disease.
(Raw fish → human gut → eggs in feces → fish)

Clonorchis sinensis. Raw fish.
Chinese liver fluke. Occasional liver disease.
(Snail → raw fish → human bile duct → eggs in feces → snail)

Adult   *Clonorchis   sinensis*   Egg

69

Dioctophyma renale. Raw fish.
Giant kidney worm disease. Occasional uremia.
(Eggs in urine → annelid worm → raw fish → human gut →
worm burrows to kidney → eggs in urine)

Diphyllobothrium latum. Raw fish.
Fish tapeworm. Occ. vitamin B_{12} deficiency, obstruction.
(Crustacean → raw fish → tapeworm in human gut → eggs in
feces → crustacean)

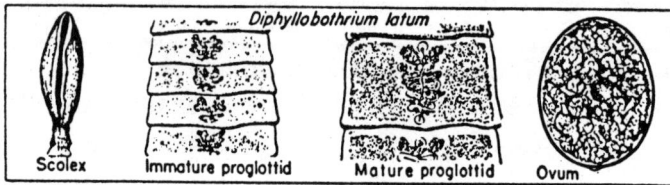

Diphyllobothrium latum

Scolex | Immature proglottid | Mature proglottid | Ovum

Echinostoma species. Undercooked snails.
Mild intestinal worm infection. Enteritis, ulceration.
(Raw snail → fish → human gut → eggs in feces → snail)

Gnathostoma spinigerum.[221]
(Undercooked fish, fowl, frogs, pork → human gut → larval migration to
skin, eye, lung, brain. Cycle stops.)

Opisthorchis species. Raw fish.
Mild liver fluke infection. Jaundice, cirrhosis.
(Raw fish → human bile duct → feces → snails → fish)

Paragonimus westermani. Raw crab.
Lung fluke disease. Bloody cough, occ. paraplegia as fluke migrates to
brain and spinal cord.
(Raw crab → human gut → lung → coughed up, swallowed → eggs in feces
→ snail → crab)

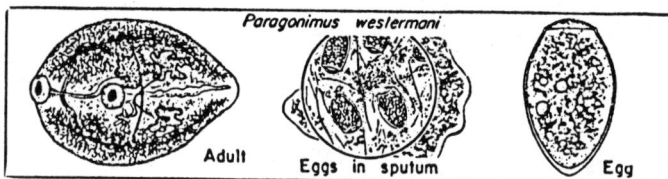

Paragonimus westermani

Adult | Eggs in sputum | Egg

Taenia saginata. Undercooked beef.
Beef tapeworm. Usually benign. Occ. brain damage from burrowing larvae.
(Encysted eggs in raw beef → human gut → intestinal tapeworm → eggs in
feces → cattle)

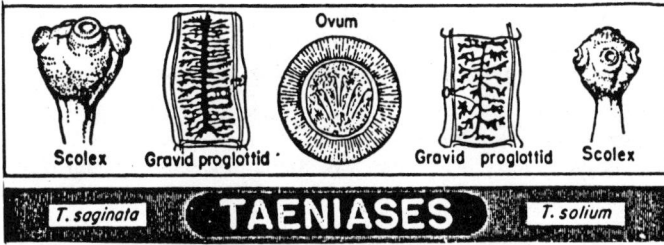

Scolex | Gravid proglottid · | Ovum | Gravid proglottid | Scolex

TAENIASES

T. saginata | T. solium

Taenia Solium. Undercooked pork.
Pork tapeworm. Same cycle as T. saginata, only pigs.

Trichinella spiralis. Raw pork, horse, bear meat.
Trichinosis, a severe roundworm infection. Pain and weakness. Calcified cysts in muscle. ~300 cases/yr. Fatality rate 5%.
(Cysts in raw meat hatch → larvae migrate into muscle, encyst there)

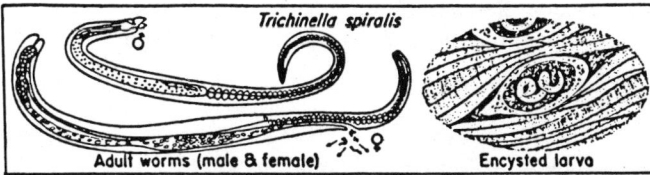

Trichinella spiralis
Adult worms (male & female) | Encysted larva

Protozoa:

Cryptosporidium. Raw milk.
Cryptosporidiosis. Diarrhea, abdominal pain.

Toxoplasma gondii. Raw meat, goat's milk.
Toxoplasmosis. Usually asymptomatic but can cause brain damage in children.

Bacteria:

Brucella species. Raw, contaminated dairy foods.
Brucellosis. Fever and malaise.

Campylobacter species. Raw milk, chicken.
Campylobacteriosis. Abdominal pain and bloody diarrhea.

Corynebacterium ulcerans. Contaminated milk.
Pharyngitis, diphtheria (rarely).
Escherichia coli, serotype 0157:H7. Raw milk and beef.
Hemorrhagic colitis. Diarrhea and abdominal pain.

71

Listeria monocytogenes. Milk, refrigerated cheese.
Listeriosis. Meningitis, pneumonia, endocarditis, abscesses.

Mycobacterium bovis. Raw milk.
Bovine tuberculosis. Similar to human TB. Slow, progressive, fatal disease
if untreated.

Salmonella species (> 1000 serotypes). Milk, poultry, eggs.
Salmonellosis. Usually a self-limiting watery diarrhea. This zebra is almost
a horse. In 1974 the organism was found in 90% of inspected chicken
carcasses.[222] About 50,000 cases are reported yearly in the U.S.[223]

Streptobacillary species. Contaminated milk.
Streptobacillary fever. Fever, malaise, endocarditis, arthritis.

Streptococcus species. Raw milk.
Streptococcosis. Fever, occ. meningitis. Fatality rate 8% for
S. suis.

Vibrio species. Usually transmitted by contaminated water, but linked to
ingestion of raw shellfish[224] in ten U.S. cases in 1991.
Cholera. Profuse, watery diarrhea, occ. death within hours.

Yersinia species. Raw milk, pork, cheese.
Yersiniosis. Abdominal pain and diarrhea.

Rickettsial: (size between a bacterium and a virus)

Coxiella burnetti. Raw milk.
Q fever. Pneumonia and endocarditis.
A great flap occurred over this one in Los Angeles in the 60's between the
health department and parents who believed raw milk was healthier than
pasteurized since the enzymes were still active. It's unlikely that enzymes
have any bearing on nutrition since they are copolymers, usually proteins,
and are digested prior to absorption. The kids would likely have been better
off without any milk.

Viral:

Hepatitis A virus. While it can be acquired in other ways, in Hawaii
shellfish are an affirmed risk factor in about 15% of cases.[225] Total U.S.
cases ~32,000 in 1989.[226]
Fever, malaise, jaundice.

Picornaviradae virus. Frozen meat.
Foot and mouth disease. Mild blistering of lips, mouth, extremities (1-2 week duration).

ORGANISMS SPREAD BY PLANT FOOD.

Parasites:

Dicrocoelium dendriticum. Ants on raw vegetables.
Dicroceliasis. Mild worm infection of bile ducts.
(Feces → snail → "slime balls" (eaten by ants) → humans accidentally eat the ants crawling on fresh vegetables)

Echinococcus granulosus. Dogs and foxes are the final hosts but eggs can contaminate the outside of vegetables.
Hydatid disease. Liver and lung cysts with jaundice and cough, often fatal.

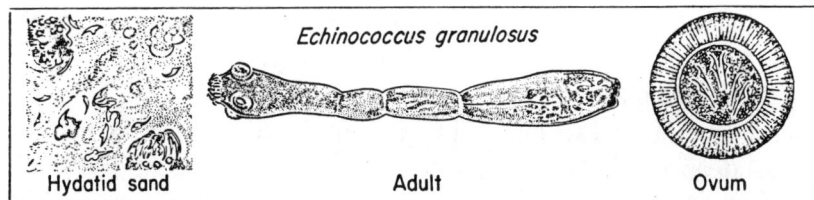

Echinococcus granulosus

Hydatid sand   Adult   Ovum

Fasciola hepatica. Intermediate form of parasite encysts on water plants.
Fascioliasis. Liver fluke disease. Jaundice and liver pain. (Herbivores → eggs in feces → snail → intermediate form encysts on plant leaves (e.g. watercress) → ingested and migrate to liver)

Gastrodiscoides hominis. Water plants.
A flatworm infection of the human cecum and colon. Local inflammation. (Eggs pass in feces → snail → intermediate form encysts on aquatic plants → humans infected by eating the plants)

Protozoa:

Entamoeba histolytica. Usually in contaminated water, but vegetables fertilized by human manure also transmit.
Amebic dysentery. Bloody diarrhea.

The score: Animal foods 28, plant foods 5.   Most of

the animal food organisms are actively exploiting the metabolic shelters of the animal hosts. The plant food organisms extract no metabolic support from the plant, and are present largely as accidental contaminants.

It can't be argued that these unpleasant guests represent a major reason to go vegan; the cholesterol and saturated fat dependably present in that daily piece of beef will plug your arteries long before the occasional beef tapeworm causes a mild intestinal malaise.

Nevertheless, there are grounds for contemplation. Most higher organisms have microbes and parasites that over a 500 million year period have adapted to their host's "internal milieu." Nature puts up "no off limits" signs; our most private and romantic parts are regarded as fair game by the gonococcus and the spirochete, but they, of course, are not transmitted by food. Of the organisms that are, it's not surprising to find that they also find places to hide in our fellow animals.

Out of 116 laboratory culture media used to grow and isolate bacteria that cause human disease, 97 contain blood, serum, brain, heart, bile, eggs, and other animal material.[227] By contrast, only 1 out of 9 media used to grow bacteria that cause plant disease uses animal material (beef extract).[228] In short, humans are unlikely to get oak wilt by eating acorns, and tapeworms can't live in trees.

Even the most fastidious vegan is a walking bacterial culture medium, a treasure trove of microorganisms looking for a break. Unlike omnivores, however, the vegan does not enhance that break by eating the stuff the bugs love best.

TOXIC CONDITIONS.

Animal Foods:

Gambierdiscus toxicus. Reef fish, cooked *or* raw.
Ciguatoxin (CTX) originates in this plankton which is eaten and concentrated 100 times in the fish.[229] CTX opens sodium channels in nerve cells causing numbness, tingling, reversal of temperature sensation, and abdominal pain. If not fatal, symptoms may persist for months. In Hawaii ~33 cases/yr.

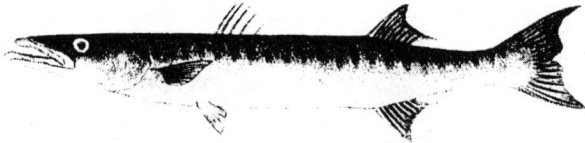

Barracuda (Sphyraena barracuda). Sporadically poisonous in a few tropical localities.

Protogonyaulax catanella. Clams, oysters, and scallops.
Saxitoxin originates in this plankton and is passed on to human gourmets. Paralytic shellfish poisoning. Fatality rate 8%.

Scombroid fish poisoning. Fish has the highest content of the amino acid histidine, of any food. Bacteria readily degrade histidine to histamine and saurine. Symptoms: Headache, peri-oral numbness, peppery taste, and a rash. Mild hives occur frequently by a similar mechanism after eating fish and shrimp.

Staphylococcus species. Food poisoning. Staph grows best in meats and dairy. It produces an enterotoxin that causes a severe, short term gastroenteritis, mostly vomiting.

Plant Foods:

Aspergillus flavus. Aflatoxin. This fungus in peanut meal stored in hot, humid places, produces a substance that induces liver cancer.

Claviceps purpurea. Ergot. This fungus may grow on rye, producing an alkaloid that stimulates smooth muscle in arterioles, intestines, and uterus. While one author suggests ergotism may have been the real cause of the Black Plague of the 14th century[230] (usually attributed to *Pasteurella pestis*), toxicity now is rare.

75

Clostridium botulinum. This bacillus produces a neurotoxin that blocks acetylcholine in nerve endings, leading to respiratory paralysis and death. Famously attributed to improper home vegetable canning, botulism has also been linked to ingestion of honey,[231] and fish intestines.[232]

While a laundry list of plant toxins could be drawn up, (e.g. toadstools, hemlock, castor beans, foxglove), most reflect innate plant metabolism rather than parasitic contamination. People generally have enough sense to avoid hemlock but they continue to dally with animal food in spite of its preponderance in the above lists.

Death cap
Amanita phalloides

Fly agaric
Amanita muscaria

FURTHER CONDITIONS ONLY AN EMERGENCY PHYSICIAN WOULD NOTICE.

Animal Foods:

We should not leave without mentioning the ubiquitous fishbone in the throat, a first magnitude nuisance for both patient and doctor, who must perform acts of hand-eye legerdemain with mirror and forceps to locate and extract the fishbone. Large pieces of meat often stick in the esophagus, requiring operative removal, while wolfed plant food usually digests enough to go down by itself.

In a cardiac arrest, the ER doc frequently gets a regurgitated display of the patient's prior meal which usually includes chunks of meat. It's less likely the patient choked on the meat ("The Cafe Coronary") than that the saturated fat and cholesterol plugged the heart's capillary circulation, usually about 3-4 hours after dinner.

Plant Foods:

While pediatric texts warn of the dangers of children aspirating and choking on beans and peanuts, this is a rarity. Kids prefer to stick these items in their noses and ears.

IX. THE FARM FOLLIES

The statistics are difficult if not impossible to interpret: the leavings of 60 years of Byzantine political meddling in a process better left to the free market. Furthermore, one must rely on figures given out by the United States Department of Agriculture, in effect asking the fox for a resumé of his activities in the henhouse. Veteran USDA employees admitted that even after 25 year's service and new farm bills every five years, they still didn't understand the system. If anything ever just grew like Topsy, it's the USDA price support program, financed by the Commodities Credit Corporation (CCC) since 1933,[233] and pushed this way and that by generations of special interest politicians. The program claims to help small farmers, but most of the help actually goes to farmers whose income already exceeds that of the average American.[234]

From the time of the Civil War to World War I, U.S. agriculture expanded due to technical advances. But as the food supply went up, prices went down. The notion of shielding farmers from market forces peaked after World War I. During that conflagration European agriculture closed down and U.S. farmers cleaned up selling crops overseas. After the war the market dropped back to normal, but the farmers argued in Congress that legislation should guarantee farmers "parity" with non-agricultural workers rather than let normal market forces reduce the total number of farmers. Special interest politicians, ever mindful of their next campaign chest, were only too happy to oblige.

Price supports take the form of "non-recourse loans" to farmers. If it's a good market year, the farmer pays off the loan and sells his crop on the free market at a price above the support price, pocketing the difference. If it's a bad year, the farmer defaults on the loan and the USDA has no recourse but to take the farmer's crop as collateral, paying him the legislated support price in the form of the defaulted loan. The crop surplus is then dumped into food programs for the needy or foreign "aid" programs[235] ($20 billion worth from 1954-

1970)[236] that frequently cripple emerging agricultural systems.

In the great 1995 flap over cutting school lunch programs, no mention was made that these are also a major USDA dumping ground for consistently fat food.

Average price supports from 1980-1991 are shown below.[237]

Commodities Credit Corporation
USDA Price Supports for Agriculture

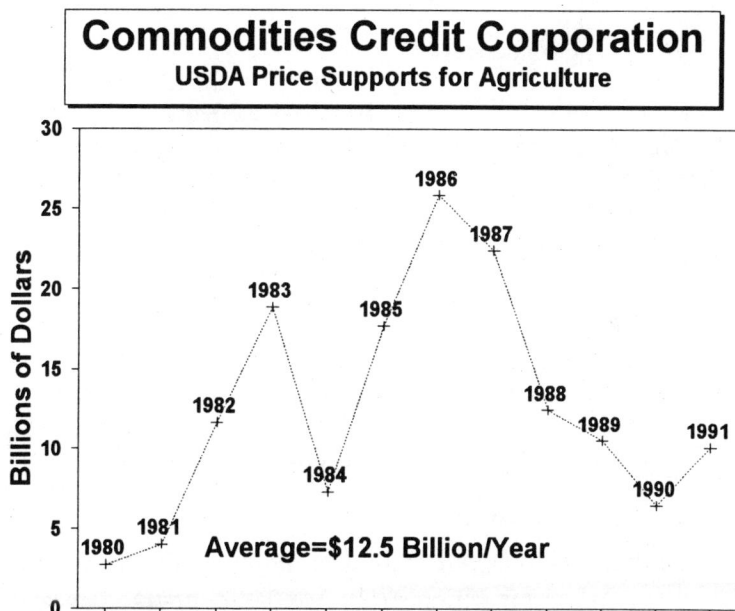

Although full understanding of USDA five-year-average crop acreage base (CAB) rules requires a command of several languages that did not originate on Earth, it appears the rules discourage crop rotation.[238] Without crop rotation more fertilizers and pesticides must be used. The USDA's Rube Goldberg school of agricultural economics then allows dairy farmers to collect indemnity payments for milk contaminated by pesticides.[239]

One thing seems straightforward, however. Fruits and vegetables, among the foods most essential to human health get no price supports:[240] "All crops may be harvested on flex acreage except...fruits and vegetables..."[241] By contrast USDA price supports and freebies go to 21 agricultural products, almost all either superfluous or actively injurious to human health, including animal feed grains, the dairy industry, sugar, and tobacco[242] in the amounts shown below:[243,244]

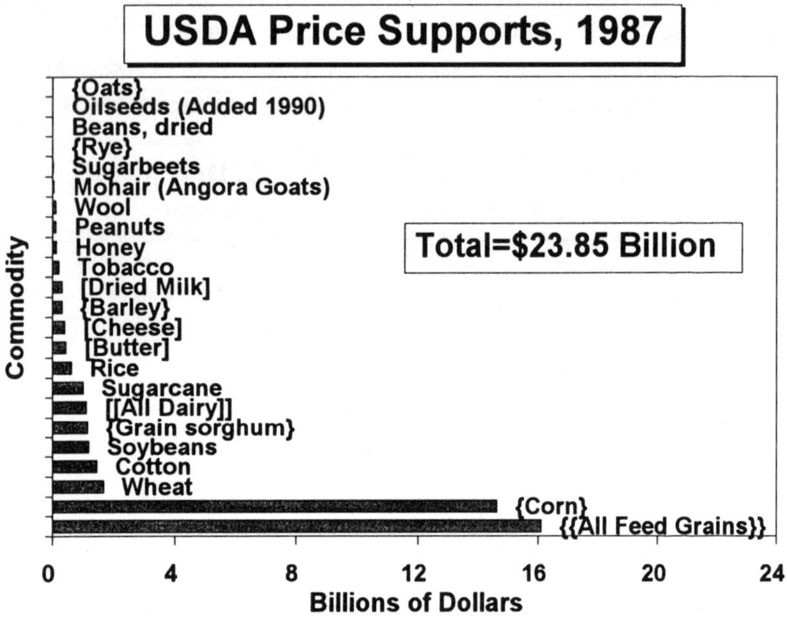
USDA Price Supports, 1987
{Oats}
Oilseeds (Added 1990)
Beans, dried
{Rye}
Sugarbeets
Mohair (Angora Goats)
Wool
Peanuts
Honey
Tobacco
[Dried Milk]
{Barley}
[Cheese]
[Butter]
Rice
Sugarcane
[[All Dairy]]
{Grain sorghum}
Soybeans
Cotton
Wheat
{Corn}
{{All Feed Grains}}
Total=$23.85 Billion
Commodity
0
4
8
12
16
20
24
Billions of Dollars

Mohair, and wool supports amount to government backing against competition from synthetic fibers. Cotton supports would appear to be more of the same but cotton seed meal becomes animal feed and cottonseed oil is used by the food industry.

Dairy prices are set above market-clearing levels. As a result, farmers produce more dairy products than the public will buy. In 1981, a $3 billion surplus was bought by the CCC, and sold for animal feed or given away. In 1986, 1.6 million cows were slaughtered in an attempt to reduce the surplus. The carcasses were dumped on the meat market and cattlemen saw *their* prices drop 15% as a result.[245] The dairy and pharmaceutical industries now want to increase production still more with synthetic bovine growth hormone, even though the dairy market is already flooded.[246]

The dairy lobby expanded its power in Washington from 1967 to 1977. With laundered political contributions averaging $6.9 million/year, the dairymen pressured for 90% parity (90% of the buying power dairy farmers enjoyed from 1910 to 1914). The recipients included Jimmy Carter (already a millionaire as a result of USDA peanut subsidies), Dick Clark, John Connally, James Eastland, Walter Huddleston, Hubert Humphrey, Lyndon Johnson, Wilbur Mills, and Herman Talmadge. At the time of his resignation, Richard Nixon, if not brought down by Watergate, would likely have faced charges from involvement not only in the Ellsberg break-in, and ITT, but also payola from the dairy lobby.[247]

Sugar has been on the dole since 1789, since the U.S. has a poor climate for sugar, and can be grown more economically in sub-tropical countries.[248] Sugar is nutritionally *worthless*: concentrated carbohydrate which should be applied to the teeth only at places where you desire holes to appear. Honey is not much better, but honey supports are almost equal to the market value of honey.[249] If tastebuds are to be appeased, fruit is a much more nutritious choice:[250,251]

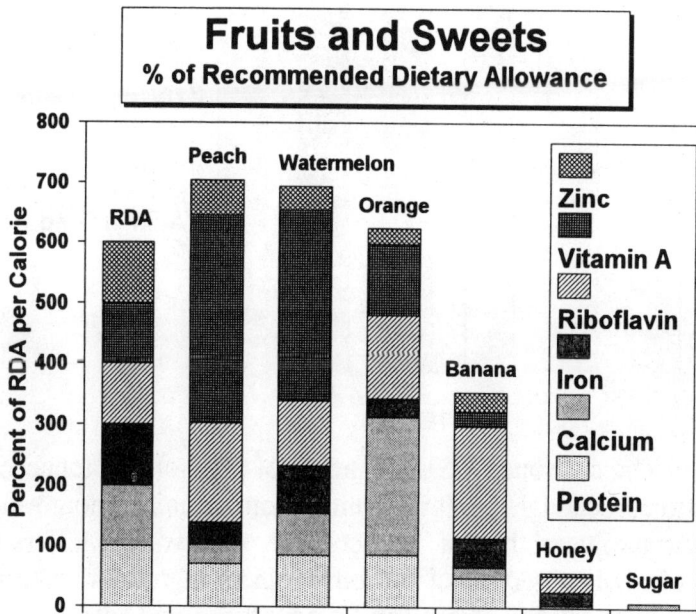

Fruits and Sweets
% of Recommended Dietary Allowance

Oil seeds (canola, flaxseed, mustard seed, rapeseed, safflower, soybean, and sunflower), were added to the support list in 1990.[252] Some of these seeds are nutritious if eaten whole, but the oils made from them are not essential to humans, and there is no evidence that pure liquid fat is of any benefit other than gustatory.

Peanuts are a reasonable food source, providing spoilage has not added aflatoxin, but most of the crop is turned into peanut oil and mash for animal feed.

Distilled spirits and beer are made from USDA price-supported feed grains. Barley and rye are the major contributors, but corn, rice, sorghum, and wheat are also used.[253,254] BATF data suggest that Uncle Sam indirectly spends about $80 million/year to make booze.

Percent Usage
USDA Price Supported Grain (1992)

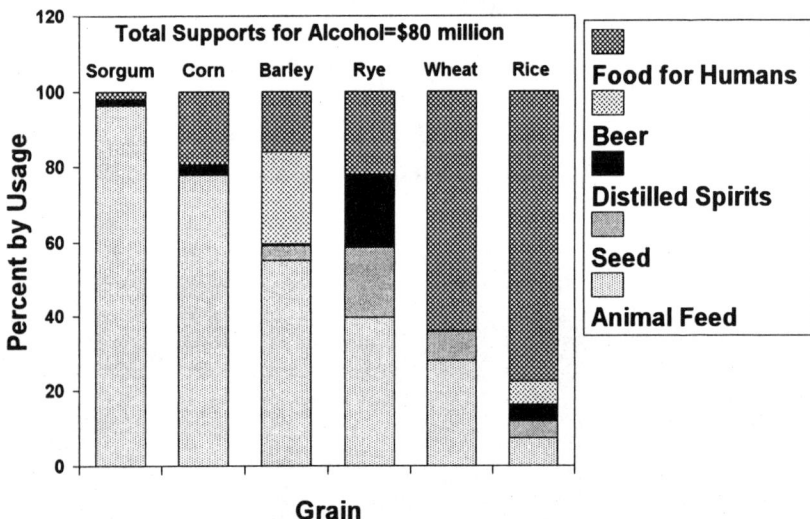

The continued USDA support of alcohol and tobacco is a national scandal. While political opportunists mount their war on marijuana, heroin, and cocaine, the two real killers (in 1990 alcohol caused $46.1 billion worth of highway crashes[255]) are not only subsidized but can be advertised and sold over the counter.

"Food processing is indispensable to animal agriculture in America," in the words of author Robin Hur.[256]   While breads, breakfast cereals, corn chips, pastries, and other grain products are ostensibly plant foods, there's a flip side.   The food processing companies buy raw material from one source, the field crop farmers,   but sell the resultant products on several markets.   Animal feed is one market:[257]

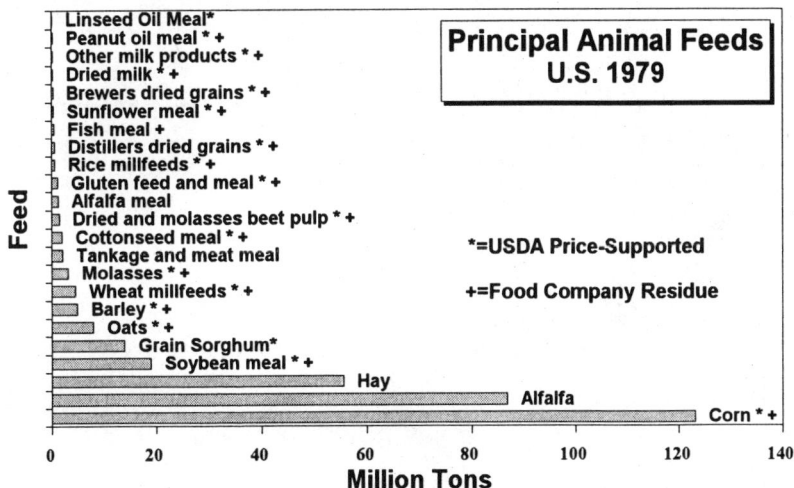

Principal Animal Feeds
U.S. 1979

Linseed Oil Meal*
Peanut oil meal * +
Other milk products * +
Dried milk * +
Brewers dried grains * +
Sunflower meal * +
Fish meal +
Distillers dried grains * +
Rice millfeeds * +
Gluten feed and meal * +
Alfalfa meal
Dried and molasses beet pulp * +
Cottonseed meal * +
Tankage and meat meal
Molasses * +
Wheat millfeeds * +
Barley * +
Oats * +
Grain Sorghum*
Soybean meal * +
Hay
Alfalfa
Corn * +

*=USDA Price-Supported

+=Food Company Residue

Feed

0   20   40   60   80   100   120   140
Million Tons

In the above graph, * denotes an animal feed that received USDA price supports, and + denotes a feed that is the residue after the food companies have worked it over, usually extracting refined grain products or pure vegetable oil for human consumption, and passing the rest on as animal feed.   Absent from the graph are horticultural crops such as apples, broccoli, or kale. These foods are specifically excluded from USDA price supports[258] and are grown primarily for human consumption, although some of the residues also become animal feed.

Top food companies start with inexpensive grain crops that often have been grown primarily for use as animal feed. As an example, USDA price supports for corn, the major animal feed grain, in 1987 came to $14.64 billion[259] but only 3% of the crop was for human consumption;[260] the rest went for animal feed.   The companies then add animal by-products, chemicals, fat, and sugar to improve salability, and sell the products as animal feed grain, fertilizer, human food, and pet food.

Food Industry Sales
1991

Company (top to bottom):
Gerber (a g)
McCormick (g)
Dean Foods (a g)
Intl. Multifoods (a f g)
Land O'Lakes (a f)
Hormel (a)
Hershey Foods (a g)
Tyson Foods (a)
Chiquita Brands (a g)
Kellogg Co. (a g)
Quaker Oats (a g p)
RJR Nabisco (a g p t)
CPC International (g)
Campbell Soup Co. (a g)
H.J. Heinz (a g p)
Nestle (a g p)
General Mills (a g)
Borden (a c g)
Ralston Purina (a f g p)
Archer Daniels (f g)
Sara Lee (a g)
Conagra (a c f)
General Foods (a g t)

a=animal food for humans

c=chemicals and fertilizer

f=animal feed

g=grain-based food for humans

p=pet food

t=tobacco

X-axis: Billions of Dollars — 0, 14, 28, 42, 56, 70

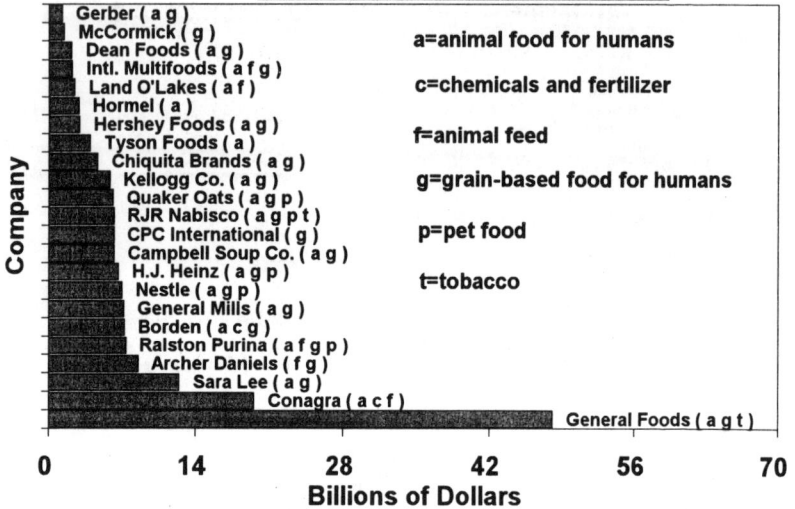

The refined oils and grain products go for human consumption. The millings go back to slop the hogs. In the processing of grains, many of the nutrients are removed. Some of them, calcium, iron, niacin, riboflavin, and thiamin, are put back in and the product is then called "enriched."[261] Many minerals and vitamins are not restored, however, and comparison of the original food, its "enriched" product, and the bran, meal, or millings left for animal feed suggests the hogs are the beneficiaries. The chart below (next page) shows that grain and seed meals commonly incorporated into animal feed actually have higher nutrient densities than their field crop sources, and that the human foods made from the same sources have less.

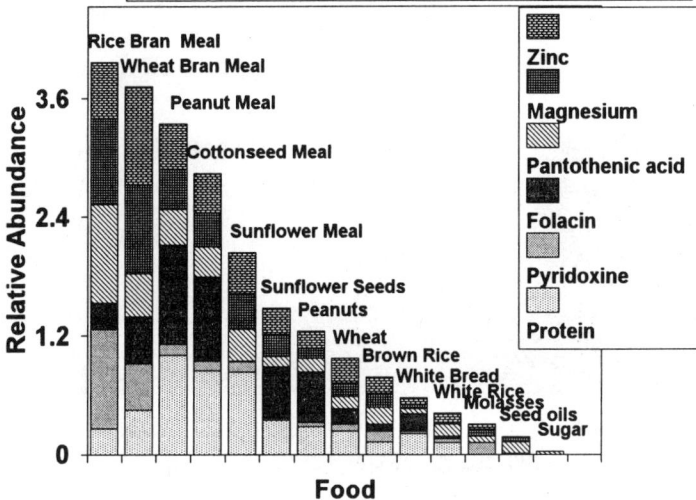

Nutrients in USDA Products
All Price Supported

Clearly, however, the feed grains (barley, corn, grain sorghum, and oats) are the big winners in the USDA sweepstakes. While the 16 billion dollar windfall might appear to benefit mostly the grain farmers, there's a flip side. Seventy percent of the feed grain crops go to feed animals[262] which are then consumed by humans. The meat industry, conspicuously absent from overt subsidies and supports, is probably the real winner. If grain farmers sold on the free market, they would charge higher prices for less feed grain, and the price of dairy, meat, and poultry, would rise, even as profits fell.

Now, dairy products are advertised on the basis of their calcium content, and meat is recommended for its protein.

Using USDA 1988 market price data[263] and USDA nutrient data,[264] the following graphs were constructed, showing the calcium/*cost* and protein/*cost* ratios for various foods. Included are free market fruits and vegetables, price-supported dairy and field crops, and other animal source foods that receive de facto supports from the price-supported feed grains. In these charts no cost adjustments have been made to reflect the tax dollars that have been used to grow the foods (next page):

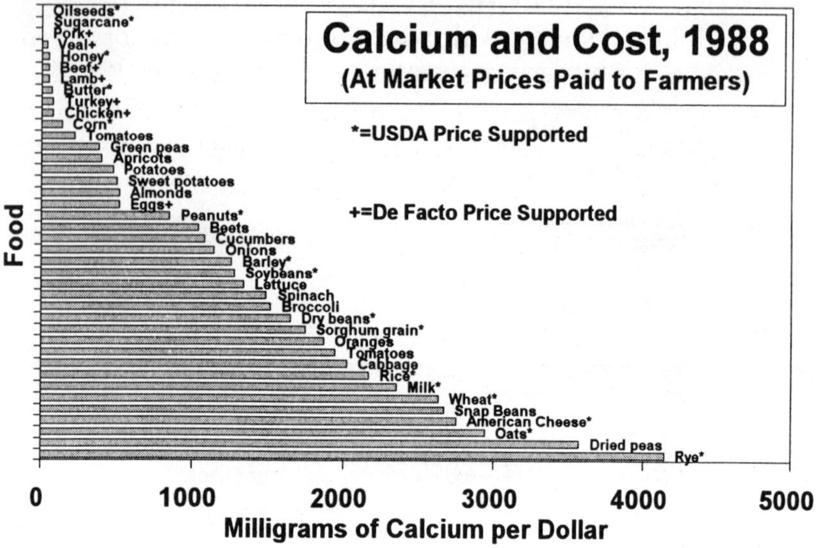
Calcium and Cost, 1988
(At Market Prices Paid to Farmers)
*=USDA Price Supported
+=De Facto Price Supported
Food
Oilseeds*
Sugarcane*
Pork+
Veal+
Honey*
Beef+
Lamb+
Butter*
Turkey+
Chicken+
Corn*
Tomatoes
Green peas
Apricots
Potatoes
Sweet potatoes
Almonds
Eggs+
Peanuts*
Beets
Cucumbers
Onions
Barley*
Soybeans*
Lettuce
Spinach
Broccoli
Dry beans*
Sorghum grain*
Oranges
Tomatoes
Cabbage
Rice*
Milk*
Wheat*
Snap Beans
American Cheese*
Oats*
Dried peas
Rye*
0
1000
2000
3000
4000
5000
Milligrams of Calcium per Dollar

Dairy products are not the cheapest source of calcium and meat is a long way from being the cheapest source of protein:

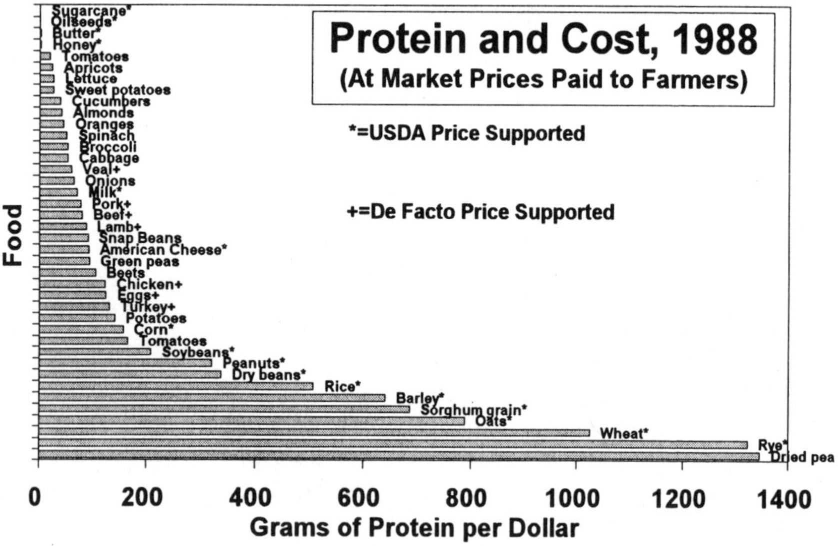
Protein and Cost, 1988
(At Market Prices Paid to Farmers)
*=USDA Price Supported
+=De Facto Price Supported
Food
Sugarcane*
Oilseeds*
Butter*
Honey*
Tomatoes
Apricots
Lettuce
Sweet potatoes
Cucumbers
Almonds
Oranges
Spinach
Broccoli
Cabbage
Veal+
Onions
Milk*
Pork+
Beef+
Lamb+
Snap Beans
American Cheese*
Green peas
Beets
Chicken+
Eggs+
Turkey+
Potatoes
Corn*
Tomatoes
Soybeans*
Peanuts*
Dry beans*
Rice*
Barley*
Sorghum grain*
Oats*
Wheat*
Rye*
Dried pea
0
200
400
600
800
1000
1200
1400
Grams of Protein per Dollar

The efficiency with which animals convert plants to animal food for human consumption varies by species.[265] The following chart indicates that chickens waste ~ 100 - 26 = 74% of the plant protein they eat to make eggs; young sheep waste ~ 100 -2.5 = 97.5% of the plant Calories they ingest to produce lamb.

Conversion Efficiency

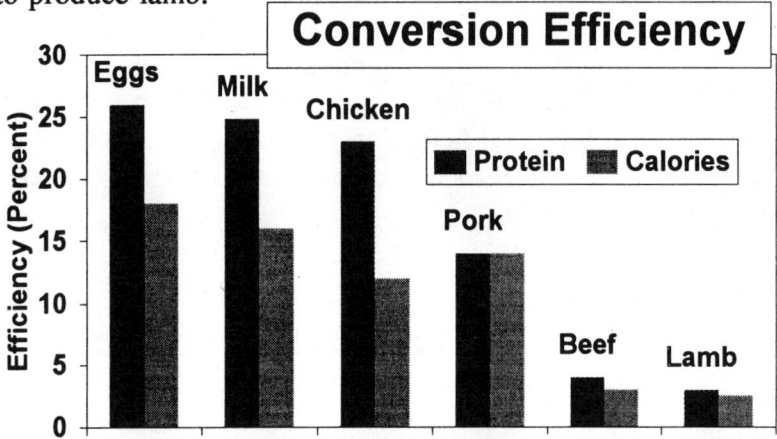

Labor costs impact on food production costs. Not surprisingly animal food is more labor-intensive than plant food.[266] (The improved efficiency of pork production since 1969 probably reflects factory farming techniques):

Labor Efficiency

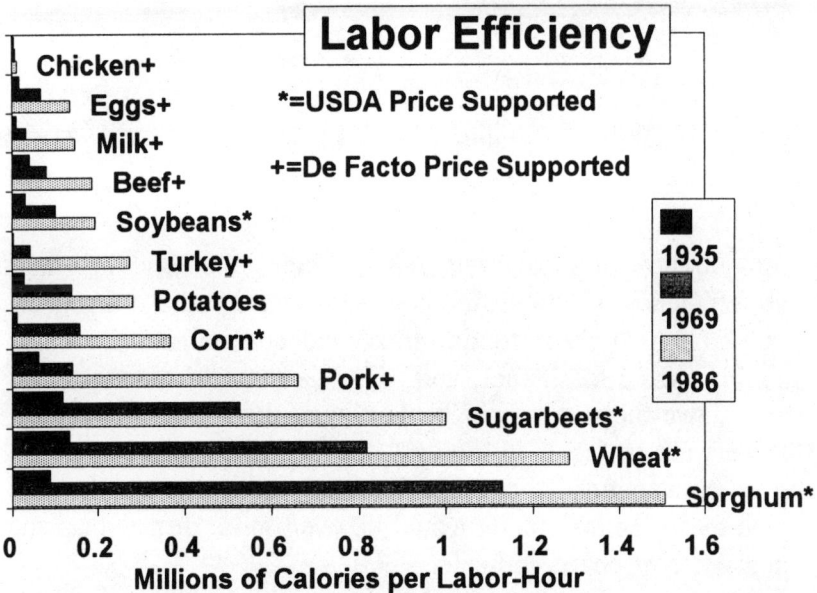

87

Cartesian rationalizations may insist that animals are mere machines, mimicking but not replicating human interests, but their mimicry includes digestion, elimination, heat loss, reproduction, and respiration, all of which waste protein and Calories at about the same rate we do for those same activities.

Grass and leaves might appear to be unlikely food sources for humans but pilot programs[267] suggest that good quality protein can be easily extracted from both. In any event, animal food and field crop protein production is a less efficient use of land than horticulture[268] (e.g. cabbage, green peas and snap beans):

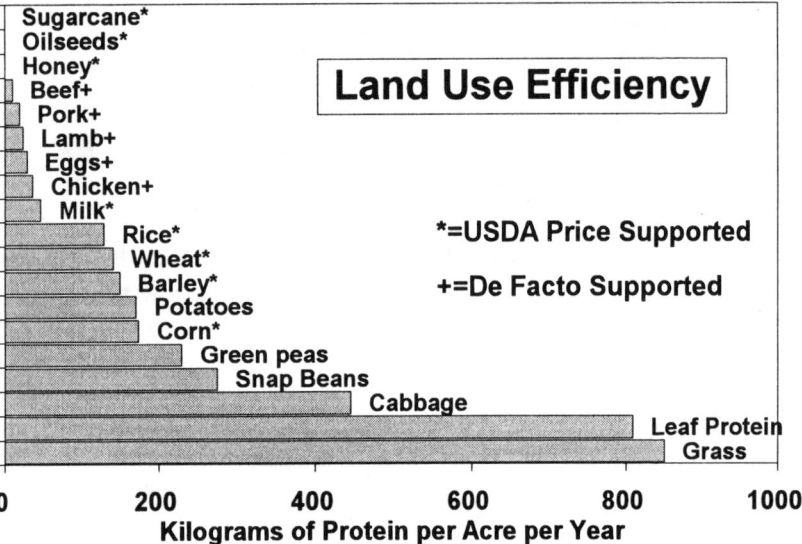

Land Use Efficiency

*=USDA Price Supported

+=De Facto Supported

Sugarcane*
Oilseeds*
Honey*
Beef+
Pork+
Lamb+
Eggs+
Chicken+
Milk*
Rice*
Wheat*
Barley*
Potatoes
Corn*
Green peas
Snap Beans
Cabbage
Leaf Protein
Grass

0   200   400   600   800   1000
Kilograms of Protein per Acre per Year

The conversion efficiency, labor efficiency, and land use efficiency of animal foods reflect, among other things, the rate at which these foods utilize and contaminate the water supply, waste fossil fuel, and degrade the environment, over and above the rate at which plant agriculture does the same. If we were to factor in the de facto feed grain price supports, plus conversion, labor, and land use efficiency costs, the picture for animal foods would be even more dismal than the nutrient/cost charts indicate.

88

By contrast, plant foods retain their nutritional and economic advantages with or without price supports.

Therefore, it appears the USDA uses tax money to support the least valuable and least nutritious agricultural products and to give de facto supports to animal foods, which would fare poorly in a free market. As one dairy apologist remarked,[269] "It seems unlikely that the major components of milk can compete directly with products of vegetable origin." The same comment applies *a fortiori* to meat.

Left in the lurch are the most nutritious foods, the vegetables and fruits, that nevertheless make it on their own in spite of a tax and price gradient that favors the supported commodities.

People no doubt have the right to make poor food choices, but other citizens should not be obliged to subsidize their food bills. Faced with retail hamburger at $35/lb,[270] many devout carnivores would finally discover the virtues of beans.

It may not always be true that ending price supports would raise prices. If, for instance, the USDA cut its price supports for sugar cane, the price of sugar would drop since this worthless product would no longer be grown in the U.S. but would be imported from tropical countries where cane can be grown for a third the cost of U.S sugar.[271] And at least one meat economist,[272] using a computer model, concluded that a gradual five-year elimination of feed grain price supports would lower the price and increase the supply of beef and hogs, although immediate elimination would decrease supplies and raise prices.

Is he right? Let us imagine an agricultural "black box," the contents of which are hidden from view. CO_2, H_2O, soil minerals, and sunlight go in one end and meat comes out the other. There is a funnel on top into which the Commodities Credit Corporation pours an average of $5 billion a year in the form of feed grain price supports.[273] The economist suggests that if the funnel and the $5 billion are only removed *slowly* that the cost of the output meat will actually decrease while its quantity increases. He may be right, but if so it should be possible to construct a perpetual motion machine along the same lines. Also if it's true, the CCC should be dismantled immediately since its $5 billion only reduces the efficiency of the black box. But it's likely that an end to feed grain price supports would invariably raise the price and reduce the supply of meat.

The question could be put to the test by eliminating price supports. If I'm wrong and the price of meat actually goes down, then everyone will still be happy; the meat-eaters will get more of their favorite product for less, and vegetarians will no longer see their taxes squandered to produce the stuff.

A campaign to abolish USDA price supports across the board would be a major step for ecology, ethics, and health. Allies could be found in a wide spectrum of analysts,[274] economists,[275] and politicians, who feel the supports have been a disaster to the U.S. economy, the small farmers they are supposed to help, and to struggling third world agricultural systems[276] as well.

Milk	Meat	Fruit-	Grain
Calcium	*Protein*	**Vegetables**	*Carbohydrate*
Riboflavin	*Niacin*	*Vitamins A*	*Thiamin*
Protein	*Iron*	*and C*	*Iron*
	Thiamin		*Niacin*

Most everyone has seen variants of the famous colored poster, shown above in line drawing. We are advised to eat foods from each of the Basic Four Food Groups to insure adequate nutrition.   The two animal food groups, milk and meat, are said to be high in calcium and protein, respectively.

If we go to USDA Handbook No.8, some of the poster foods and some of their nutrients look like this:

Table 1.-Composition of Foods
100 Grams, Edible Portion.

Food	Energy Calories	Protein Grams	Calcium Mgs
Beef, Sirloin	313	16.9	10
Bread, Whole Wheat	241	9.1	84
Broccoli	32	3.6	103
Chard, Swiss	25	2.4	88
Cheese, Swiss	370	27.5	925
Hamburger, Regular	286	24.2	11
Milk	65	3.5	118
Rice, Brown, Ckd.	119	2.5	12

Obviously cheese and milk are winners in the calcium department. Hamburger and cheese are good protein foods, while chard and broccoli aren't. If we load *all* the foods[277,278,279,280] shown in the poster into a computer spreadsheet and sort for the foods with the highest calcium content we get the graph below.

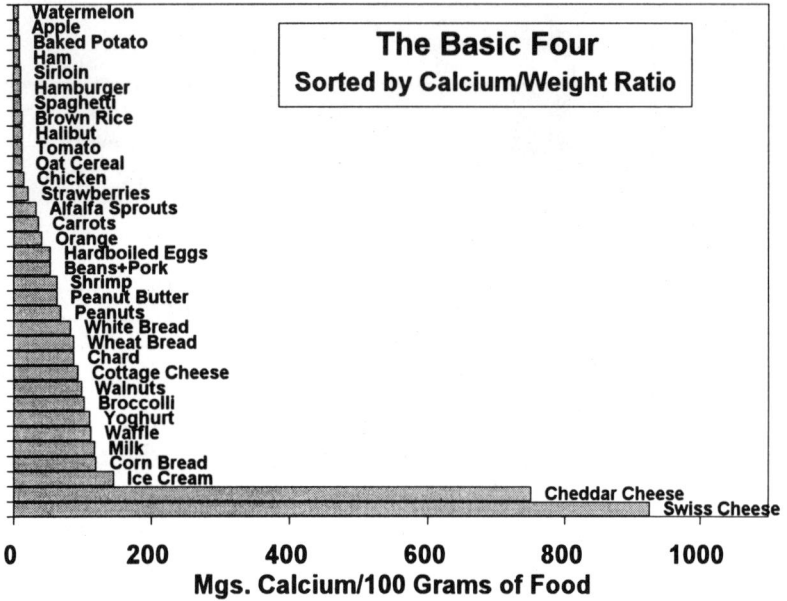

The Basic Four
Sorted by Calcium/Weight Ratio

Watermelon
Apple
Baked Potato
Ham
Sirloin
Hamburger
Spaghetti
Brown Rice
Halibut
Tomato
Oat Cereal
Chicken
Strawberries
Alfalfa Sprouts
Carrots
Orange
Hardboiled Eggs
Beans+Pork
Shrimp
Peanut Butter
Peanuts
White Bread
Wheat Bread
Chard
Cottage Cheese
Walnuts
Broccolli
Yoghurt
Waffle
Milk
Corn Bread
Ice Cream
Cheddar Cheese
Swiss Cheese

0   200   400   600   800   1000
Mgs. Calcium/100 Grams of Food

Then we sort for foods with the highest protein content and get the graph on the next page:

Apple
Watermelon
Strawberries
Orange
Carrots
Tomato
Chard
Brown Rice
Baked Potato
Yoghurt
Alfalfa Sprouts
Oat Cereal
Milk
Broccolli
Ice Cream
Spaghetti
Beans&Pork
Corn Bread
Wheat Bread
White Bread
Waffle
Hardboiled Eggs
Cottage Cheese
Walnuts
Ham
Sirloin
Shrimp
Halibut
Hamburger
Cheddar Cheese
Peanuts
Swiss Cheese
Peanut Butter
Chicken

| 0 | 5 | 10 | 15 | 20 | 25 | 30 | 35 |

Grams Protein/100 Grams of Food

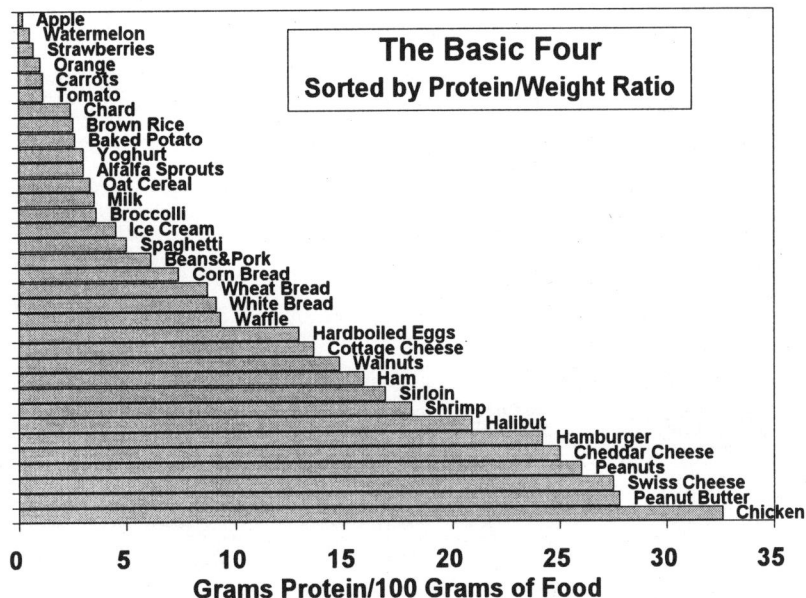

It certainly looks as if the two animal food groups do have unique properties. The milk group dominates the calcium sort and the meat group dominates the protein sort, as advertised.

However, *the foods have been sorted by nutrient/weight ratio.* Suppose we sort for foods with the highest calcium/Calorie ratio instead. Significant changes occur. Broccoli and chard move ahead of cheese. If, in fact, one sorts the entire USDA data base by calcium/Calorie ratio,[281,282] about 10 leafy greens make the list ahead of the first dairy product.

The vertical dotted line at 33.3 mg/100 Cal is the ratio needed in the overall diet to meet Recommended Dietary Allowances (RDAs) of 800 mg calcium and 2400 Calories (next page):

93

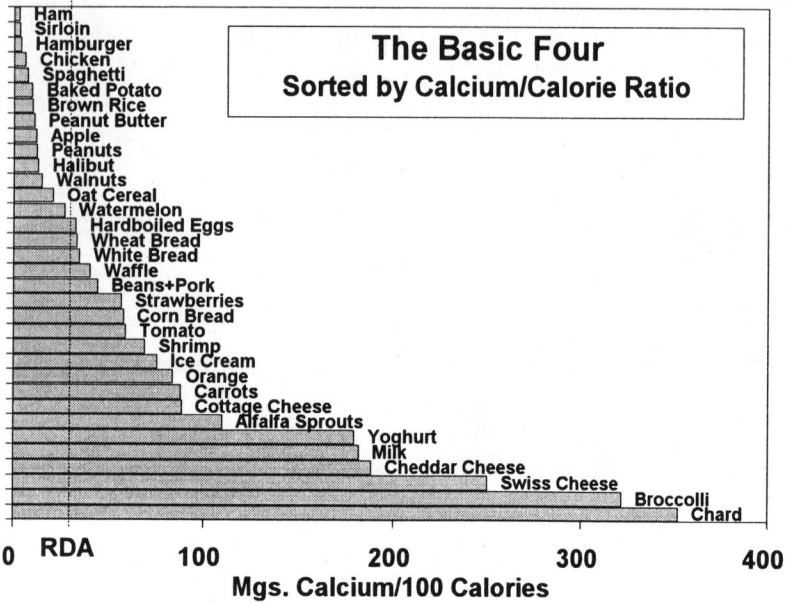

The Basic Four
Sorted by Calcium/Calorie Ratio

Ham
Sirloin
Hamburger
Chicken
Spaghetti
Baked Potato
Brown Rice
Peanut Butter
Apple
Peanuts
Halibut
Walnuts
Oat Cereal
Watermelon
Hardboiled Eggs
Wheat Bread
White Bread
Waffle
Beans+Pork
Strawberries
Corn Bread
Tomato
Shrimp
Ice Cream
Orange
Carrots
Cottage Cheese
Alfalfa Sprouts
Yoghurt
Milk
Cheddar Cheese
Swiss Cheese
Broccolli
Chard

0   RDA   100   200   300   400

Mgs. Calcium/100 Calories

Sorting by protein/Calorie ratio produces more surprises, and vegetable foods (broccoli, alfalfa sprouts and chard) are scattered high among the animal foods.

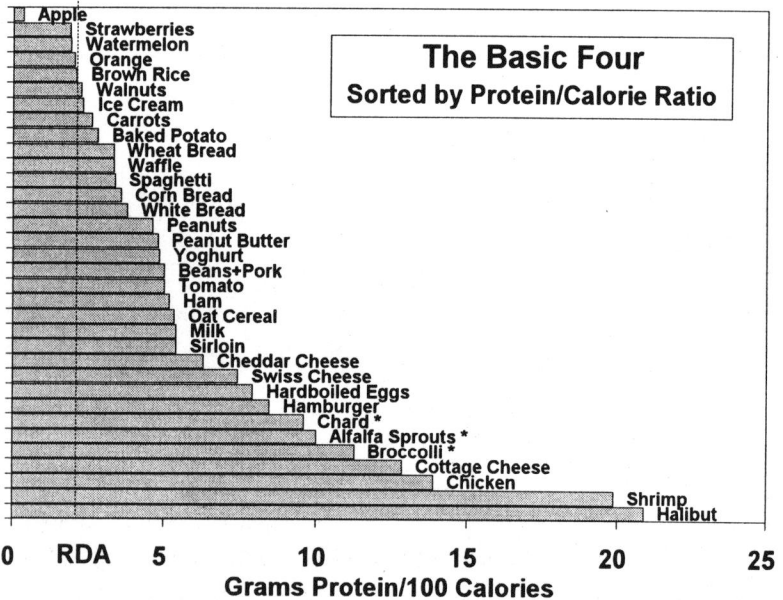

The Basic Four
Sorted by Protein/Calorie Ratio

Apple
Strawberries
Watermelon
Orange
Brown Rice
Walnuts
Ice Cream
Carrots
Baked Potato
Wheat Bread
Waffle
Spaghetti
Corn Bread
White Bread
Peanuts
Peanut Butter
Yoghurt
Beans+Pork
Tomato
Ham
Oat Cereal
Milk
Sirloin
Cheddar Cheese
Swiss Cheese
Hardboiled Eggs
Hamburger
Chard *
Alfalfa Sprouts *
Broccolli *
Cottage Cheese
Chicken
Shrimp
Halibut

0   RDA   5   10   15   20   25

Grams Protein/100 Calories

94

The vertical dotted line at .023 gm/Cal is the ratio needed in the overall diet to meet Recommended Dietary Allowances (RDAs) of 56 gm. protein and 2400 Cal (~ 10% of Calories from protein). All the foods to the right of the line exceed the protein requirements, some by wide margins. If the entire USDA database is sorted by protein/Calorie ratio, only some fruits, nuts, and junk foods fall to the left of the dotted line.

Of some interest to protein-seeking vegans and Natural Hygienists is the fate of peanut butter, peanuts, and walnuts which are now below the leafy greens. The reason for this fall from grace is the same thing that drops sirloin, ham, and cheese. They're high in fat. Fat is lighter (specific gravity is .913-.945)[283] than water, the chief constituent of fruits and vegetables, so fatty foods will show up well in a nutrient/weight sort, but since fat has 9 Calories per gram, as opposed to 4 Calories per gram of carbohydrate or protein, these foods do poorly in a nutrient/Calorie sort.

"The job's not over until the paperwork is done," as the cartoon says, but the USDA never finished its paperwork. The USDA No. 8 sample, finished and rewritten, looks like this and chard and broccoli turn out to be pretty good foods after all:

Table 1. Composition of Foods per 100 Calories

Food	Weight Grams	Protein Grams	Calcium Mgs
Beef, Sirloin	31.9	5.4	3.2
Bread, Whole Wheat	41.5	3.7	34.9
Broccoli	312.5	11.2	321.9
Chard, Swiss	400.0	9.6	352.0
Cheese, Swiss	27.0	7.4	250.0
Hamburger, Regular	35.1	8.5	3.9
Milk	153.8	5.3	181.5
Rice, Brown, Ckd.	84.0	2.1	10.1

The Basic Four poster also invites us to believe animal foods are a serious source of vitamins and iron. The stacked bar graph below shows the relative abundance of these substances, sorted by nutrient/weight ratio, and mathematically adjusted to keep all figures visible on the graph. Hamburger appears to have lots of iron, as suggested by the poster, and milk is a good source of riboflavin:[1]

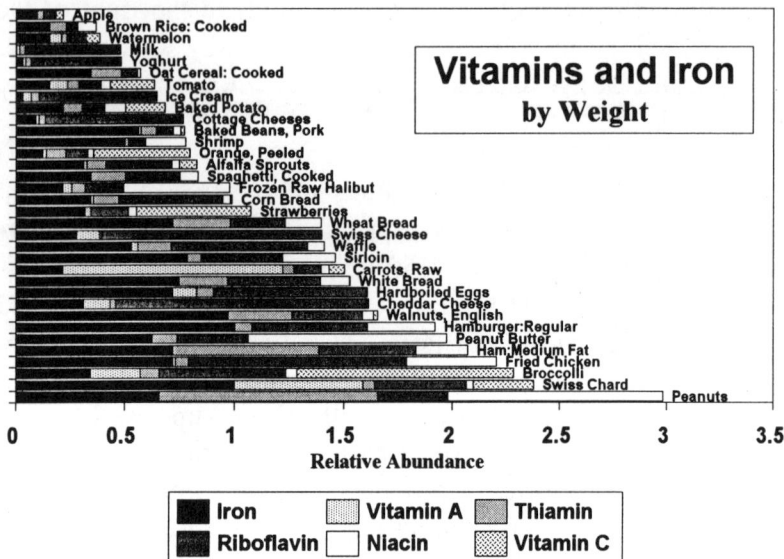

If we sort by nutrient/Calorie ratio, a different picture emerges. Dairy foods are no longer a remarkable source of riboflavin. Meats do not score well in the niacin, iron, and thiamin departments. Fruits and vegetables lead the way in all six nutrients (next page):

---

[1]Author's Note: This busy stacked bar graph was chosen to avoid six separate bar graphs. Since there is a wide variance between 4000 IUs of Vit A and 2 mg. of riboflavin, if all six secondary nutrients mentioned in the poster are to be visible in the same graph, the ranges for each nutrient must be normalized to 1 by dividing each nutrient value by the largest number appearing in that nutrient column. If one food led in all six nutrients, it would score a relative abundance of 6.

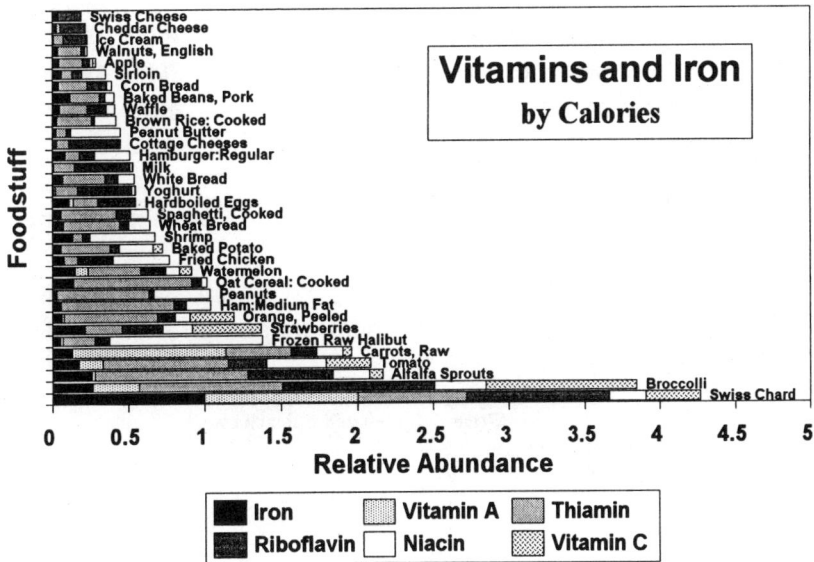

Vitamins and Iron
by Calories

Foodstuff (y-axis): Swiss Cheese, Cheddar Cheese, Ice Cream, Walnuts, English, Apple, Sirloin, Corn Bread, Baked Beans, Pork, Waffle, Brown Rice: Cooked, Peanut Butter, Cottage Cheeses, Hamburger:Regular, Milk, White Bread, Yoghurt, Hardboiled Eggs, Spaghetti, Cooked, Wheat Bread, Shrimp, Baked Potato, Fried Chicken, Watermelon, Oat Cereal: Cooked, Peanuts, Ham:Medium Fat, Orange, Peeled, Strawberries, Frozen Raw Halibut, Carrots, Raw, Tomato, Alfalfa Sprouts, Broccolli, Swiss Chard

Relative Abundance (x-axis): 0, 0.5, 1, 1.5, 2, 2.5, 3, 3.5, 4, 4.5, 5

Legend: Iron, Vitamin A, Thiamin, Riboflavin, Niacin, Vitamin C

Q.E.D., if foods are sorted and preferenced by nutrient/Calorie rather than nutrient/weight ratios, animal foods lose their clout and the whole "Basic Four" concept evaporates.

Well, which sorting method is right? There's no doubt weight is a quick way to find out how much of a given food you've got, but there's no RDA for weight in the diet since weight is not a metabolite or nutrient but a means of measurement. People do not eat until a certain weight of food has been consumed but rather until Calorie and nutrient requirements are satisfied. Acquisition of Calories is arguably the main reason for eating in the first place; the body is quick to send hunger signals if insufficient food energy has been taken in to run its metabolic pathways.

A complicated system of chemoreceptors throughout the body are believed to send nutrient and Calorie information to the hypothalamus which then regulates feeding behavior.[284] Nerve fibers in the throat and intestines monitor the Caloric and nutrient content of every morsel eaten which helps to determine the satiety point.[285]

It may well be that people eat what they want to eat regardless of what is advised, but if advice is to be given it should be physiologically sound. Now, a bowl of soup has about the same nutritional value as its dry ingredients, but under nutrient/weight sorting rules, the soup runs a poor second because of the additional weight of water. Let us here introduce, as an alternative system of nutritional analysis, the concept of "Percent of (RDA per Calorie)." It is that portion of the RDA of a given nutrient to be provided by each Calorie of the given food.

We will compare[286]a piece of sirloin steak, fresh spinach, and spinach with an equal weight of added water ("spinach soup").

	Sirloin	Spinach	Spinach soup
% of Calories from:			
Carbohydrate	0	49	49
Fat	29	11	11
Protein	71	40	40
Nutrient - Percent of (Recommended			
Daily Allowance per Calorie)			
	(%)	(%)	(%)
Calcium	10	1633	1633
Cholesterol	376	0	0
Fiber	0	1187	1187
Folate	68	12737	12737
Iron	503	3585	3585
Magnesium	132	2978	2978
Potassium	329	3679	3679
Phosphorus	518	807	807
Riboflavin	273	1470	1470
Thiamin	112	691	691
Vitamin A	0	8868	8868
Vitamin B12	2474	0	0
Vitamin B6	341	1297	1297
Vitamin E	0	2429	2429
Vitamin C	0	6172	6172
Zinc	805	467	467

There are stretch receptors in the stomach (that has a capacity of about one liter) to signal satiety by detecting volume. In order to fulfill the day's requirements of about 2400 Calories, one could easily consume 2.85 pounds of sirloin (1.29 liters) and still be short on calcium, fiber, folate, and vitamins A, C, and E. The chemoreceptors would be advising further food consumption to make up the shortfalls and the stomach would be reporting plenty of room, but one would already be at 376% of a *maximum* RDA (300 mg) for cholesterol (at 1128 mg) and close to 30% of Calories from fat.

Or one could take a stab at 2400 Calories of spinach for the day's food intake which would be 22 pounds or 9.3 liters. From personal experience I can say this is an experiment you won't want to try. The limiting nutrients (save vitamin B_{12} which is a given) are zinc and protein which are nevertheless at about 400 "percent of (RDA per Calorie)." If one ate about 1/4 of the 22 pounds (5.5#, or 2.32 liters) over the course of two meals, one would still meet RDAs for all nutrients with a full stomach, but with a shortage of 3/4 the day's Calorie requirements. Calories, not nutrients, are the limiting intake on a whole-food vegan diet which may explain why vegans are generally healthy though slender.

On the other hand, nutrients, not Calories and not fat, are the limiters for those who follow the "Basic Four." Obesity is with us always, in part because of mathematically flawed nutritional advice.

In proper nutritional analysis the weight of food is irrelevant. But your body has an intuitive understanding of Calories and will demand that you eat enough of them. Most people can count on the fingers of one finger the number of U.S. citizens they've seen recently who looked as if they didn't meet their Calorie requirements. If each food and each Calorie meets 100% or more of the RDA per Calorie for each nutrient, your nutritional status is automatically assured, and you're probably eating mostly vegetables, not much fat, and no cholesterol.

Food grouping started out innocently enough in 1897 when W.O. Atwater, in *Food and Diet Yearbook of the USDA*,[287] tried to advise Americans how to make the best of their traditional meat-based diets. Over the years there have been two dozen food group schemes[288,289] listing anywhere from 3 to 11 "Basic Food Groups." A ten group scheme in 1941 included water as a food group; many others have listed fat and sugar.   Since then there have been another half dozen food group schemes, all financed by animal food interests and backed   by respected nutritionists[290] who, in other ways diverse, all failed to let on that sorting foods by nutrient/weight ratio is fundamentally unsound.

Does it matter? The "Basic Four" poster shown above, that says "National Dairy Council" on the back in small print, was obtained from a hospital dietician who keeps sheaves of them on hand for patient education.   A trip to the State Health Department produced an assortment of 4,5, and 9 food group posters.   Two required school of nutrition textbooks at the local university include the "Basic Four,"[291] one with a five page color spread.[292]

In recent years there has been mention of "Nutrient Density" which is nutrient/Calorie analysis with RDAs installed in both numerator and denominator.[293]   A few authors[294,295] have utilized this powerful antidote to food industry flim-flam. "The recommendation that nutrient labelling be provided in relation to Calories has obvious merit," in the words[296] of Mark Hegsted, M.D.

But suggesting nutrient/Calorie analysis to the animal food industry produces much the same effect as approaching Dracula with a white stake since when Nutrient Density flies in one window, the animal foods fly out the other, taking with them most of the fat and sugar bon-bons as well.   The "Basic Four" materialize only if foods are sorted by nutrient/weight ratio which is an ideal strategy to sell animal food, which is a great way to keep excess Calories, cholesterol and saturated fat in the diet, which is a splendid way to grow an arteriosclerotic, obese, cancer-ridden nation, which is what we have.

XI. WHO PAID THE PIPER?

"No company or industry group can afford to teach the lesson 'Eat less of what we make' even if that lesson is nutritionally sound[297]."

-Joan Dye Gussow, Ed.D.

Previous writers[298,299,300] have documented the political pressure applied via the USDA by the egg, dairy, meat, and poultry industries, against lower cholesterol and dietary fat recommendations. It appears the USDA, whose original charter specified only the promotion and sale of U.S. agricultural products,[301] has also had a major role in nutrition education,[302] hence, also a major conflict in interest:

Federal Funding for Nutritional Education Research

	FY '79 $Million	FY '80 $Million
U.S. Department of Agriculture	8.40	6.28
U.S. Department of Health and Human Services	.45	8.7
Other Federal agencies	.21	.94
	9.06	15.92

Harvard is the home of the first school of nutrition in any medical or health school in the world, according to Frederick Stare, M.D. His autobiography, *Adventures in Nutrition*, reveals that the Basic Four Food Group scheme was devised at the Harvard Department of Nutrition[303] in 1955 and by 1957 had replaced 1943's Basic Seven,[304] in the USDA's meandering and cabalistic system of numerology. The department, begun in 1942, was short on funds so the author solicited support from outside sources.[305] By 1986 he had raised $20,640,347 from private and government agencies and over 100 industrial benefactors.[306]

In Stare's words:[307] "Money Talks!" This revelation not only failed to raise eyebrows but was praised by one of the book's reviewers.[308] A "scurrilous attack, " *Harvard's Sugar-*

Pushing Nutritionist, in the August 1978 Saturday Review[309] also listed most of the following contributors and noted that Stare had not yet advised against the use of DDT, diethylstilbestrol in cattle feed, food additives and colorings, pesticides, saccharin, soft drinks, sugar, or white flour. Among the funding sources were the following:

HARVARD DEPARTMENT OF NUTRITION
Funding 1942-1986
Source: *Adventures in Nutrition* Appendix 6

FOOD COMPANIES:

Ajinomoto Co. of Tokyo
American Meat Institute
Armour & Co.
Beatrice Food Co.
Birds Eye (Division of General Foods)
Borden Co.
California & Hawaii Sugar Co.
Campbell Soup Co.
Carnation Co.
Coca-Cola Co.
Coca-Cola Foundation
Dairy Council of California
Florida Sugar Cane League, Inc.
Frito-Lay, Inc.
General Foods
General Mills
Gerber Baby Food Company
Hartford Foundation (A & P Foods)
H.J. Heinz
Hershey Foods
Hunt-Wesson Foods

International Sugar Research Foundation
Kellogg Company
Kraft Corp.
McDonald's Corp
National Biscuit Company
National Confectioners Association
National Dairy Council
National Dairy Products
National Livestock & Meat Board
Oscar Mayer Co.
Oscar Mayer Foundation, Inc.
Pet Milk Co.
Pillsbury Co.
Special Dairy Industry Board
Sugar Association, Inc.
Sugar Research Foundation
Swift & Company
Swift and Company Foundation
Tuna Research Foundation

An early graduate student was Mervyn Hardinge, M.D., of Loma Linda University. His landmark *Nutritional Studies of Vegetarians* first appeared in 1954 in the American Journal of Clinical Nutrition. The series continued through 1966, appearing also in the Journal of the American Dietetic Association with Stare as co-author. Although these technical articles exonerated vegetarianism and revealed a number of advantages, in his latest book Dr. Stare continues to find no intrinsic harm in chips, cupcakes, french fries, hamburgers, hot dogs, soft drinks and sugar.[310]

*"Milk has been called
the perfect food. "*

The statement as it stands is unquestionably true. Milk *has* been called the perfect food, but who called it that and how much were they paid? Harvard may have been the first school to dabble with food industry money, but it was not the last. Michael Jacobson, of The Center for Science in the Public Interest, found six other nutrition professors at the Universities of California, Iowa, Massachusetts, Minnesota, Oregon State, Virginia Polytechnic, and Wisconsin accepting grants and assorted freebies from Campbell, General Mills, Institute of Shortening and Edible Oils, Kellogg, Kraftco, McDonald's, the National Dairy Council, Nestlé and other drug, food, soft drink and food vending machine companies. He was unable to get dollar amounts from any of the parties except Wisconsin ($635,390), and two of the professors refused to respond at all.[311]

Jacobson also tracked the pre- and post-administration careers of top FDA and USDA officials in the period 1970 to 1985. Of 33 officials, 8 came *from* the food industry, but 22 went *to* the food industry on relinquishing their government posts. Most of them went either into the meat biz or joined the sugar pops folks, although one individual joined the Cling Peach Association. There was a strong cross-over effect between the drug and food industries.[312]

A Harris poll in 1977 showed that food manufacturers were highest on a list of industries Americans would like to see investigated,[313] although the drug industry often runs a close second.

Other sources of funds for the Harvard school of nutrition were the following drug companies:

Abbott Laboratories	Mead Johnson Research	OTHER:
Ayerst Laboratories	Merck, Sharp, & Dohme	
Burroughs Welcome & Co.	Miles Laboratories	Council for Tobacco
Griffith Labs.	Parke-Davis & Co.	Research
Hoffman LaRoche	Pfizer, Inc.	Tobacco Industries
Eli Lilly & Co.	Searle Laboratories	Research Foundation
Marion Laboratories Center	Upjohn Co.	

Consumer Reports has commented recently on the pernicious effects of drug advertising on science.[314] Pharmaceutical houses exploit the urgent human wish that health be restored with no more effort than the popping of pills into the mouth, and by financial leverage alone, select those experts who support this fantasy to serve as media spokesmen. Therefore it's not surprising the dreaded "V" word seldom appears even in reputable publications like The Journal of the American Medical Association (JAMA), or the New England Journal of Medicine (NEJM), although the context in which it does appear is more likely to be favorable than unfavorable, as in the past.

Less reputable journals arrive on the doctor's desk at the rate of ~ a dozen a month. They are freebies from the drug industry with cover-to-cover drug ads. The average throwaway contains mostly rehashes of material doctors are taught in medical school, and therapeutic options are virtually limited to drugs and surgery. This is a technique for brainwashing doctors, but the journals are expensive and the costs are passed on to consumers.

A recent Medline search on the word "Vegan" found 38 articles, which is roughly 38 more than were available 38 years ago, so the cause is not hopeless, just slow. Included were Barsotti's 1991 article showing reduced proteinuria and maintenance of normal serum albumin in nephrotic patients on the vegan diet,[315] Kjeldsen-Kragh's 1991 article showing remission of arthritis on the vegan diet,[316] and Lindahl's 1985 article showing clinical and biochemical improvement in 92% of asthmatic patients placed on a vegan diet.[317]

Nutrition journals occasionally drop the "V" word. The American Dietetic Association, "recognizes a growing body of scientific evidence...between a plant-based diet and the prevention of certain diseases,[318]" and in 1990 approved the formation of the Vegetarian Nutrition Dietetic Practice Group within the ADA.[319] However, a recent list of ADA scholarships, showed at least 16 out of 28 were funded by drug and food companies, with distinctly non-vegetarian financial interests.[320]

The American Journal of Clinical Nutrition has devoted two supplementary issues to the First and Second International Congresses on Vegetarian Nutrition.[321] The first Congress was supported by Loma Linda Foods, S.E. Rykoff, Sanitarium Foods, and Worthington Foods. *Am J Clin Nutr* runs elegant scientific articles, but nothing in the editorials suggests that there are fundamental errors in American nutritional advice or that a global policy change in favor of vegetarianism is in the works. Perhaps a list of continuing sponsors explains why:

Source: Facesheet from unidentified Am J Clin Nutr review:

American Society for Clinical Nutrition Sustaining Associate Members

Abbott Laboratories	Lederle Laboratories, Inc.
Best Foods	Miles Laboratories
Bristol-Meyers and Mead Johnson	Proctor and Gamble Company
Campbell Institute for Research and Technology	Ross Laboratories
Clintec Nutrition	Sandoz Nutrition
General Foods Corporation	The Coca-Cola Company
General Mills, Inc.	The NutraSweet Company
Gerber Products Company	The Pillsbury Company
Hoffmann-La Roche, Inc	The Quaker Oats Company
Kendall McGaw Laboratories	Wyeth Laboratories

"The American Society for Clinical Nutrition is pleased to acknowledge the generous support of these organizations to selected, educational activities of the society."

Well, what's wrong with having food and drug companies fund nutritional education? After all, few would complain if IBM kicked in for courses on semi-conductors, or if Boeing gave grants for airfoil research. In the hard sciences the same answers drop out regardless of funding sources, but nutritional education is not about launching a V2 at Peenemünde. It's not rocket science, and while the answers may be okay, the <u>questions</u> have been censored by economic pressure. Esoteric nutritional research of little practical value finds easy funding, but studies illuminating the advantages of vegetarianism, for the most part do not. There's no money in demonstrating that inexpensive vegetable diets are the healthiest, and as noted above, "Money talks!"

In the end, establishment nutritional advice does little more than reinforce the dietary errors people *prefer* to make. After rationalizing away the ecological and nutritional calamities induced by animal agriculture, one animal science writer showed his true colors: "No cereal platter...can ever inspire the toast or impart the status symbol of a roast of beef or a sizzling steak."[322]

If nutritionists were to come out in favor of nutrient/Calorie sorting, nutrient density, nutrient indexing, or any other scheme in which Calories rather than weight appear in the sorting denominator, the apparent complexities of balancing nutrient requirements against excess Calorie, cholesterol, and fat intake would disappear, animal source food would vanish from dietary recommendations, nutrient requirements would be met automatically, and nutritional advice would finally reduce to:

"Eat as wide a variety of plant foods in as unprocessed a form as possible."[323]

-*Susan Havala R.D.*

XII. THE MADISON AVENUE CHA-CHA

"Governments lie; the press catches them at it. "

-Anon.

Where's the Beef?
The Incredible edible egg.
Milk. It's fitness you can drink.
Beef Gives Strength.
Enjoy the best! Iowa corn-fed beef.
How to live high on the hog and steer
clear of the fat.
Somehow, nothing satisfies like beef.
America, you're leaning on Pork.
Come to Marlboro country.
You've come a long way, baby.

If logic were the criterion, the agricultural revolution would have put an end to the animal food habit 10,000 years ago, but human inertia is a powerful deterrent to change. In the modern age, advertising is another major obstacle, since the media routinely suppress vegetarian opinions in fear of losing food advertising revenues. In this area, the lies are *not* exposed by the press.

Advertising began 3000 years ago with the selling of slaves, cattle, and imports. By 1758 Samuel Johnson observed that, "Advertisements are now so numerous that they are very negligently perused, and it is therefore become necessary to gain attention by magnificence of promise and by eloquence sometimes sublime and sometimes pathetick."[324]

Things have only gone from bad to worse since then. The current U.S. outlay for advertising runs about 2.39% of the GNP or ~ $145 billion[325], more than twice as much as the next ten countries combined and up from about $10 billion in 1950. Distributions vary depending on the media. Local

107

newspapers account for 25% of U.S. ad expenditures and 17% of food marketing expenditures.[326] TV, newspapers, radio, and billboards attract the rest.[327]

The *generic* advertising of food products is funded by commodity check-off programs, which date back to 1880 with state taxes given over for agricultural promotion.[328] This wasn't enough, so several commodity groups organized voluntary programs with advertising funds contributed by the farm producers. Under this system, "free riders" who refused to pay their share, but benefitted from everybody else's ads, became a problem. State governments then obligingly stepped in with legislation for nonrefundable advertising assessments, that are deducted from the prices farmers receive when they sell, and are regarded by docile farmers as a tax write-off or an investment. Putative "free riders" no doubt view it as another strong arm act by the government. Costs follow:[329,330]

Generic Advertising 1982-1990
Authorized by Federal Statute (USA)

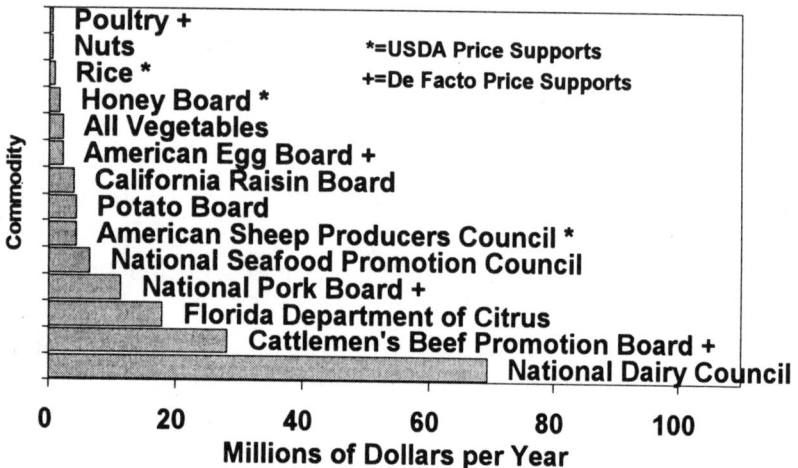

*=USDA Price Supports
+=De Facto Price Supports

Commodity

Poultry +
Nuts
Rice *
Honey Board *
All Vegetables
American Egg Board +
California Raisin Board
Potato Board
American Sheep Producers Council *
National Seafood Promotion Council
National Pork Board +
Florida Department of Citrus
Cattlemen's Beef Promotion Board +
National Dairy Council

0   20   40   60   80   100
Millions of Dollars per Year

Milk marketing orders, which "constitute a government sanctioned monopoly designed to give producers greater control over prices, income, and product distribution,"[331] finally led to the Dairy and Tobacco Act of 1983 which mandates a collection of $.15/lb of fluid market milk from dairy farmers. The industry spends $145 million/year on advertising and another $55 million/year on "education and research," for a total of $200 million/yr[332] including the generic ads.

In 1988, the Mid-Atlantic Milk Marketing Association had its "educational" wrists slapped. The Baltimore Vegetarians (now the Vegetarian Resource Group) brought MAMMA's "Milk Has Less Than 4% Fat," campaign to the attention of the Consumer Protection Division of the Maryland Attorney General, who exacted a penalty of $3500 from MAMMA for "consumer education," and a promise not to do it again.[333] While milk *is* only 4 grams fat per 100 grams of milk (hence 4% fat by weight), that 100 grams carries 70 Calories. Each gram of fat carries 9 Calories so the milk is actually 4x9/70=51% of Calories from fat. Using Dairy Council logic, a simple way to reduce fat content still more would be to thin it out with water ten times, then it could be claimed to be ".4% fat milk." Alas, it would still be 51% fat by Calories, and so dairy interests always present nutritional "education" in nutrient/weight terms.

The Maryland ruling did not spread out of state, and since then, the fast food joints have picked up on the dairy industry's mathematical flim-flam. McDonald's "91% fat free hamburger" is actually ~ (100-91)(gm) x 9(Cal/gm) / 180 (Cal)=81/180=45% of Calories from fat,[334] and the "93% fat free chicken" now being hyped by the chicken chains is ~ (100-93)x9/155=40% of Calories from fat.[335] The genetic engineering of low fat, low cholesterol beef, is a waste of time from a scientific viewpoint, since saturated fat and cholesterol are essential to the cell membrane integrity of any viable food animal. From the sales viewpoint, however, the beef, pork, and chicken people could solve their fat problem at no cost at all, by following dairy's lead. Just mix in an equal weight of water, and the 91% fat-free hamburger becomes 94.5% fat-free hamburger soup. The 93% fat-free chicken becomes 96.5% fat-free chicken soup.

Ah, the miracles of advertising are like the loaves and the fishes!

Fundamental to all animal food advertising is the confuse-o-gram, example shown below:

Living With Osteoporosis Sources of Calcium (This Patient information has been made available through a grant from Roerig) ***	Portion	Calcium (mg)
T-bone steak	12 oz	32
Round steak	3 oz	5
Pork chop	1 chop	7
Fried chicken	1/2 chicken	61
Fish (herring)	3 oz	63
Fish (snapper)	3 oz	34
Applesauce	1/2 cup	5
Banana	one	7
Cherries	1 cup	16
Fruit cocktail	1/2 cup	6
Pineapple	1 slice	6
Fried egg	one	26
Hard boiled egg	one	28
Omelet (butter, milk)	three eggs	141
Poached egg	one	28
Scrambled egg	one	47

This meaningless, but strangely typical, list appeared in a throw-away medical journal.[336] The text stated, "The chart shows foods which are good sources of calcium." Variable volume and weight measures are used, so no ranking is possible. Also, it should be noted that whenever the terms "portion," or "servings," appear in place of the word "Calories," a generous "portion" of balderdash is about to be "served." Adding Calories from USDA #8, and some real heavy hitters (*), the whole effort is hoisted on its own petard with a quick calcium/Calorie sort (next page):

SOURCES OF CALCIUM (REVISITED)		
	Calories	Calcium (mg)
ADDED:		
Seaweed, (ogo or limu) *	100	1062
Bok Choy *	100	1055
Turnip greens *	100	921
Collard greens *	100	559
Cheese, Parmesan *	100	302
Cheese, Swiss *	100	254
Kale *	100	228
Romaine lettuce *	100	227
Milk, whole *	100	194
Broccoli *	100	164
ORIGINAL:		
Omelet (butter, milk)	100	45
Scrambled egg	100	44
Fish (snapper)	100	40
Fish (herring)	100	36
Poached egg	100	34
Hard boiled egg	100	33
Fried egg	100	28
Fruit cocktail	100	15
Pineapple	100	14
Cherries	100	13
Applesauce	100	10
Banana	100	7
T-bone steak	100	5
Fried chicken	100	5
Round steak	100	5
Pork chop	100	2

Clearly, if anyone did take the first list to heart, they *would* have to learn to "Live with Osteoporosis," since there wouldn't be much calcium in their diet. However, poetic justice was at least rendered, since the Dairy Council is usually the prime offender in the *calcium* confuse-o-gram, and its product was originally omitted.

Current USDA nutrient tables are set up much like confuse-o-grams, which is not surprising in view of the USDA's protective and paternalistic relationship with the animal food industry. USDA #72, *Nutritive Values of Foods*, abounds with cans, containers, cups, gallons, loaves, oz, packets, pieces, servings, slices, tbsps, tsps, wedges, and finally variable gram weights. However, there are no standardized USDA "nutrients per 100 Calorie" tables from which idle curiosity and a thumb could quickly ferret out the most nutritious foods, which for the most part would not be dairy and meats, but leafy green vegetables, which give the most nutrients for the fewest Calories.

The Beef Industry Council likes *fat* confuse-o-grams. Beef ads leave weight and nutrient data hanging in the air, apparently on the assumption that readers don't own calculators. On the left is the hype, on the right the percent of Calories from fat.

Beef. Real Food For Real People. Source: U.S.D.A. Handbook No. 8-13		FAT Percent of Calories Source: Pocket Calculator	
TOP ROUND 5.3 gms total fat* (1.8 gms sat. fat) 162 calories	**29**	EYE OF ROUND 5.5 gms total fat* (2.1 gms sat. fat) 155 calories	**32**
ROUND TIP 6.4 gms total fat* (2.3 gms sat. fat) 162 calories	**36**	SIRLOIN 7.4 gms total fat* (3.0 gms sat. fat) 177 calories	**38**
TOP LOIN 7.6 gms total fat* (3.0 gms sat. fat) 172 calories	**40**	TENDERLOIN 7.9 gms total fat* (3.1 gms sat. fat) 174 calories	**41**

The Food and Nutrition Board has done a little cha-cha of its own to stay out of print with an RDA for fat, but anything over 30% Calories from fat is too much for the McGovern Committee,[337] whose advice was thoroughly disturbing to the "fat lobby" back in 1977.[338] Anything over

10-20% is probably too much for persons interested in fitness.

OTHER PLAYERS
****
RADIO COPY: National Pork Producer's Council. 12/30/86

SFX: TELEPHONE RINGING IN RECEIVER.
MAITRE D': Allo. Chez Blanc restaurant.
JUNE: Hello, this is June Jenkins...
ANNOUNCER: It's no surprise that white meat dishes are popular. What is surprising is that the white meat in this restaurant is pork. The other white meat. Pork is nutritious and surprisingly low in calories (sic) and cholesterol...
JUNE: Well, I guess I understand that. I'll tell Harry to pick up an order from your restaurant tonight.
MAITRE D': I can tell him for you. He iz here now, dining with your lovely daughter.
JUNE: We don't have a daughter.
SFX: PHONE CLICKS.
ANNOUNCER: Pork. The other white meat. A message from America's pork producer's.

Poor June. Dirty Harry has run off with another lady because June never learned how to cook a pig. This radio copy was scrutinized by a U.S. Senate hearing on health and nutrition claims in advertising.[339] Neither pork nor chicken (the first white meat) is a big time fat buster, but animal food aficionados do get their pick: too much fat or too much cholesterol, or too much of both (next page):

113

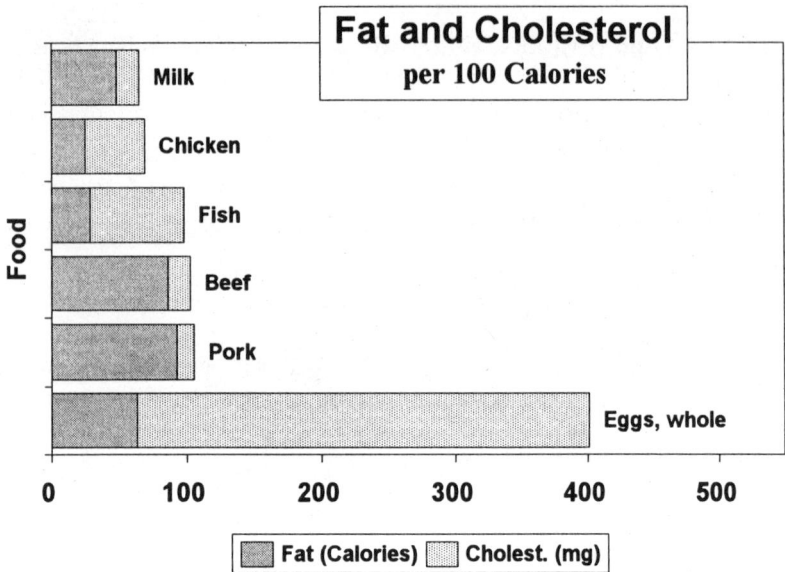

Fat and Cholesterol
per 100 Calories

Food

Milk
Chicken
Fish
Beef
Pork
Eggs, whole

Fat (Calories)   Cholest. (mg)

The total of $750 million/year for commodity advertising is dwarfed by the $9 billion for brand name food advertising:[340]

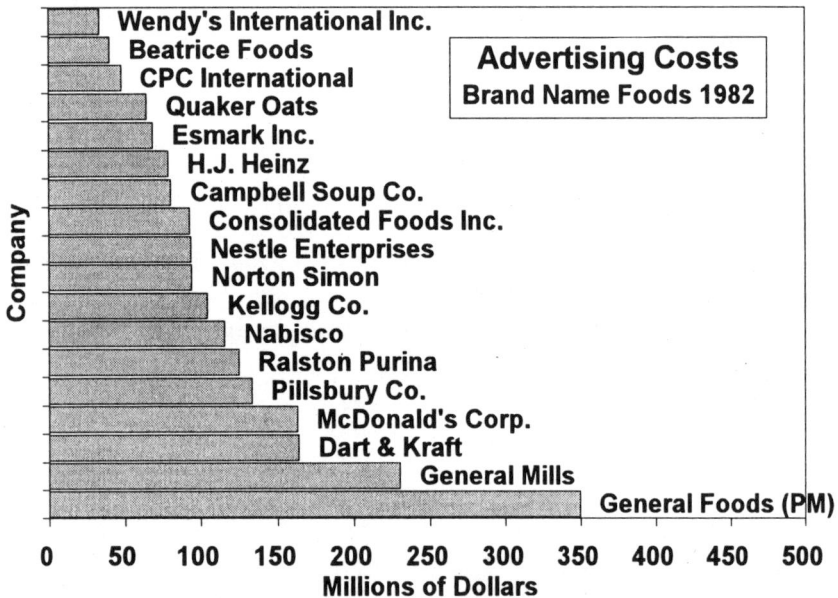

Company

Wendy's International Inc.
Beatrice Foods
CPC International
Quaker Oats
Esmark Inc.
H.J. Heinz
Campbell Soup Co.
Consolidated Foods Inc.
Nestle Enterprises
Norton Simon
Kellogg Co.
Nabisco
Ralston Purina
Pillsbury Co.
McDonald's Corp.
Dart & Kraft
General Mills
General Foods (PM)

Advertising Costs
Brand Name Foods 1982

Millions of Dollars

While the Potato Board generic ads came to $5.7 million in 1988, the potato chip companies sank $46 million into pushing a product that, due to the fat layer on the fried chips, has roughly a quarter of the nutrient/Calorie ratios of a baked potato. One might reasonably argue that the more something has to be advertised, the more likely it's bad for you.[341]

Fast food advertising on television runs up a tidy bill by itself:[342]

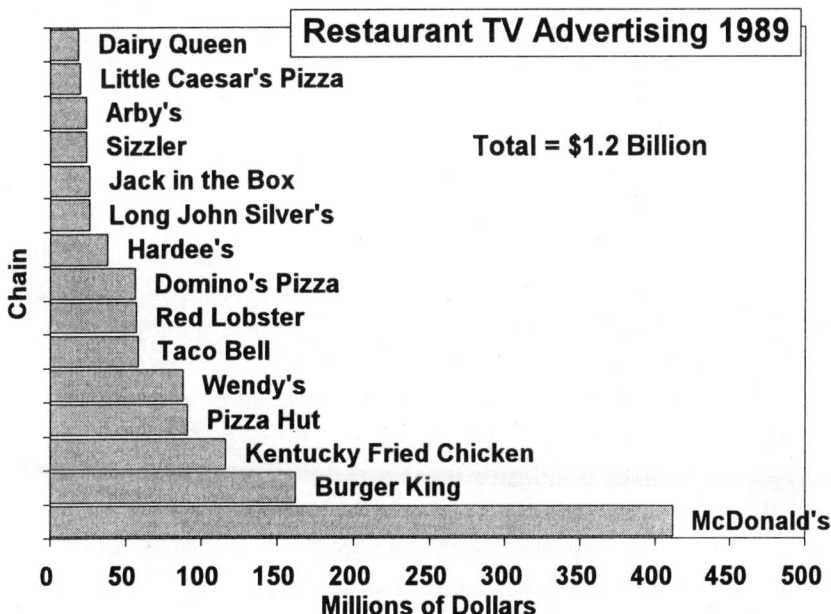

Restaurant TV Advertising 1989

Total = $1.2 Billion

(Chain, from top to bottom: Dairy Queen, Little Caesar's Pizza, Arby's, Sizzler, Jack in the Box, Long John Silver's, Hardee's, Domino's Pizza, Red Lobster, Taco Bell, Wendy's, Pizza Hut, Kentucky Fried Chicken, Burger King, McDonald's)

Millions of Dollars: 0, 50, 100, 150, 200, 250, 300, 350, 400, 450, 500

So, what to do about the imbalances of dairy, egg, fast-food, junk-food, meat, and poultry advertising? One solution would be for the fruit and vegetable growers to advertise more aggressively. However, while plant foods netted $11.8 billion in sales in 1987, the small growers won't kick in for generic advertising. They feel "it would be difficult to devise an equitable method to assess fees from producers of the approximately 162 different fruits and vegetables grown and commercially marketed in the United States."[343] The growers also believe "the nutritional benefits of fruits and vegetables are already well known,"[344] so why waste the money? Except for the California Raisin Board and the Florida Citrus Board, the plant food growers seem reluctant to involve themselves in nutritional politics, advertising, or education. The Potato Board, an exception, mounted an "advercation" campaign in the 80's to counter the notion that potatoes are fattening.[345] Using cookbooks, food page editors, magazine articles, and TV, the Potato Board was able to improve the public perception of potatoes as a nutritious food from 55% in 1973 to 81% in 1975, honest advertising for a change. But in essence, most food advertising goes for foods that have a negative impact on health.

OTHER STRATEGIES:
****

Cigarette ads are uniquely obnoxious. Recent articles in the Journal of the American Medical Association concluded that Camel's "Old Joe," was recognized by 91.3% of 6-year-old children,[346] and was "far more successful at marketing cigarettes to children (grades 9-12) than to adults (ages > 20)."[347] Taxpayers are gouged three times: first, tax dollars are used to administer USDA tobacco administration programs. Next, the tobacco industry takes a tax deduction on its ~ $2.5 billion/yr advertising bill which forgives about 35% or $870 million.[348] Lastly, we all chip in to pay the ~ $65 billion/yr medical bills[349] for the citizens who get taken in by those virile cowboys from Marlboro Country and the glamorous courtesans in the Virginia Slims ads. (Curiously, smoking is a serious risk for both male impotence and wrinkled female skin).

Much the same arguments apply to the animal food industry. First, our taxes are used for outright supports to the dairy industry, and as de facto supports for the meat and poultry industries, into which taxpayers pour ~ $5 billion/yr for feed grain.[350,351] This financial break allows the animal food interests to fund the tax-deductible nutritional education/propaganda that leads the public to make further use of disastrously unhealthy food that could not even hold its own on a free market. Lastly, our taxes go to pay the ~ $123 billion medical bills for all the heart attacks, cancers, and related calamities that inevitably follow.

Cigarette advertising again provides a model for strategy. JAMA's call for an outright ban on cigarette advertising is attractive, and lawyer John Banzhaf, of Action on Smoking and Health (ASH), argues that commercial speech is *not* protected by the first amendment.[352] However, when cigarette broadcast advertising was banned in 1971,[353] the tobacco companies, previously airing 80% of their ad dollars on TV, hardly blinked. With the $1.5 billion/yr savings in advertising costs,[354] they diversified. R.J. Reynolds bought up Nabisco and Philip Morris took over General Foods, so the remaining media, which in some cases devote as much as 70% of space to advertising,[355] must now cave in not only on the issue of animal food and packaged junk-food but also on the tobacco issue.

Currently, there are a number of lawsuits pending against tobacco companies, charging wrongful death from heart attack, lung cancer, oral cancer, etc. If one of these suits succeeds, the tobacco industry will fall, but so will the judicial system, that would overnight be jammed with back-to-back liability suits. Worse, if cigarette companies can be held liable for the damage caused to people foolish enough to use their product, then bicycle, motorcycle, and skateboard manufacturers, to name a few, will also go out of business. In essence, we will have illegalized risk taking.

However, advertising costs are currently tax deductible. U.S corporation taxes, adopted in 1909 and personal income taxes, adopted in 1913,[356] may be unconstitutional to begin with. Arguably, if we are to have income taxes, they should be flat rate taxes, lower, and with none of the deductions that make the IRS such a lucrative maze for bureaucrats and the cunning entrepreneurs who find ways around the bureaucrat's rules.[357] Arguably, of the items that are currently deductible, the first to lose that status should be business expenses for advertising and promotions. *If they can't tell the truth, why should we pay them to teach?* Without tax deductibility, advertising expenditures would shrink and the surviving media could tell both sides of vital issues such as the effect of smoking and diet on human health. Parsimonious advertising might finally come down to "A has product B to sell at price C and with desirable features x, y, and z."

Opponents would be the ~ 4000 ad agencies,[358] who in the last 10 years lost 13% of their business to direct marketing and junk mail, but who still get 15% commissions on media billings.[359] The library contains shelfloads of books on advertising which fall into two main camps: authors who *do* advertising and authors who want to do something *about* it. Some of the former discuss sophisticated mathematical models correlating product sales with advertising input,[360] but seem aimed mostly at convincing sponsors that their ads are working at all.

A good deal of effort could have been saved here; the estimated increase in beef sales of .28 lb/household/mo. after the "Beef: Real Food for Real People" promo,[361] reflects human gullibility, not partial differential equations.

Some of the latter books, although written by admen[362] who believe the U.S. economy would collapse without their services, admit that 80% of the public believe advertising dishonest and degrading. One brand new ad writer, asked if wasting her Ivy League education was distasteful, replied with a question: "Did you ever eat a pigeon?"

The alcohol, junk food, and tobacco industries would also protest a "no ad deductions" policy. Most of the food that is heavily advertised has been adulterated, chemicalized, sugared, salted, and packaged for the profit of the manufacturers rather than the nutritional benefit of the buyer. If the policy spread beyond health-related commodities, other complainants would likely be makers of inferior products, since the superior products sell themselves anyway.

Allies would be consumers, who should experience a drop in prices, taxpayers weary of subsidizing their own deception, and activists like Adbusters[363] who feel that the commercial priorities of advertising have almost destroyed culture.

In any event, price-supported and ad-deducted animal

food interests currently shape medical and lay opinion by simply backing authorities who favor the use of drugs and animal foods, and suppressing equally informed individuals who feel that most disease is the result of lifestyle error, preventable and often correctable by exercise, a vegan diet, and no recreational drugs.

Doubtless, citizens have a right to eat as high off the hog as they please, but they also have the obligation to pay the full cost of the hog, including the growing costs, advertising costs, and lastly their own medical costs.

XIII. DOES DIET AFFECT BEHAVIOR?

Alcohol is involved in about 64% of all murders, 41% of assaults, 34% of rapes, and 29% of all other sex crimes.[364] Intake of alcoholic beverages[365,366] parallels animal fat[367] consumption, so the answer to the title question is: probably yes.

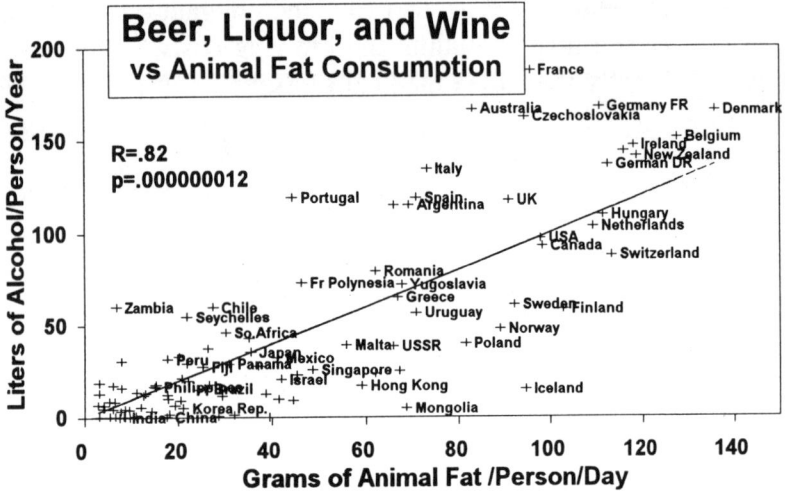

Beer, Liquor, and Wine vs Animal Fat Consumption

R=.82
p=.000000012

(Y-axis: Liters of Alcohol/Person/Year; X-axis: Grams of Animal Fat /Person/Day)

Countries plotted: France, Australia, Czechoslovakia, Germany FR, Denmark, Ireland, Belgium, New Zealand, German DR, Italy, Portugal, Spain, Argentina, UK, Hungary, Netherlands, USA, Canada, Switzerland, Romania, Fr Polynesia, Yugoslavia, Greece, Uruguay, Sweden, Finland, Zambia, Chile, Seychelles, Sq.Africa, Norway, Malta, USSR, Poland, Japan, Mexico, Peru, Panama, Singapore, Israel, Hong Kong, Iceland, Philippines, Brazil, Korea Rep., Mongolia, India, China

The correlation coefficient (R) is .82 and the p value is much less than .01, indicating that the correlation of alcohol and fat intake is not a mathematical accident. There are 106 data points, each represented by a + , but not all the country names can be shown without overlap. The rich nations do the drinking. Is it because only they have the extra cash to buy alcohol, or does the insoluble fat in their diets cry out for a solvent: alcohol?

Diet may also affect sexual behavior.

Most of the higher plants and animals on Earth reproduce sexually, all arose within the last half billion years. By mixing their genes, two individuals can increase the gene variance in their offspring.

Death, the giant of evolution, then wields a merciless scythe that cuts down the poorly adapted variants, leaving rapid opportunities for the fit variants to expand and evolve even more.

The advantages of sexual reproduction extend into several additional areas. In vertebrates, a protective environment for the offspring is provided by the sexual bonding of the parents. Many bird species are monogamous. Mammals carry the process a step further: the female carries the fetus in her body until it's ready for the world and then feeds it with the milk from her modified sweat glands.

By exploiting their sexuality, human females not only improve their own reproductive chances but their children's survival chances as well. The evidence suggests that a positive feedback loop is in effect. Women trade off sex for male assistance, which is given by those males most driven by sex, who endow the offspring with similar features. The offspring reinforce the loop by their own mating selections.

Sexual pair bonding also endows individuals with personal survival advantages; marriage and parenthood are associated with greater longevity and good health.[368] The bonding is catalyzed by the sex hormones, which are all derived from cholesterol.[369]

DERIVATION OF A FEW SEX HORMONES

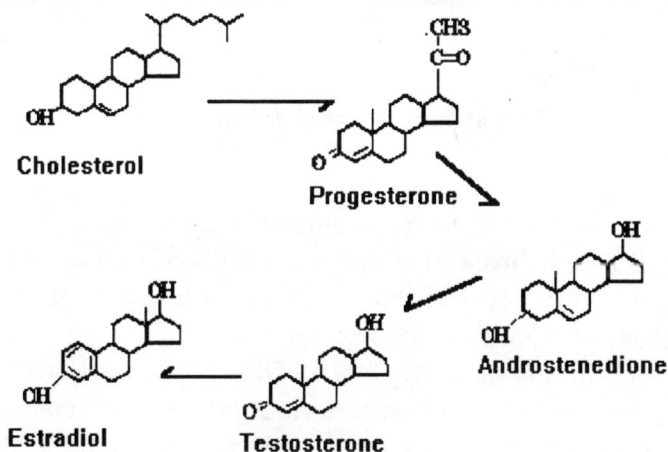

Cholesterol

Progesterone

Androstenedione

Estradiol

Testosterone

Most vertebrates mate once a year,[370] the event being timed to give the new offspring an optimal seasonal environment. But many of the primates have no particular breeding season,[371] and in humans the female can be receptive 365 days out of the year. We might as well stop disparaging sex on the grounds that "it's animalistic"; compared to us, the other animals have taken vows of chastity.

Sterol hormones are insoluble in blood, so they are carried through the circulation bound to transport proteins. Once unbound they freely cross the plasma membranes of all cells but only encounter receptors in their target cells. The hormone-receptor complex then binds to DNA in the cell nucleus, changing its genetic structure and influencing prenatal brain and genital development as well as postnatal behavior.[372] The female hormones progesterone and estradiol[373] have higher values and ranges that vary with the menstrual cycle and pregnancy.

Human Serum Sex Hormone Ranges (in nanograms per 100 milliliters)

	Male		Female	
	Low	High	Low	High
Androstenedione	75	205	85	275
Estradiol	100	600	300	350000
Progesterone	5	50	150	20000
Testosterone, free	9	30	0.3	1.9
Testosterone, total	350	800	10	60

Units:
Milligram (mg)=10^-3 gm   Nanogram (ng)=10^-9 gm
Microgram(ug)=10^-6 gm   Picogram (pg)=10^-12 gm

A basket load of animal studies and a few human studies[374] indicate that testosterone and similar androgenic hormones are responsible for the sex drive and the aggressive behaviors of both males and females.[375]

In the U.S. in 1991, 78% of persons arrested for murder, robbery, and other serious crimes were male. Eighty-two percent of all other arrestees were also male,[376] 98.7% of the rapes were by males, and it's anybody's guess how the implied 1.3% of rapes by women were accomplished. The only areas in which the ladies excelled were prostitution

(65.9%) and juvenile runaways (56.7%).

Several studies suggest that vegetarians and vegans run lower total and bound estrogen and progesterone[377] (female) and testosterone[378] (male) levels than do omnivores[379] although the unbound (active) hormone levels are about the same. This is part of the reason why they also have lower rates of hormone-dependent breast[380,381] and prostate cancers.[382] Most research indicates that the higher hormone levels in omnivores are due to increased reabsorption of endogenous hormones secreted into the gut, a phenomenon brought about by low dietary fiber. However, there is nothing in the literature to rule out the possibility that some of the effect is due to increased synthesis of hormones resulting directly from dietary cholesterol.

Since females have a fraction of the testosterone level of males, and since female hormones such as estradiol and progesterone lead more to nurturing behavior than sexual arousal in women, there's a mismatch in sex drives. Prostitution, the oldest profession, and rape, a form of violent theft, probably reflect this. Monetary transactions in which the bartered item is valued equally by both parties seldom occur, and one seldom steals what is freely given. Feminists often claim that rape is entirely a matter of male aggression and dominance, but what would happen to the incidence of prostitution and rape if male and female sex drives were equal?

The following graph[383] is compatible with the notion that since animal fat consumption increases sex hormone levels, it also aggravates the sex drive mismatch (next page):

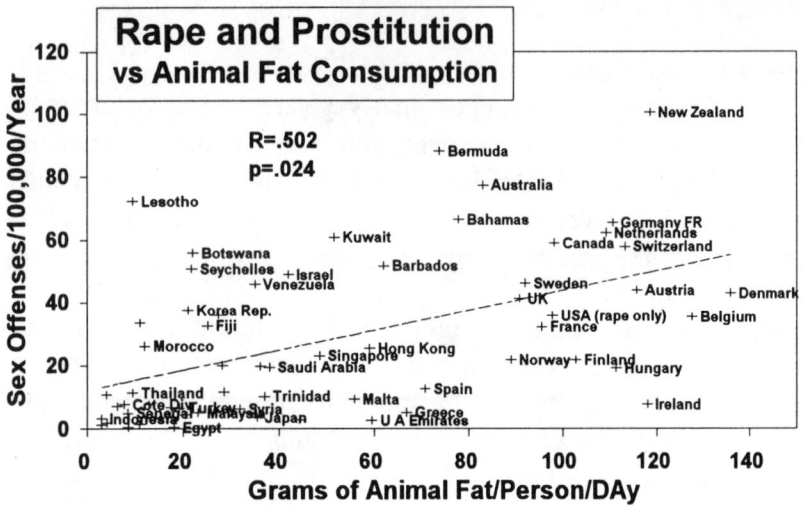

Rape and Prostitution vs Animal Fat Consumption

R=.502
p=.024

(Y-axis: Sex Offenses/100,000/Year; X-axis: Grams of Animal Fat/Person/DAy)

Data points include: New Zealand, Bermuda, Australia, Lesotho, Bahamas, Germany FR, Netherlands, Canada, Switzerland, Kuwait, Botswana, Seychelles, Israel, Venezuela, Barbados, Sweden, Austria, Denmark, UK, Korea Rep., Fiji, USA (rape only), France, Belgium, Morocco, Singapore, Hong Kong, Saudi Arabia, Norway, Finland, Hungary, Thailand, Spain, Cote D'Iv, Trinidad, Malta, Greece, Ireland, Egypt, Indonesia, Japan, Malaysia, Syria, U A Emirates

Sociobiology is a recent branch of scientific theory that more or less postulates that humans are simply life support systems used by their genes to get themselves into the next generation. It's not a comforting idea, but the theory has developed elegant mathematical formulations that predict animal behavior on the basis of genes. Humans have 46 genetic chromosomes in 23 matched pairs. Females have two X chromosomes; males have an X and a Y. Fetuses default to female unless they have the testis differentiation factor (TDF) encoded by a gene on the short arm of the Y chromosome[384]; in this case the fetus becomes a male.[385]

This genetic difference leads to different reproductive strategies as well. Here is a nearly perfect sociobiological expression of raw male reproductive strategy:

"They fought against Midian, as the Lord commanded Moses, and killed every man...'Now kill all the boys and kill every woman who has slept with a man, but save for yourselves every girl who has never slept with a man.'"

-Deuteronomy[386] 31:7 and 31:17.

As that great Bible fan, Mark Twain, once said, "Man is the only animal that blushes—or needs to." The reproductive objective here is obvious; however, one cannot imagine a female Moses telling her Amazon warriors to "Kill all the women, all the men who may have slept with a woman, and all the little girls, but keep the little boys for yourself." Since women can rarely manage more than one baby a year, there is little advantage to multiple matings and only marginal advantage to destroying other females and their offspring. Female strategy depends on cooperation and on attracting a dependable male who will stay around to help with the chores, which may include fending off large, muscular, predacious males. Those up to the task often turn out to be large, muscular, and predacious themselves. Feminists who despair of macho male behavior should blame it on the reproductive choices of their female ancestors.

"Men are the result of a vast breeding experiment run by women."

-Anon

While there are many confounding social factors, here's another correlation between diet[387] and sexual conflict:[388]

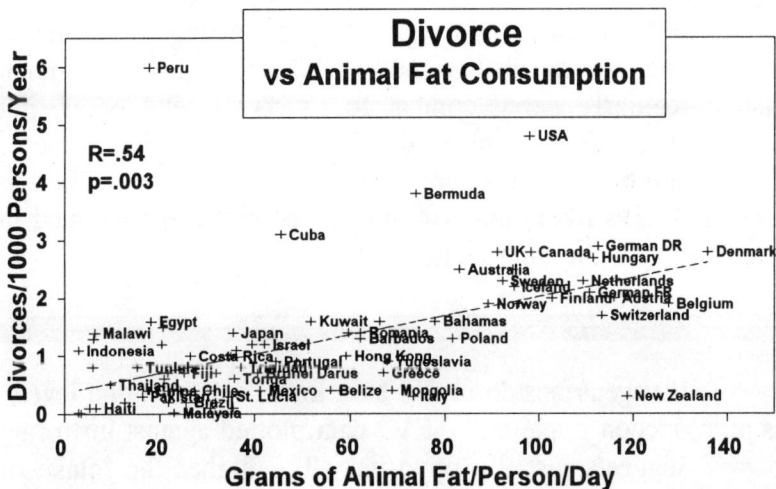

Divorce vs Animal Fat Consumption

R=.54
p=.003

(y-axis: Divorces/1000 Persons/Year, x-axis: Grams of Animal Fat/Person/Day)

Data points include: Peru, USA, Bermuda, Cuba, UK, Canada, German DR, Hungary, Denmark, Australia, Sweden, Netherlands, Iceland, Norway, Finland, Austria, Germany, Belgium, Switzerland, Egypt, Kuwait, Bahamas, Malawi, Japan, Israel, Barbados, Poland, Indonesia, Costa Rica, Portugal, Hong Kong, Yugoslavia, Tunisia, Fiji, Ireland, Brunei Darus, Greece, Thailand, Chile, Mexico, Belize, Mongolia, Pakistan, Brazil, St. Lucia, Haiti, Malaysia, New Zealand

Somewhat less robust but nevertheless suggestive, is this correlation of war[389] and animal protein consumption:

Wars and Civil Wars
From 1816 to 1980

R=.35
p= .005

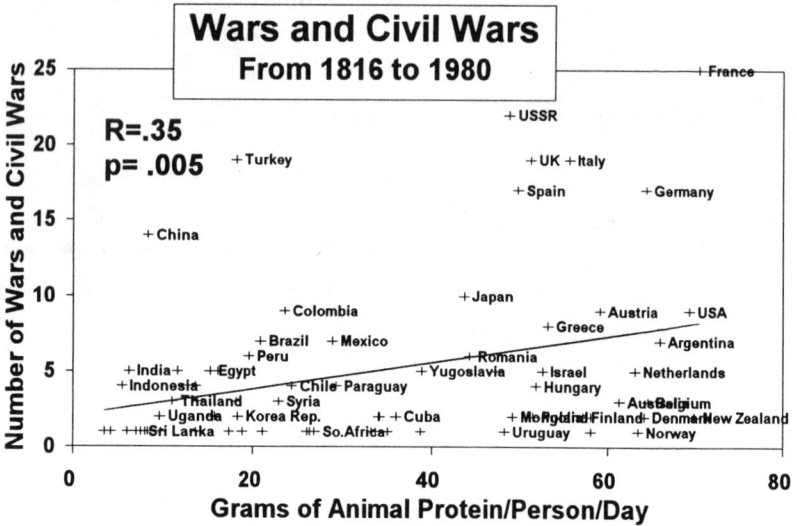

Population pressures and territorial ambitions drive most wars, but the "Moses effect" may also be operative. Many male animals fight each other at mating time but the losers generally trot off into the woods, largely intact. Human males regularly carry combat to its mortal end point, not infrequently taking many of the female war prizes with them. Twenty million humans died in WWI and about 36 million in WWII.[390] It's likely that 100 million people will have died in the wars[391] of the 20th century.

If vegetarians do in fact have lower sex hormone levels, is reproduction impaired? FAO data plotted against birth rate data[392] suggests just the opposite. The higher the intake of animal source food, the lower the birth rate.

This graph is nothing to brag about. The countries having all the kids are hovering on the brink of economic disaster and can't *afford* meat. Unless they find a way to cut their birthrates, there will be more appeals to feed the starving faces on TV. Nevertheless, there's nothing here to suggest that low animal food intake leads to reproductive problems:

Birth Rate vs Animal Fat Consumption

R=-.77
p= <<.0001

(Y-axis: Births/1000 Inhabitants/Year, ranging 0 to 60)
(X-axis: Grams of Animal Fat/Person/Day, ranging 0 to 140)

On the other hand, infertility clinics are doing a brisk business in the U.S. In 30-40% of cases the problem is in the man, in 50-60% of cases in the woman, in 5% no cause can be found.[393] Male infertility may be due to inadequate sperm motility or to a low sperm count. The average sperm count in the 60s was 60 million per milliliter. It has since dropped to 20 million.[394] Ongoing male contraceptive research found that 52 weekly injections of 200 mg testosterone shut off sperm production in 70% of male members of a study population.[395] High levels of testosterone slow the release of two pituitary hormones; follicle stimulating hormone (FSH) and luteinizing hormone (LH) that trigger the production of sperm in the testes. Perhaps high testosterone levels are helpful in the bedroom but not in the nursery.

Disturbances in fertility, fetal sex organ development, and adult gender identification in both animals and humans have recently been correlated with environmental contaminants such as DDT and PCB, that interact with hormone receptor sites.[396] The widespread medical use of diethylstilbestrol (DES) from the '40s to the '60s to prevent miscarriage caused an increase in vaginal and possibly testicular cancer in the children.[397]

127

Male fetuses exposed to female hormones become feminized. Female fetuses exposed to male hormones become masculinized.[398] As a result, exposed fetuses of both genders demonstrate homosexual mating behavior in later life. Scientific writers[399] are beginning to link the unwise use of sterols and sterol mimics to escalating human sexual dysfunction and gender orientation problems.

Impotence is a problem in the U.S., affecting an estimated 10 million[400] males, many of whom take it with poor grace that their plumbing no longer stands up to expectations. Out of 440 men studied for impotence,[401] the frequency of organic impotence rose from 49% to 100% in those individuals who were smokers,[402] diabetic, hyperlipidemic, and hypertensive. Vegans have a low incidence of all these risk factors, and a Medline search for "impotence, vegetarian, vegan" turned up no references. If impotence is a problem for vegetarians and vegans, it has thus far escaped detection. Smoking and nonsmoking impotent patients do not differ in terms of their hormonal profile.[403] It's unlikely that low testosterone levels are by themselves a common cause of impotence[404] unless combined with obesity,[405] in which case there may be an association. However, obese vegans are rare.

The age of puberty has been falling steadily in developed countries at the rate of 1-3 months per decade for the past 175 years.[406] It appears to have dropped at the same time that fat consumption was going up. One author[407] suggests that in prehistoric times when the food supply was scarce, stored fat was essential for reproduction. Further analysis indicated that girls do not reach menarche until their percent of body fat is high enough to support a successful pregnancy. Since vegan fat intake is low, it's possible that vegan girls will tend to mature later than omnivores, but is this a disadvantage? Are there any advantages to early puberty and late menopause, both characteristics of omnivores? One might argue the advantage of a longer reproductive life, but is there any advantage to children having babies they can't take care of? Is the number of babies born as important as the quality of life provided by their parents? Do we need a larger population than we have?

Female fertility seems a bit more hormonally fragile[408]than male fertility. A Medline search for "infertility, vegetarian, vegan," turned up some references pertaining to women. Both underweight and obese women are at risk for infertility.[409] Vegans and vegetarians are at some risk for underweight,[410] but not as much as omnivores are for obesity. Obese women are at greater risk for reproductive problems[411] and infertility,[412] with or without polycystic ovarian disease.[413] Normal weight and vigorous exercise for less than an hour a day correlates with good female reproductive health,[414] but vegetarians are at some risk for menstrual irregularities[415,416] and women who are also heavily involved in long distance running sometimes become amenorrheic,[417] anovulatory, hypoestrogenic, and osteoporotic.[418] After cutting back on the miles and regaining normal periods, they recover lost bone mass.[419] Of ancillary interest, it has shown that even post-menopausal women can recover up to 3.8% of forearm bone mass density by weight lifting.[420] Another author suggests that a natural progesterone skin cream derived from yams can also recover bone mineral density.[421] The alleged adverse effect of prolonged exercise on women has been challenged,[422] but to put this complex issue in perspective, perhaps it should be recalled that the first Marathon runner immortalized himself by dropping dead at the finish line.

In short, slender vegetarian women who also engage in competitive athletics should probably regard loss of ovulatory and menstrual function as a warning that they're overdoing it; otherwise, there is little evidence that vegan and vegetarian men and women are at risk for infertility or sexual dysfunction, and considerable evidence that omnivorous men and women *are*, in spite of higher total sex hormone levels.

CULTURAL CONSIDERATIONS:

In the age of theatrical overkill, macho violence sells at the box office. The old Batman defeated his opponents with gymnastic feats and a reasonable physique. Stallone approaches his foes not only with muscles that would make a gorilla feel inadequate, but half an ammo dump on his shoulders. Sexual content is dominant in the U.S. media, with particular emphasis on the female form. The only detectable difference between the covers of women's magazines and men's magazines is that in the former, the models keep their clothes on. TV soap operas feature fictitious sexual exploits in the lives of imaginary people, and newspaper columns report their antics in idolatrous detail. Apparently someone watches the soaps and reads the synopses; one suspects that many devotees are chubby omnivores thinking more about sex and enjoying it less. Perhaps someone will eventually summarize the tragic marital effects of women scarfing down meat like football players, while desperately hoping to retain the slimness desired by their spouses. If they switched to whole vegan food, most of these ladies could drop their weight without ever reading another diet book, improve their chances in the mating market, turn off the TV, and get on with their own love lives.

But humans are probably the most sexually active species on the planet with or without the lamb chops. Hypersexuality has paid off handsomely in terms of family bonding and social organization, but with increasing animal food consumption, the already hypertrophied human hormone system is thrown into overdrive. The result is a morbid preoccupation with sex and violence, impairment of reproductive function, amplification of the unavoidable gap between male and female reproductive strategies, and a resultant increase in conflict between the sexes and within and between nations.

While these considerations may make life less tranquil for individuals, the overall effect is quite different; societies seem to thrive on conflict. If the level of murder and mayhem can be held below the threshold of mass extinction, warfare promotes science, technology, and even the arts. Aggression advances national interest as long as it doesn't destroy the nation first. Without the "raging male hormones" underlying the World Wars (with the support of admiring female hormones, it should be noted), we'd be flying about in Curtiss Jennies, not 747s. With less machismo on the part of Tybalt, Romeo would have finally assisted Juliet with the diapers, and we would have been deprived of at least a dozen masterpieces (Shakespeare, Tschaikowsky, Prokofieff, Berlioz, etc.)

XIV. WHAT'S REALLY WRONG WITH THE U.S. HEALTH CARE SYSTEM?

"Medical insurance costs so much...it takes a fatted calf every month!"
- An Iowa farmer complaining on National Public Radio
(NPR) 3/19/93, without a trace of the irony.

For starters it's not health care, it's disease care.

Secondly, the goals of the system have not been properly defined. Is it supposed to fix healthy people who have been broken? Or is it supposed to keep everyone alive forever? If it's the latter, why hasn't some grandiloquent Lyndon Johnson assigned a "Task Force" to lead a "War on Death"? There would be an expensive search for "the death gene." And if the death gene exists (highly unlikely), and we eliminate it, what then? If the earliest life form had been immortal, the only extant life would be a solitary three-billion-year-old bacterium.

> *"Yes, death indeed is quite a friend;*
> *it shows how fragile health is.*
> *Oh, what a friend we have in death;*
> *especially someone else's."*
>
> *-JB*

Is there any chance that a "War on Death" would be any more successful than Johnson's "War on Poverty?"[423] Or Nixon's "War on Cancer?" Somewhere along the line *that* "Task Force" picked off a sampan or two[424] (childhood cancers, stomach cancer), but the enemy carriers and battleships[425] (cancer of the breast, prostate, intestine, lung, and liver) are still hiding under ancient biplanes towing banners that read "Beef - Real Food for Real People", "Pork - the Other White Meat", "Milk - It Does a Body Good", "Come to Marlboro Country", and "This Bud's for You." The United States Department of Agriculture price-supports the planes, and the Internal Revenue Service tax-deducts the banners.

Presently the U.S medical budget runs about 12% of the gross national product.[426] Although there has been a 27-year

132

increase in life expectancy at birth since the turn of the century, Thomas McKeown, M.D. has made a strong case that most of the increase was brought about by improved sanitation and better food distribution as a result of "the second agricultural revolution" of the 19th century. In his words: "The health of man is determined essentially by his behaviour, his food, and the nature of the world around him, and is only marginally influenced by personal medical care."[427] McKinlay and McKinlay[428] analyzed American health statistics and concluded that no more than 3.5% of the decline in mortality since the turn of the century could be attributed to medical intervention.

While life expectancy at age 65 has gone up five years since 1900, annual medical costs per capita have risen from $25 (1930) to $1200 (1988-inflated). In the graph below,[429] national health care costs as percent of GNP are compared to increased life expectancy.

U.S. Life Expectancy
vs Health Care Cost

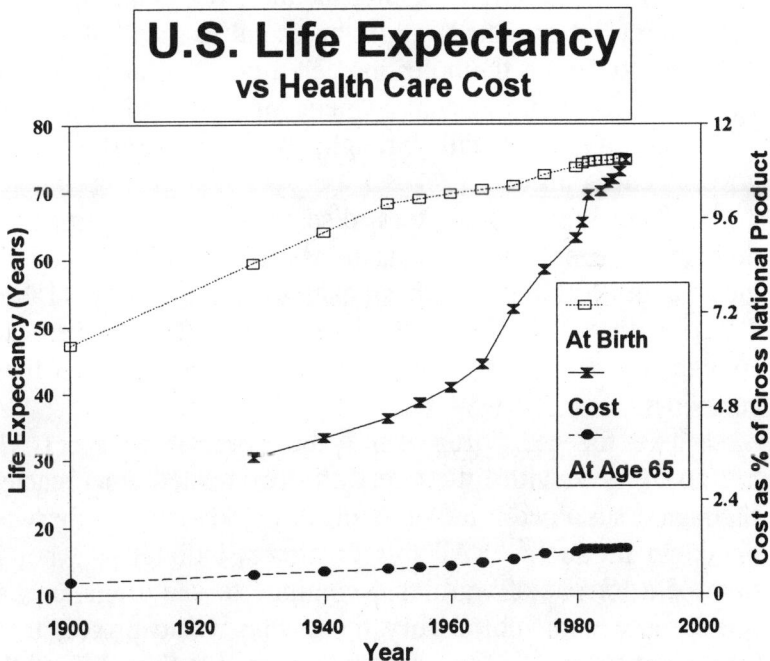

The major increases in longevity occurred before medical costs went through the ceiling, so the present costs do not appear to be a superlative example of a bargain.

Workers in the Clinton "Health Reform War Room" (usage courtesy of NPR 10/13/93) are unlikely to reduce the burden, since they have skillfully sidestepped some fundamental problems.

A. DEFINITION PROBLEMS

It's widely argued that the government's medical interventions are there to provide a "safety net" for those who can't afford care. But there *is* no safety net, and the use of the term in the context of disease care is a tendentious semantic manipulation. A true safety net keeps the trapeze flyer from hitting the floor.

Every time. And it works.

But in the circus of life, *all* the flyers wind up on the floor, safety net or not. It might be useful to speak of a safety *sieve* and to design the holes in such a way that only the most egregious lack of personal hygiene or advanced age would allow the flyers to fall through, but that's not what the government is up to.

The government sees disease as a capricious and democratic event and intends to tax the healthy to pay the medical bills of those who smoke, drink, consume 41% of Calories from fat,[430] and use hard drugs. If that were not enough, this same government actively finances the first three behaviors.

As for the "drug war," the government spent $12 billion in 1992 with little effect on drug-related emergencies, although it sustained a lucrative black market for an otherwise worthless product.[431] All this to protect individuals who, in spite of a torrent of warnings, continue to use drugs anyway and to defy with mortal fury those who would protect them from themselves.[432] They accounted for less than 1% of the drug-abuse deaths,[433] much less than alcohol and tobacco users (next page):

Drug Abuse Deaths
As Percent of Yearly Total

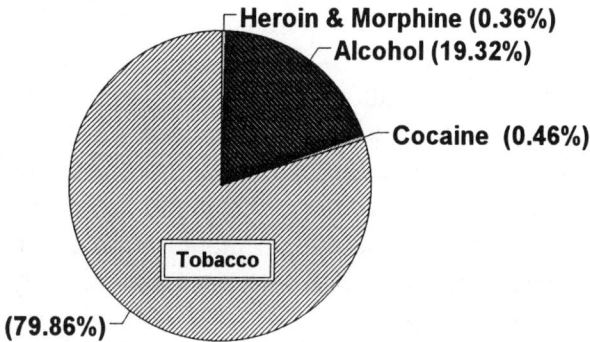

Heroin & Morphine (0.36%)

Alcohol (19.32%)

Cocaine (0.46%)

Tobacco

(79.86%)

"Health care" is being hyped as a "human right" to citizens unaware that the first term is an oxymoron, and the second is a legal fiction. If you really have health, you don't need any care. And do we have a "human right" to food and shelter?

The Soviet Union tried that one, and after numerous lethal purges, wars, tens of millions of deaths, constant shortages and dissatisfaction, communism finally collapsed from its own sheer ideological defects.

But food and shelter *are* essential to human survival. Medical care is *not*. Sixty million years of primate, hominid, and human evolution proceeded without antibiotics, doctors, or magnetic resonance imagers.

There are documented cases of humans who actually make it through a long, healthy, and productive life without ever seeing a physician. They fall asleep in their nineties and don't wake up, and the autopsy report reads, "Patient dead, cause unknown...." If medical care disappeared overnight, the overall effect on humanity might not be measurable except for a return to the folds of Darwinian selection, a change that might be applauded by future generations.

B. VALUATION PROBLEMS

Let us postulate that all therapeutics are bogus until proven otherwise. If public funds *are* to be used to pay for private therapeutics, which therapeutics should be covered first?

Surely, civilization should be able to guarantee treatments that are both effective and cheap. A child who falls and breaks an arm should not have to go through life with a crooked arm because no orthopedist could be found. A stone sober, alert, quick-reflexed athlete should not die of a ruptured spleen because a drunk hit his car and no surgeon was available. And while the cause of rheumatic heart disease probably has more to do with diet, sanitation, and general hygiene, an inexpensive shot of penicillin will abort the opportunistic streptococcal infection that causes the permanent auto-immune valvular damage in the heart.

At the other end of the continuum we have the coronary artery bypass graft (CABG), and two choices: Choice One: Quit smoking, start exercising, go on a vegan diet and watch while your serum cholesterol drops, your coronary arteries open up,[434] and your coronary heart disease (CHD) gradually vanishes - cost $0.00.

Choice Two: Lie down on a table, have your sternum split, your heart stopped, other vessels used to bridge your plugged coronary arteries, your heart started again, your chest closed with permanent steel wires, run a 1.8% chance of dying in the OR, spend a week recovering in the hospital,[435] and face a 15% chance the grafts will plug up again[436] if you keep smoking, sitting on your duff, and eating grease deep fried in hot fat - cost $40,000. The roto-rooter approach to CHD is a waste of time unless a vegan diet is instituted first. If it is instituted, the need to call a plumber will diminish rapidly.[437]

Some cardiologists are still telling their patients that Choice One is ineffective, although a host of studies show that CHD can be regressed in primates and rodents,[438] and at least two studies have shown that it can be regressed in humans also.[439] Other cardiologists admit CHD is regressible but state that a vegan diet is "impractical."

Two responses to this one are in order: first off, it's not the doctor's job to tell his patient what's practical. It's his job to tell the patient what's possible and let the patient decide what's practical. Secondly, if the patient were charged the full cost of the CABG, he might find the vegan alternative a whole lot more practical than he thought. But the patient usually prefers that his fellow citizens cough up the shekels for the CABG and doctors, drug companies, the government, hospitals, insurance companies, "progressive" politicians, and surgical supply houses all shout hosannahs of affirmation.

A Few Medical Costs
Some Conditions Preventable by Diet

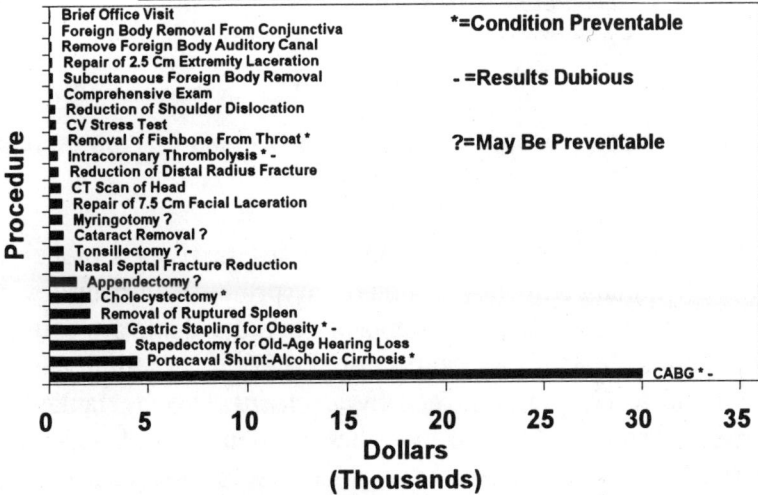

Procedure	
Brief Office Visit	
Foreign Body Removal From Conjunctiva	*=Condition Preventable
Remove Foreign Body Auditory Canal	
Repair of 2.5 Cm Extremity Laceration	
Subcutaneous Foreign Body Removal	- =Results Dubious
Comprehensive Exam	
Reduction of Shoulder Dislocation	
CV Stress Test	
Removal of Fishbone From Throat *	?=May Be Preventable
Intracoronary Thrombolysis * -	
Reduction of Distal Radius Fracture	
CT Scan of Head	
Repair of 7.5 Cm Facial Laceration	
Myringotomy ?	
Cataract Removal ?	
Tonsillectomy ? -	
Nasal Septal Fracture Reduction	
Appendectomy ?	
Cholecystectomy *	
Removal of Ruptured Spleen	
Gastric Stapling for Obesity * -	
Stapedectomy for Old-Age Hearing Loss	
Portacaval Shunt-Alcoholic Cirrhosis *	
	CABG * -

Dollars (Thousands): 0   5   10   15   20   25   30   35

In the above graph a few therapeutic regimens are compared for effectiveness, cost, and preventability.[440] Fixing a broken arm costs about $433. It's effective and cheap, and the condition is usually accidental. The CABG lies at the other end. It has not been shown to extend life (although it reduces the frequency of angina), it's expensive, and CHD is surely the most preventable disease known to mankind. One could fill in the graph with many choices until it became unreadable, but the concept is simple. Some diseases are accidental, the lightning bolts hurled by a demented Zeus but repairable by scientifically enlightened mortals. Other diseases people bring upon themselves, largely by following lifestyle and dietary patterns, which, though socially acceptable, are fatally flawed.

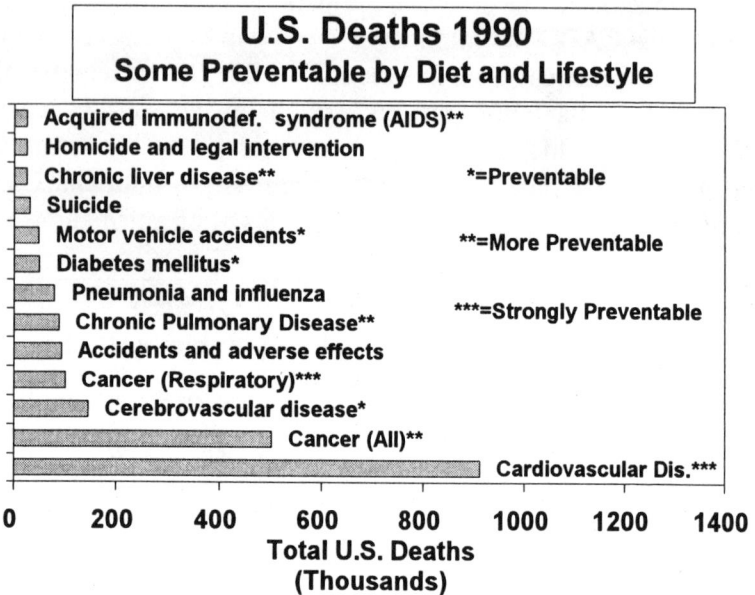

U.S. Deaths 1990
Some Preventable by Diet and Lifestyle

Acquired immunodef. syndrome (AIDS)**
Homicide and legal intervention
Chronic liver disease**   *=Preventable
Suicide
Motor vehicle accidents*   **=More Preventable
Diabetes mellitus*
Pneumonia and influenza
Chronic Pulmonary Disease**   ***=Strongly Preventable
Accidents and adverse effects
Cancer (Respiratory)***
Cerebrovascular disease*
Cancer (All)**
Cardiovascular Dis.***

0   200   400   600   800   1000   1200   1400
Total U.S. Deaths
(Thousands)

Surely if the government is to use taxpayer's money to care for human ailments, it should pay primarily for the Jovian lightning bolts. However, it appears that accidents are causing only about 7% of the deaths, or 5.77% if we eliminate the 50% of MVAs caused, not by *accident*, but by tanked-up drivers. Probably 50% of the other accidents are also alcohol-related, in which case the real accidents only cause about 3.48% of the deaths.[441] Of course, we can run the figure back up a bit by including the Saturday Night Knife and Gun Club under the heading "Homicide and Legal Intervention," but most of these frolicsome clients, a standard feature in urban emergency rooms, are also tanked, as are many of the suicides. As noted in Chapter IX, distilled spirits and beer are made from USDA price-supported feed grains at a cost to taxpayers of about $80 million/year.

Most of the remaining medical costs are going to the treatment of degenerative diseases that result from other lifestyle errors also underwritten by the USDA's price-support policies.

C. FINANCIAL PROBLEMS

The public debt[442] increases each year, reflecting the federal deficit[443] of the previous year.[444] Each U.S. war also increases the debt substantially.

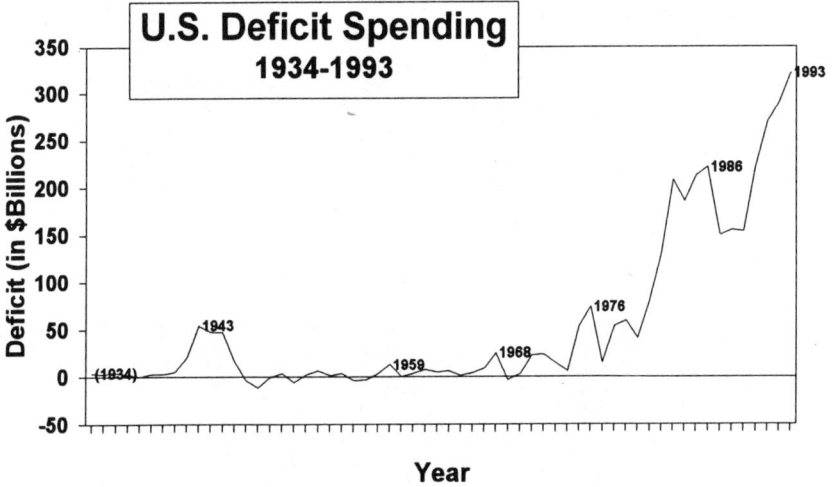

U.S. Deficit Spending 1934-1993

Arguably, this is a way a of shifting our own financial responsibilities onto the shoulders of our grandchildren, but sooner or later the system must break down.

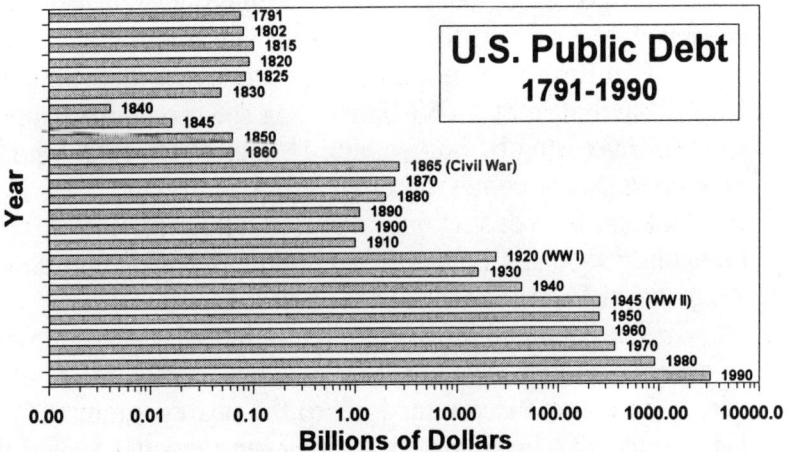

U.S. Public Debt 1791-1990

139

Alcohol advertising amounts to $1.2 billion/year.[445] The Internal Revenue Service allows tax deductions for advertising, so taxpayers in effect are paying about a third of the bill, or $360 million/year for the flapdoodle put out by the booze companies.

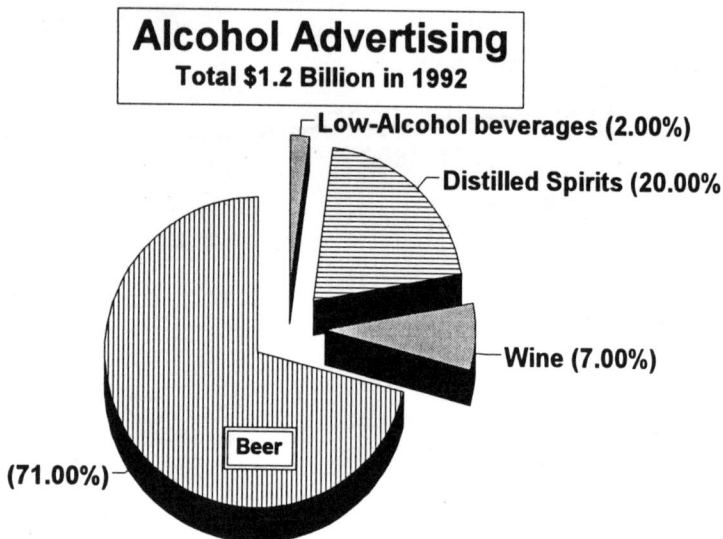

Alcohol Advertising
Total $1.2 Billion in 1992

Low-Alcohol beverages (2.00%)

Distilled Spirits (20.00%

Wine (7.00%)

Beer

(71.00%)

Alcohol, food, and tobacco advertising comes to about $5.757 billion/year.[446] The pharmaceutical industry does a $63 billion/year trade,[447] and its $5 billion/year advertising budget has almost persuaded both patients and physicians that the only conceivable treatment for any ailment is a drug.

Fertilizer and pesticide sales were over $28 billion in 1992,[448] and at least $.658 billion was spent on advertising.[449]

Advertising by horticultural food crop growers, who get no USDA help, comes to only $.245 billion/year.[450] If all advertising tax deductions were disallowed, the loss to horticulturists would be more than compensated by the reduced competition from the rest of the food industry.

The Food and Drug Administration (FDA), supposedly riding herd on dishonest advertisers, actually *requires* labels in which fat content is rounded off to the nearest gram.[451] "No Fat Yogurt" can be found, in which even the label admits that there are 2 grams of fat in a 220 Calorie serving, or about 8% of Calories from fat (10.2% if the 2 grams were actually rounded off from 2.49, as they probably were.) Plain yogurt is about 30% of Calories from fat, but when sugar and fruit are added, the denominator is conveniently juggled. The infamous "93% fat-free hamburger," that is actually 35% of Calories from fat, is another FDA triumph. The new "Nutrition Facts" food labels hailed by FDA chief, David Kessler, as a way to make "informed choices," become usable facts only after the consumer applies a calculator to the fat and Calorie data. There are many who would be pleased if the FDA, the USDA, and the entire advertising biz[452] were fricasseed and served *en flambé*.

When water subsidies for cattle ranchers ($1 billion/yr),[453] grazing breaks on Western public lands ($.058 billion/yr),[454] advertising deductions for the health sensitive products mentioned above, and USDA price supports are added together, the total is only about $18 billion/year, hardly enough for the Pentagon to buy a left-handed monkey wrench for a Lockheed C-5A.

But wait; there's more. That $18 billion goes through a little biological photo-multiplier, and when it comes out, we've got an additional $123 billion medical bill for the diseases caused by animal food consumption. Tobacco runs up $65 billion[455] and alcohol another $100 billion,[456] so we're up to $306 billion. If the USDA, the cause of it all, were itself phased out, there would be further savings of $63 billion dollars/year,[457] much gnashing of teeth, but also a return to an agricultural free market. The grand total of $369 billion exceeds the estimated 1993 deficit. Readers who feel the USDA is irreplaceable should consult *The Farm Fiasco* by James Bovard.[458]

One might suggest to the distinguished Solons that withdrawing financial support from the enterprises that make people sick might kill two birds with one stone, the deficit *and* the medical bills. Unfortunately, the Solons are accepting bribes from concerned parties,[459] whose agendas, though generally not supportive of the Clinton "health care

141

reforms,[460"] are blind to the problems outlined above.

Political Action Contributions
1981-1992

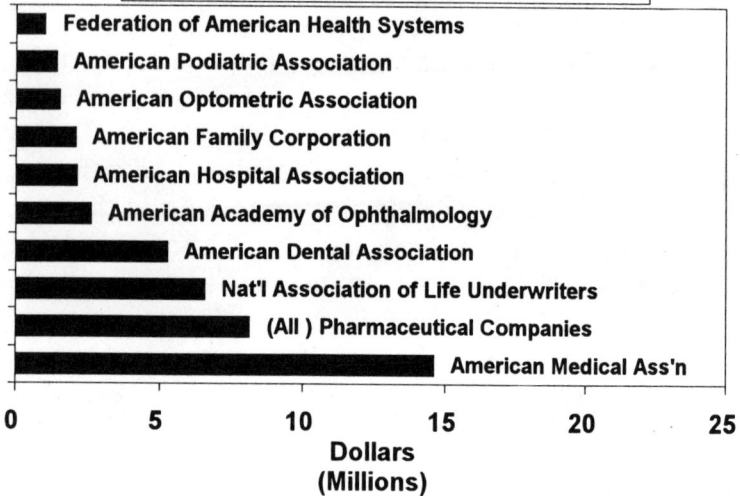

■	Federation of American Health Systems
■	American Podiatric Association
■	American Optometric Association
■	American Family Corporation
■	American Hospital Association
■	American Academy of Ophthalmology
■	American Dental Association
■	Nat'l Association of Life Underwriters
■	(All) Pharmaceutical Companies
■	American Medical Ass'n

```
0        5        10       15       20       25
              Dollars
             (Millions)
```

Some have suggested "sin taxes" on alcohol, tobacco, and animal source food to be dedicated to the care of the users. But to make "instant pork," one need only take dedicated tax moneys and pour in the U.S. Congress. Total abolition of these items would cause a civil war, but it's completely reasonable to demand that the U.S. government cease and desist from *supporting* them with our taxes.

D. BUZZ WORD PROBLEMS

"Preventive medicine" has a fine ring to it, and is increasingly heard in the halls of Academe, as well as in Hillary's "task force." But very little is really being done to prevent disease. Those yearly physical exams, EKGs, and proctoscopic exams serve only to detect disease early in its course. If mammography detects your breast cancer before it can be palpated, there may be an improvement in survival rate, but nothing to compare with not getting it at all.

The" price of prevention" in the usual sense of mass screening programs may be more costly than treating individual disease[461] although workplace incentives for exercise, diet, and no smoking can reduce a company's medical bills up to 20%.

E. MOTIVATION PROBLEMS

There are several factors that have always inhibited a truly preventive approach to human health. First of all, there's no money in it. If a physician tells a patient to stop smoking and drinking, exercise regularly, and quit all animal food, and if the patient actually takes that advice, the only winner will be the patient. The physician may see the patient for an occasional injury, but gone will be the lucrative repeat visits for cancer and rumors of cancer, diabetes, hypertension, obesity, vascular disease, and the weakness woes. Are M.D.s actively suppressing this advice? It's probably not that simple.

"The distinctive feature of Homo sapiens is the desire to take a pill."

-Anon

The descendants of Hygeia have always fared poorly in the market against the descendants of Aesculapius; the conditions necessary for health have been known to every generation and are known today. The problem is that most humans would rather be boiled in snake oil than give up their bad habits and accept full responsibility for their own health. Around this uniquely human failing have grown up the animal food industry, which panders to a physiological fat addiction probably bred into us by ancestral famines, and the pharmaceutical industry, which purveys palliative remedies for the preventable conditions caused by that addiction. Doctors at worst are like heroin dealers; they didn't really create the demand or grow the stuff, they just prescribe it.

F. CATEGORY PROBLEMS

Honolulu street scene: a man pushes a baby carriage five feet into a crosswalk, then leaves the carriage and walks

143

back to the curb to retrieve a piece of wind-blown paper. An oncoming motorist brakes, the father returns, pushes on to the other side, and a passing police officer stops the motorist and tickets him for driving without a seat belt. Lewis Carroll did not write this scenario. Government rules put the motorist in the same risk category with the jay-walker and his hapless baby.

Because of the increased cost and complexity of medical technology, few people can afford fee-for-service medicine, so medical insurance is a logical option. But many health insurance plans suffer from a fatal flaw. By charging the same rates for everyone, sickness is actually encouraged and health is penalized. *Nowhere* in the medical system is there a financial inducement to health. Doctors, drug companies, hospitals, and politicians depend financially on human illness, and many patients exploit minor illness for secondary gain. Healthy, fit, young people who seldom utilize medical services often pay the same rates as those who believe a stay in the hospital is equivalent to a visit in exotic lands.

A number of variable rate insurance schemes have been used. One company charges higher rates for smokers, since they're at greater risk for everything. But how does the company find out who smokes, and who doesn't? A "smoker's questionnaire" only rewards dishonesty.

Another approach is to copy the automobile insurance companies and make health insurance experiential. The more you visit the doctor, the higher your rates go. Since many omnivores wind up with obesity, hypertension, CHD, diabetes, or cancer, a "meat-eater's questionnaire" could be dispensed with and dietary status would be largely self-revealing by higher utilization rates.

The Cato Institute suggests employer-funded Medical Savings Accounts (MSAs), similar to tax-free IRA accounts, in which workers would "effectively be spending their own funds for non-catastrophic health care," thus restoring market incentives to control costs.[462] However, while seven states have now provided for MSAs in their income tax codes, federal tax law discriminates heavily against them in favor of traditional third-party insurance which "insulates consumers from the cost of their health care decisions."

A legendary Chinese system is sometimes mentioned: the doctor is only paid when the patient is well. But how many patients will admit they're well if telling the truth results in a doctor bill? Furthermore, wellness has little to do with doctors, and almost everything to do with lifestyle, diet, and exercise. Doctors are most useful in treating accidental conditions, and for these, they can easily be paid.

G. EMPIRE-BUILDING PROBLEMS

Other players emerge. There is now a little growth industry apparently determined to classify every human character disorder as a disease. "Alcoholism" is a splendid example. There are genetic predispositions to the inappropriate metabolism of ethanol, and on the basis of this, "specialists" in the "treatment" of "alcoholism" raid the treasury for funds. Authors[463] who point out that one cannot be alcoholic if alcohol and the volitional act of imbibing it are both absent get the silent treatment from the press and withering attacks by academics claiming special expertise in the field.[464] Neither side has apparently noted that there are few, if any, alcoholic vegetarians and that a common finding at meat-centered restaurants is a beverage list recommending which form of alcohol to consume with which fat-laden meat dish.

There's no limit to the money that can be thrown into the treatment of such "diseases"[465] as alcoholism, anorexia-bulimia, cyclothymia, gambling, hyperactivity, obesity, obsessive-compulsive disorder, PMS, sexual addiction, and smoking for which the best treatment is peer pressure and a personal determination to change. However, each time disease status is achieved, costs are passed to the taxpayers, while the disease entrepreneurs become tenured. Skinnerian behaviorists[466] to a man, they believe humans to be will-less automatons but miss the point that if we are all causal robots in a pre-determined world, then there's no sense trying to treat *anything*, since all outcomes are already foreordained.

H. UTILIZATION PROBLEMS

A segment of the U.S. population now regards the human body as a two-legged automobile. If something malfunctions, they take it to the mechanic. If the mechanic fails to fix it, a lawyer is then brought in to "fix" the mechanic. A scalpel left in a surgical abdomen is no doubt cause for legal action, but failure to eliminate low back pain is not.[467] The physician did not create back pain, the Great Zuzu did. Why not sue Zuzu? A hefty part of the medical budget represents unnecessary tests[468] done to keep the physician out of range of another of Zuzu's mistakes: the legal profession. Lewin-VHI, a health care consulting firm, suggests that eliminating malpractice-defensive medicine could save more than $38 billion over the next five years.[469]

Because of the illusion that medical care is free, Health Maintenance Organization (HMO) patients will often demand unnecessary X-rays, an abuse that could cause some genetic problems in the next century. For instance, falls from a crib hardly ever cause a skull fracture, but anxious parents may insist on an X-ray, doubting the physician's judgement and apparently failing to understand that greater knowledge is needed for the same physician to read the X-ray after it's ordered than is needed to order it. Some parents seem to feel x-rays are therapeutic. Perhaps passing high energy photons through the brain will increase the child's intelligence?

"Better safe than sorry," says the parent after the X-ray is read negative. Of course,"better safe than sorry!" And better heads than not-heads, if you don't like tails. This nonsensical tautology is also extensively used by the walking well, arriving in the ER after a minor traffic crunch in which not even the car received visible damage. Further unnecessary x-rays are taken, that in the great majority of cases are of interest only to dueling liability lawyers.

One radiology text suggests that most ankle, bone survey, coccyx, lumbar spine, nasal bone, rib, sinus, and skull[470] x-rays are unnecessary, and that 30% of them are done for medico-legal reasons, not for good patient care.[471]

Americans now use lawyers to solve their medical problems and doctors to solve their legal ones, with no obvious overall benefit to either their health or wealth.

Laboratory exams account for 25-30% of all health care costs.[472] In one hospital there was an 82% variance in ordering criteria among staff physicians. The high utilizers did not improve their quality of medical care, shorten hospital stays, or reduce mortality.[473]

The common cold is caused by any of a myriad of viruses in the nose. Viruses are not affected by antibiotics, but when a patient gets penicillin for a cold, and the cold clears up as it always does with or without penicillin, that patient then joins the First Church of Penicillin, and henceforth will always demand penicillin when a cold comes along. Church members will complain loudly if the useless antibiotic is not given, but if it is given, doesn't work, or causes a serious drug reaction, there will be nary a peep. "Do something, Doctor!" is a cry dear to Church members, even if what's done makes the problem worse.

Members of the Society for the Medical Performing Arts, a related group, like to call the ambulance for trifling problems. ER physicians dread the sound of an ambulance coming up the driveway, not for fear of dealing with a serious case, but because about half the time a patient is only using the ambulance to make *le grande* entrance, after which he can hustle the hospital for a dubious admission. In Arizona in one year[474] there were 5,500 unnecessary "code 3" (lights and siren activated) ambulance calls with a $1 million bill to the state. In a Connecticut study,[475] patients with private insurance made appropriate use of ambulances in 77.8% of cases, patients with Medicare did so in 65.8% of cases, and patients with Medicaid did so in 14.7% of cases. Approximately 20% of the observed misuse was related to alcohol intoxication.

Ivan Illich[476] has pointed out that the sound of a siren in developing countries stifles the community's instincts to charitably take care of its own. In the U.S., that which began as charity now suffers thoughtless and selfish exploitation by the recipients.

147

One patient, after treatment for constipation, was asked why she had dialed 911 to get to the ER. "It was an emergency to me!" she replied indignantly. Well, yes, ma'am, but how emergent would you have defined it if you had to pay the ambulance driver before you got on board? And how many physicians can spend an hour haggling with the lady after disallowing her free ambulance trip, knowing she will likely invent further symptoms to justify it?

During a tour in Vietnam in 1967 I took care of bleeding civilian war casualties brought to the ER by hired pedicab. In this country constipation arrives by tax-supported state-of-the art ambulance.

There are related and similar defects in workman's compensation programs. A cook who works for someone else will try for a week off after a 1 cm first degree burn. A cook who has his own business and a family to support will pitch out the doctor's work slip and go back to work with a broken leg. The system is rewarding those who magnify their illness. Many workers feel cheated if they don't take their full allotment of sick time and will exploit symptoms that others would hardly notice. Perhaps employers should simply tack on an extra week of vacation and give the employee the option of using it to play sick or take off for Acapulco.

The 1991 total employer's cost of workers' compensation was $62 billion, up $7 billion (12.5 percent) from 1990.[477] A recent report by the General Accounting Office indicates that fraud may account for as much as 10% of all health care costs.[478] Physicians are key players, but for the majority not actively padding the books, exposing compensation fraud is painful and occasionally hazardous; no bonus points are awarded. Fraud is predictable whenever the government decides that funds are to be taken from group A and given to the more deserving members of group B.

"If you have chest pain, see your doctor," is advice that floods emergency rooms with "the worried well," afraid they're having a heart attack. Psychiatric illness was present in up to 50 per cent of new patients attending a chest pain clinic.[479] In another study 40% of young adults presenting with chest pain were deemed to have no disease and to require no follow-up.[480]

Americans have lost confidence in their health. To some extent this is the result of over-sell by the medical profession, but there's no reason they should have any confidence, either. They're overweight and out of shape, and they consume 500 mg cholesterol/day. The un-diagnosable chest pains may simply be a subtle and ischemic warning from nature that unless dietary habits are changed, there *will* eventually be a heart attack.

I. PATERNALISM PROBLEMS

"All systems are evil. All governments are evil. Not just a trifle evil. Monstrously evil. "

-John Gardner, *Grendel*[481]

The widely lamented 39 million medically uninsured Americans[482] are not proof that universal medical coverage is essential, but, rather, evidence that human existence is possible without *any* coverage. However, advocates of universal medical insurance[483] make unwarranted and hidden assumptions that they never reveal, namely that since we're all eventually going to get dead, we're necessarily going to get sick first, and therefore the young and healthy should sacrifice their own family finances to foot the bills for the old. It's also assumed that we'll all want our chronic or terminal illness given aggressive and expensive treatment rather than inexpensive hospice support or merciful euthanasia, and that we are all so afraid of death that we're willing to bankrupt the country and saddle our grandchildren with paralyzing debt in order to fend it off. Those who do not agree with these assumptions will be taxed exactly as if they did.

There are solutions to most of the problems of life, but not by the government. The government *is* the problem.[484] While piously proclaiming "health for all," it uses our taxes to finance the very substances that cause disease. Then it abrogates the decision-making process by throwing life's *bon vivants* into the same insurance pot with the most abstemious health kooks (e.g., this author and most of this book's readers). That's probably rooted in some religious injunction to be one's brother's keeper, but the injunction is a cruel one, since it relieves brother of the vital necessity of learning to be his own keeper.

If the government got out of the "Health Care" biz, individuals could pick the healer of their choice, or none at all, and pay for the healer's service in accord with what it's worth. Medical insurance plans, a form of gambling in which you bet you'll get sick and the plan bets you won't, could compete in the free market with other companies and offer or not offer coverage for various "alternative healing" systems, that in turn would compete with M.D.s.

A free market process would then quickly establish that an experienced board certified trauma surgeon is the person to see after a bad auto crash. An orthopedist makes sense for a broken femur, and other surgical sub-specialists also do an honest day's work. But for the majority of currently fashionable degenerative diseases, a switch to an athletic, drug free, vegan lifestyle makes better sense than any nostrums in or out of the medical establishment.

SUMMING UP

The U.S. "Health Care" system is in trouble because:

1. The demagogues running it prefer catchy phrases (e.g., "'health care' is a 'human right'") to plain English. The public has grown accustomed to government gobbledegook and also speaks it fluently.

2. Politicians are driven not by principle but by pressure, much of it generated by the very agricultural interests that create disease.

3. The system itself, that seldom produces either true cures or life everlasting, has been over-valued by anxious unwell people who are indeed at high risk for disease and early death, in part because of item 2.

4. Nowhere in the system is there a financial incentive for good health. Lacking this, patients over-utilize prepaid medical services with enormous wastage. Drug companies, hospitals, labs, and physicians then over-charge for useless procedures, while the legal profession finds sustenance under every rotting stump.

XV. FISH OIL FLIM-FLAM

In 1976 researchers began to note that Eskimos have a low incidence of coronary heart disease (CHD) in spite of high (420-1650 mg/day) cholesterol intakes.[485] They eat a lot of fish. Since then over 576 articles have appeared in 155 journals[486] extolling the virtues of fish oil as a preventive for CHD.[487] Fish oil is high in Omega-3 (ω3) fatty acid (FA) and this leads to high levels of eicosopentanoic fatty acid (EPA) and the high EPA levels depress blood platelet clotting tendencies[488] and thus lessen the chance of clots in the coronary arteries.

Trouble is, fish oil is a two edged sword. It cuts the chances of a heart attack but it increases the risk of cerebral hemorrhage[489](CH). By thinning the blood, which protects against clots in the 3 mm diameter coronary arteries in the heart, it increases the chance that delicate 0.5 mm cerebral arteries will pop and bleed into the brain.

Unfortunately, there's a good deal of biochemistry involved here, but perhaps pictures will help. A few key fatty acids look like this:

Linoleic Acid (LA) 18:2ω6

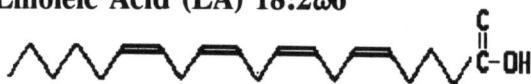

Arachidonic Acid (AA) 20:4ω6

α-Linolenic Acid (ALA) 18:3ω3

Eicosopentanoic Acid (EPA) 20:5ω3

Docosahexaenoic Acid (DHA) 22:6ω3

Each angle, end point, or "C" represents a carbon atom and the single connecting lines are (saturated) chemical bonds. The double lines represent (desaturated) double bonds in which a hydrogen atom has been knocked off the carbon on each end of the bond. A good deal of professorial infighting clouds the question of which end to count from but the winning side seems to be counting from the left, so linoleic acid (LA) with eighteen carbons and two double bonds, the first one (the ω) six carbons from the left, is an 18:2ω6 fatty acid. α-linolenic acid (ALA) is an 18:3ω3 and arachidonic acid (AA) is a 20:4ω6. It used to be held that AA is an essential fatty acid but it's now known humans can synthesize it from linoleic acid. Cats cannot and must get it from their flesh diet, further evidence that humans, unlike cats, are not serious meat-eaters.

Given LA or ALA, humans and many other animals can enzymatically elongate the acids (add on by two carbon increments), and desaturate the products (remove hydrogen atoms to form double bonds), which results in a zoo full of variant FAs.[490] From dietary ALA humans can synthesize the other ω3 fatty acids themselves.[491] Two of the most important ones are EPA, a 20:5ω3 FA, and docosahexanoic acid (DHA) a 22:6ω3 FA.

EPA and DHA are present in high quantity in fish oil but only because the bottom rung in the marine food chain is plankton which contain algae. Green plants and most algae contain intracellular organelles called chloroplasts. Chloroplasts contain chlorophyll to trap solar energy, but they also synthesize ALA which is the starting point for all the other ω3 fatty acids in both marine and terrestrial food chains.[492]

Fish oil is high in EPA and DHA only because the tiny fish ate the algae and the bigger fish ate the smaller fish, synthesizing and concentrating the other ω3s at each cannibalistic step.

Since the agricultural revolution 10,000 years ago, ω3 fatty acids have been marginal in the human diet. Why? Because the ag revolution stressed grains, which were cheap and therefore accelerated human population growth. Grains are good sources of LA (18:2ω6), but with the exception of flaxseed, grains and seeds do not have much ALA (18:3ω3), which is found in more plentiful supply in the more expensive and perishable leafy green vegetables such as kale, spinach, or taro leaves.

The following graph[493] shows that the linolenic (ALA)/Calorie ratio is not highest in fish or fish oils but in plant foods. Flaxseed oil comes in first, but in addition to being a good ALA source, it is also a truly spectacular laxative.

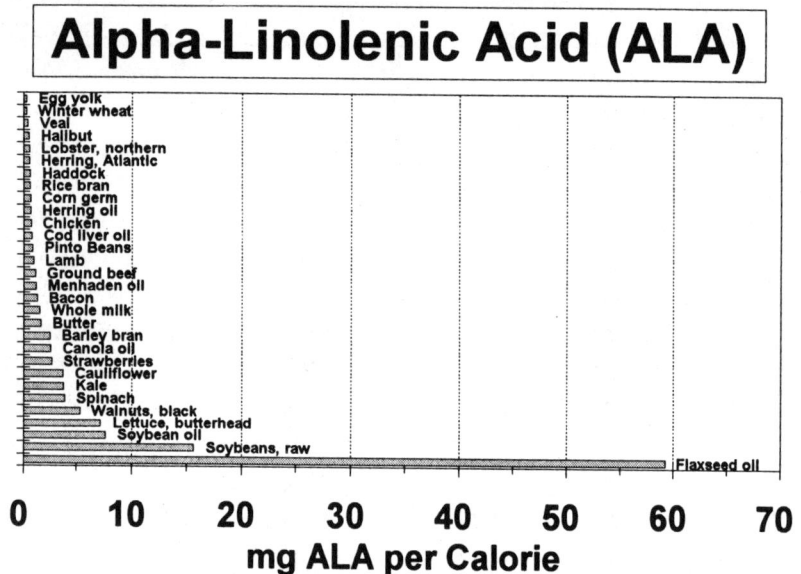

Alpha-Linolenic Acid (ALA)

Egg yolk
Winter wheat
Veal
Halibut
Lobster, northern
Herring, Atlantic
Haddock
Rice bran
Corn germ
Herring oil
Chicken
Cod liver oil
Pinto Beans
Lamb
Ground beef
Menhaden oil
Bacon
Whole milk
Butter
Barley bran
Canola oil
Strawberries
Cauliflower
Kale
Spinach
Walnuts, black
Lettuce, butterhead
Soybean oil
Soybeans, raw
Flaxseed oil

| 0 | 10 | 20 | 30 | 40 | 50 | 60 | 70 |

mg ALA per Calorie

The ω3:ω6 FA ratio in the human brain[494] is about 1:1. During most of human evolution[495] the dietary ω3:ω6 FA ratio was also about 1:1 but in the present U.S. diet it is about 1:10. The next table shows that vegetables have higher ω3:ω6 fatty acid ratios than grains. While the USDA grants horticulture no price supports, vegetables are once again shown to have better nutrient value than barley, corn, rice, rye, and wheat, which the USDA in fact does support.

Vegetables and Grains sorted by ALA:LA Ratio

Food Name	ALA:LA
SPINACH—FROZEN—BOILED—CHOPPED	5.148
CAULIFLOWER—RAW—BOILED—DRAINED	3.294
LETTUCE—ICEBERG—RAW—LEAVES	2.333
BEANS—FRENCH—COOKED—BOILED	1.728
SQUASH—SUMMER—BOILED—SLICED	1.682
BEANS—NAVY—SPROUTED—BOILED	1.354
KALE—FROZEN—BOILED—DRAINED	1.296
BEANS—BLACK—COOKED—BOILED	0.834
RICE—WILD—COOKED	0.795
SEAWEED—SPIRULINA—DRIED	0.657
CRESS—GARDEN—RAW	0.500
POI—TARO ROOT PRODUCT	0.448
RICE—WHITE—SHORT GRAIN—COOKED	0.212
FLOUR—RYE—DARK	0.164
WHEAT GERM—CRUDE	0.137
BARLEY—PEARLED—LIGHT—COOKED	0.109
WHEAT BRAN—CRUDE	0.082
PEPPERS—HOT CHILI—RAW	0.051
OATS—WHOLE GRAIN—UNCOOKED	0.046
WHEAT—HARD RED—WINTER	0.044
CORN BRAN—CRUDE	0.032
CORN—SWEET—CANNED—VACUUM PACKED	0.029

Leafy greens are probably the best overall food choice, not only for linolenic acid but for protein, calcium, iron, vitamins, and trace minerals. There is a reason for this: plant leaves are the biochemical "guts" of the plant. The stem supports the plant, moves it to face the sun and also transfers nutrients absorbed from the earth by the roots. Seeds and nuts store DNA, proto-nutrients, and fat for the plant's reproductive cycle. But all the photosynthetic and biosynthetic chemical reactions that sustain both plant and animal life occur in the leaves. Sutton's law says, "Go where the money is." Nutritionally speaking, the money is in the leaves, so if it's green and it tastes good, eat it.

Soybean oil is also a good source of ALA; unfortunately, it is almost always hydrogenated in the American diet, as a look at almost any bag of chips, popcorn, or other snack food will show. Hydrogenated ALA is no longer linolenic acid but a mixture of *cis* and *trans* fatty acids produced by heat and metal catalysts rather than by *cis*-specific enzymes. *Trans* fats elevate cholesterol levels and get into cell membranes with dubious results.[496]

HOW ABOUT INFANT NUTRITION?

DHA is a major player in the cell membranes of the central nervous system (CNS). Human adult brains can probably move dietary ALA across the blood-brain barrier, and hand it over to the astrocytes (CNS support cells) which then transform it into DHA and pass it on to the brain cells (neurons). Either that or the DHA is made from ALA in the liver and moved to the brain.[497] However, infant livers and brains can't do this and depend critically on adequate dietary DHA.

DHA is present in cow's milk but so are a number of adverse elements such as antigenic proteins that cause a glossary of pediatric illness.[498] Primarily because of iron absorption problems, The American Academy of Pediatrics Committee on Nutrition discourages the use of cow's milk before the age of one year,[499] but there are better reasons.

So the next possibility for infant nutrition is soy formula. Isomil, Nursoy, Prosobee, and Soyalac are frequently prescribed for cow milk kids who come in with marathon "colds," chronic diarrhea, rashes, and big tonsils. These formulas, free of cow milk, casein, and whey, have been formulated carefully but they're missing at least one thing. They don't have DHA because no plant synthesizes DHA or any of the other elongated ω3 FAs. A recent study showed that breast-fed infants have an eight point IQ edge over formula-fed kids[500] at age 8. It's partly due to the fact that in addition to maternal antibodies, the psychological benefits of mother-child bonding, and tailor made proteins, breast milk also contains DHA.

In spite of this, some mothers continue to bottle- feed. Enter, once again, the fish oil. Fish oil is loaded with DHA so one simply takes fish oil and adds it to soy formula that can be delivered in a tidy Victorian bottle. The fish-oil supplemented premature infant at the age of one year displays slightly better visual acuity, relative to formula kids,[501] and this is thought to be consistent with the notion the infant brain and retina needs DHA. Unfortunately, the infant's physical growth has been retarded apparently because the DHA interferes with the utilization of AA that is needed for growth. Exeunt fish oils.

So we come again to the old riddle. Why do humans cling so desperately to the bad idea of eating animal food, and then practice damage control by eating reduced amounts or different *types* of animal food? There are now eight studies in the literature, including the Ornish study, showing that lowering serum cholesterol regresses CHD.[502] The solution to both CHD and cerebral hemorrhage is to go vegan and cut all the cholesterol out of the diet, not to eat fish oil and trade off CHD for CH. The solution to infant nutrition is not to dodge the adverse effects of cow's milk by adding fish oil to otherwise deficient plant-based formulas. The solution is for women to breast-feed their infants and perhaps continue for three years, or until by mutual consent weaning occurs.

The fish oil flim-flam is founded on the customary error: sorting and preferencing foods by nutrient/weight ratio rather than nutrient/Calorie ratio. One hundred grams of menhaden fish oil may indeed have a lot of ω3 FA, but the oil is 100% of Calories from fat, and it contains 521 mg of cholesterol to boot. One hundred Calories of spinach has 3.16 times as much ALA as 100 Calories of menhaden oil, .0017 as much fat and a cholesterol content so low it cannot be detected by USDA assay methods and is hence reported as zero.

Finally, a recent Harvard study confirmed that there is no reduction in coronary risk from eating large amounts of fish.[503] Too bad. The miracle cure folks were making big progress. In a century they went from peddling snake oil to fish oil.

XVI. HISTORY OF A CAMPAIGN

"Cattle industry in uproar in the isles," read the headline in the 3/24/91 *Honolulu Star-Bulletin & Advertiser.* In 1991, members of the Vegetarian Society of Honolulu (VSH), founded by Elaine French in 1990, became aware that the Hawaii Legislature was allocating public moneys to quell the uproar. This chapter outlines our efforts to block funding. Vegetarians across the country might use similar campaigns to persuade other state legislators and eventually federal legislatures to appropriate public moneys in a more appropriate fashion.

Background:
    As of 1991 there were three major meat producers in the State of Hawaii. Big Island Meat was a division of Hamakua Sugar Co. and had a 67-acre feedlot with a capacity of 7500 animals and an adjacent slaughterhouse on the northeast coast of Hawaii. Conditions were wet, young cattle grew slowly, and the Hamakua Sugar Co. owed $100 million to the state.[504] The owner had managed to corner the two worst nutritional products in Hawaii: sugar and meat. Eventually the company sold off most of its land to pay its debt and the slaughterhouse went up for grabs. On 2/23/94 the owner was fined $200,000 for polluting the ocean with sugar effluent.[505]
    Hawaii Meat Company was owned 83% by Parker Ranch on the Big Island but it maintained a 124-acre feedlot with a 14,000 head capacity in Campbell Industrial Park on the West end of Oahu. Cattle from the feedlot were sent to a slaughterhouse on Middle Street in Honolulu. The feedlot closed in 1991 after abortive attempts by the state to condemn it and then buy it back for $57 million. The slaughterhouse also closed and was replaced by the Kalihi-Palama bus facility of Honolulu City and County.
    Kahua Meat Company was associated with the Kahua Ranch, also on the Big Island, and maintained the Kahua slaughterhouse in Ewa on Oahu which was dependent on Hawaii Meat's feedlot to maintain a "critical mass" of slaughter animals necessary for efficient operation.
    The State of Hawaii imports 80% of its beef from the mainland but also leases 168,000 acres for pasture. Big Island ranchers currently ship many of their cattle either to Oahu or to the mainland for slaughter. Hawaii cattle are free of brucellosis and anaplasmosis and are favored imports to Canada,[506] where they are finished, slaughtered, and not infrequently their meat sent back to Hawaii. Consumption per capita[507] of

Hawaiian beef and pork[508] fell by ~ 15% and 27% during the past decade. Figures suggesting a constant intake of these products in Hawaii were extrapolated from mainland figures[509] not from local food disappearance data.

In 1993 these bills originated in AGR, the House Agriculture Committee (Chair: Marshall Ige, Vice-Chair: Avery Chumbley):

HB (House Bill) 422 (M. Ige, A. Chumbley): State funds to resuscitate the feedlot in Campbell Industrial Park. During an AGR hearing on 2/3/93 the Vice President of the Kahua Meat Company echoed his testimony[510] from 2/11/92 against Senate Bill SB 2606 that had proposed $30,000 to plan more livestock facilities on Oahu. He also mentioned that "the slaughter business is not a money making business" and that "the neighbors object...when we slaughter hogs in the middle of the night." He gave only lukewarm support to the bill and a hog producer feared the facility might not accommodate his hogs. When the perplexed chairman asked what would happen if the meat industry lost government support there was a short silence during which a testifying VSH member interjected, "The health of the people would improve." There wasn't much laughter.

"State raids airport-system funds: Officials snatch $65 million for purchase of a racing facility and Hawaii Meat feedlot" was the incidental headline in the Honolulu Star-Bulletin on 12/23/93. While this questionable assault on airport bonds went through, the feedlot remained closed.

HB 915 (M. Ige): $5 million in general obligation bonds for the design and construction of a cattle slaughterhouse on the island of Oahu.

HB 1209 (M. Ige): Allocating ~ $209,000 for the slaughterhouse on the Big Island Meat Company at the old Hamakua sugar plantation.

HB 1239: Appropriating $50,000 to a study of waste recovery from cattle manure.

The bills passed out of AGR with $1.00 appropriations.

More Background:
In 1946 the Board of Commissioners of Agriculture and Forestry of the Territory of Hawaii reported expenditures of $960,698. Statehood came in 1959 and in 1960 the Hawaii Department of Agriculture and Conservation spent a total of $2,055,401. In 1993 the Department listed total expenditures of $15,663,759 with the heaviest outlays for general administration, milk commodities, pest control, and plant and animal quarantine,
Since 1974 the State of Hawaii's Agricultural Parks Program, initiated by Act 222 of the 1986 Legislature,[511] has funded six parks. 1991 Hawaii agriculture value was $554 million,[512] about 2.5% of the Gross State Product. Furthermore, Hawaii's 1,200,000 human population could be fed on the agricultural output of about 2.8% of the state's land area, while 40% is actually zoned for agriculture. Cattle roam on a quarter of the state's land.[513] If sugar production is phased out it can be replaced by diversified agriculture, golf courses, or housing developments. The record since the 1970s suggests that regardless of zoning laws, developers will acquire and exploit land. Arguably the state should dedicate agricultural land in order to prevent human overcrowding and environmental problems. With its varied altitudes and climates almost anything can be grown in Hawaii, so agricultural export could be an economic alternative to people import.

A new specter arose.

Awaiting approval from the governor's office in 1993 was the Environmental Impact Statement (EIS) for the Kahuku Livestock Agricultural Park which the Hawaii Department of Agriculture estimated would cost $38,759,000. It would maintain 2000 dairy cows in a one acre free-stall dairy barn, with a state-of-the-art milking parlor. The cows would not be free range, and would be subject to the usual American dairying practices: male calves and old cows to the slaughterhouse.

VSH member Katalina Lambert attended the EIS

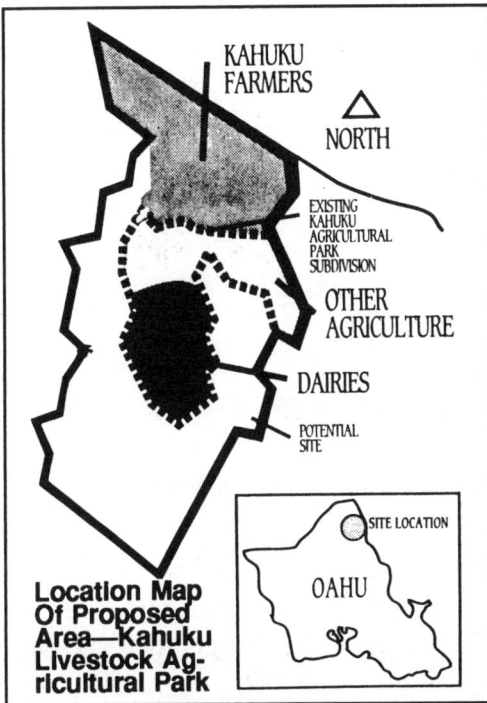

KAHUKU FARMERS

△ NORTH

EXISTING KAHUKU AGRICULTURAL PARK SUBDIVISION

OTHER AGRICULTURE

DAIRIES

POTENTIAL SITE

SITE LOCATION

OAHU

Location Map Of Proposed Area—Kahuku Livestock Agricultural Park

meeting at the Kahuku Senior Center, 1/28/93 and reported the startup costs might be even higher, beginning with 1992's $13,000,000 fee simple land purchase from Campbell Estate. Problems with waste disposal, groundwater contamination, odor and disease vector control, and storm water runoff might take another $40,000,000 of State funds and while the dairy operators were supposed to pay at least $8,000,000 of the costs, the taxpayer outlay might still have run as high as $45,000,000. Many Kahuku citizens expressed displeasure with the plan and several VSH members submitted adverse testimony which was included in the EIS.

The Hawaii Department of Agriculture, recognized our objections to state support for the dairy industry, but nevertheless concluded that "there is a demand for about 40,000 gallons of milk per day in Hawaii," and that milk provides "a healthy food alternative for consumers." We responded with a virtual glossary of pediatric illness[514] associated with dairy food.

In addition to being the most expensive Ag Park yet funded by the state, the proposed Kahuku dairy would also have had the lowest monetary output/input ratio, assuming that Oahu's present 7500 milk cows are producing milk at a value of about $21.9 million/year and the 2000 Kahuku cows would give (2000/7500)*21.9=$5.84 million/year.

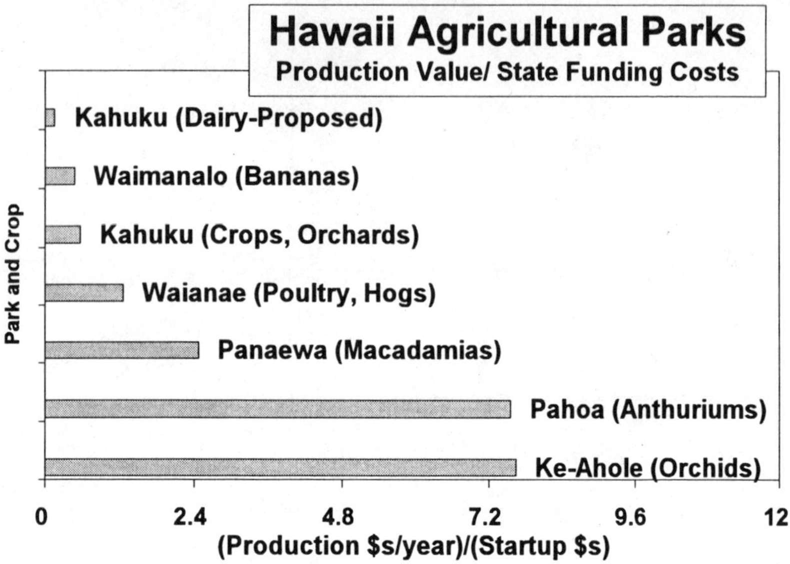
Hawaii Agricultural Parks
Production Value/ State Funding Costs
Park and Crop
Kahuku (Dairy-Proposed)
Waimanalo (Bananas)
Kahuku (Crops, Orchards)
Waianae (Poultry, Hogs)
Panaewa (Macadamias)
Pahoa (Anthuriums)
Ke-Ahole (Orchids)
0
2.4
4.8
7.2
9.6
12
(Production $s/year)/(Startup $s)

From the VSH standpoint there was a favorable outcome. The Department of Agriculture[515] reported that the Kahuku park is "indefinitely deferred due to lack of interest by the dairy industry." The land will now go to diversified agriculture, mostly nurseries and vegetables. Pig farming will probably not be included since local residents object to the smell.

In 1993 the House Agriculture Committee was back at it again:

HB 424 (M. Ige) titled: "Relating to agriculture."

1.$500,000 to construct a slaughterhouse on Molokai.

2.$200,000 to *study* the feasibility of a rendering plant on Molokai.

3.$250,000 to construct a cattle facility, rendering facility, and meat processing facility on Maui.

4.$50,000 for a cooling facility in Ka'u on the island of Hawaii.

HB 2417 (M. Ige, A. Chumbley): "There is established in the state treasury, the meat processing facility loan revolving fund to provide loans for...any qualified owner of a meat processing facility who is unable to obtain sufficient funds at reasonable rates from private lenders." This was deferred in House AGR hearing on 2/3/94.

HB 2879: Yearling Beef (M. Ige): This one was almost too silly for even the Hawaii legislature. It appropriated "out of the general revenues of the State of Hawaii the sum of $45,500...for fiscal year 1994-1995...to the study, promotion, and marketing of Hawaiian yearling beef...which contained a lower amount of fatty and saturated fatty acids, and a higher amount of the beneficial omega-3 fatty acids. Thus grass-fed yearling beef could be marketed as a healthier choice for consumers who eat meat."

In fact, all omega-3 fatty acids originate from alpha-linolenic acid (ALA) which is synthesized only in the chloroplasts of green plants.[516] The ALA content per Calorie of kale is about 3-1/3 times that of beef,[517] the Calories from fat about one fifth and the cholesterol content zero. From dietary linolenic acid humans can synthesize the other omega-3 fatty acids themselves.[518] No subsidies for kale or taro (an equally healthy and locally grown food) are in the works.

HB 3006: "Whenever milk is required ...to be destroyed by a dairy farmer because of alleged contamination and it is later found not to be contaminated, the department...shall reimburse the dairy farmer for the value of...the milk."

HB 3263:"Exempts from the income tax and general excise tax law for 10 years all new dairy farm operations with at least 300 cows."

Concerned VSH members contacted key legislators and some gave adverse testimony at AGR committee hearings. The bills from both years got through AGR but all failed to pass the House Finance Committee (FIN) whose chairman Calvin Say stressed austerity in the 1994 Hawaii Budget Bill HB 2500. All of these bills are thus dead and cannot carry over to the 35th Hawaii Legislature in 1994-95.

Having been shut out in the House the meat interests took a new tack. AGE, the Senate Agriculture Committee originated two bills to buy or construct slaughterhouses on Oahu and Molokai.

Senate Bill SB 2876 (G. Hagino): "Appropriates $450,000 to the Department of Agriculture for the purchase of the Kahua slaughterhouse in Ewa, the only operational USDA-approved facility on the island of Oahu that has the capacity to slaughter approximately 28,000 hogs and 5,000 cattle annually. The Kahua Meat Company, owner of the Kahua slaughterhouse, has announced the closure of this facility as of November 30, 1993...the livestock industry will require the State's assistance to purchase the Kahua slaughterhouse and to construct a new slaughterhouse to maintain the viability of the livestock industry."

The Dean of the UH School of Tropical Agriculture testified[519] in favor of SB 2876 saying,"The consumers want 'hot pork' delivered to the market immediately on slaughter. The slaughterhouse also provides an effective waste-disposal service...spent dairy cows are best disposed through humane slaughter rather than further overloading Oahu's waste-disposal services." Note the implication that the government, not the free market, should provide what the people want. Note the inseparability of meat production and dairy operations. Note also the oxymoron "humane slaughter."

Department of Agriculture Chairperson Yukio Kitagawa had supported a forerunner bill, HB 2897, in 1992. Nevertheless, he probably shot down S.B. 2876, by testifying that while he shared concerns about the viability of the Oahu livestock industry, "market forces...must be viewed as strong enough to permit the problem to be mitigated by the private sector." He also suggested a conflict in having the Department not only buy the slaughterhouse but subsequently regulate its slaughter activities.

Then came the curve ball:

S.B. 2010 (R. Baker, G. Hagino): "There is appropriated out of the general revenues of the State of Hawaii the sum of $500,000 for the construction of a slaughterhouse on (the island of) Molokai." This one passed AGE (Chair: G. Hagino, Vice Chair: D. Ikeda) and went through WAM, the Senate Ways and Means Committee (Chair: D. Ikeda, Vice Chair: G. Hagino) like a dose of salts.

On the Senate floor the only opposing vote came from Senator Rick Reed, a vegetarian. Reed was quoted in the Honolulu Star Bulletin 2/20/94 saying, "If we're really so arrogant... as to protect people from themselves...we should not ban guns, we should ban beef."

SB 2010 was next transformed into a CIP (Capital Improvement Project), Maui Subsidy 401C. Cathy Goeggel of VSH and Animal Rights Hawaii (ARH) happened upon this devious truth more or less by chance and two weeks too late. CIPs are not routinely heard by FIN, so in this guise SB 2010 escaped the adverse public testimony of a House FIN hearing.

At that point VSH members collected 380 signatures in less than a week opposing this appropriation and sent copies to all 35 members of FIN and WAM. When we attended their conference committee meeting on 4/27/94, SB 2010 was "in limbo" and presumably dead. We had received replies from four legislators thanking us for our input, and there was an informal "proviso" that the private sector would have to contribute some of the money or the CIP would be dropped. Two days later, after a "last minute consideration" between FIN and WAM, it was back in the budget as CIP 24C for Maui County, free of the proviso. A $90,000 appropriation that came out of nowhere for an "Oahu Meat Processing Center," was also inserted into HB 2500, the 1994 Hawaii Budget Bill, by unidentified members of the House.

HB 2500 then went to Governor Waihee for his signature, followed closely by a copy of our petition. Although he had the option of a line item veto of the Molokai

Slaughterhouse CIP 24C and the "Oahu Meat" appropriation he did not exercise it, so $590,000 in tax moneys were diverted from education and public services to subsidize the cattle industry.

Final score: out of 13 batters only one crossed the plate and that partly because we didn't know that in political baseball, the runner (SB 2010) can bypass second base, slide into third, change uniforms twice, become invisible for two weeks, then get up and steal home, followed by the water boy (the $90,000 "Oahu Meat Processing Center") who darted from the dugout just as the ump called the game.

In the course of scolding our legislators, VSH members brought up salient points:

Elizabeth Anderson, opposing SB 2010 and SB 2876 said, "As we all know, the cost of living in Hawaii is quite high, but I can accept that cost. However, with public funds as tight as they are, I can think of countless better uses for my tax dollar."

One legislator mentioned the hardship that would come to law abiding and upstanding ranch families if the bills were blocked and a VSH writer responded, "Extending this argument the U.S. government should have reinstituted slavery and paid the law abiding and upstanding slave owners for their losses after the Civil War. Most of the ethical arguments vegetarians use are the same ones used by the abolitionists of the last century if you merely substitute the word animal for slave."

Peter Burwash, vegetarian motivational speaker and CEO of the world's largest tennis organization had this to say about SB 2010: "Meat causes heart attacks, cancer, and numerous other diseases. Our monies should go toward promoting healthy foods. Why do we have to pay so much for fruits and vegetables here when we can grow virtually anything on our islands? I cannot think of one positive reason to build a slaughterhouse...we are concerned with decreasing violence yet the government will...give money to an endeavor that is full of violence to innocent creatures."

Opposing SB 2876 and SB 2010 a VSH writer said: "Owners of land zoned for agriculture may pay only $9 per acre per year in taxes. If the land lies fallow, taxes may go up as high as $125, a fourteen-fold increase.[520] Seen in this light the slaughterhouse appropriations are simply additional monetary giveaways to wealthy landowners who raise cattle on marginal land primarily as a tax dodge."

Ruth Heidrich, Ph.D., a 13-year breast cancer survivor who attributes her health and the acquisition of all her age group's running records in Hawaii to her vegan diet, had this to say about the Kahuku dairy park: "A study recently published through Harvard University cites the correlation between dairy products and childhood onset diabetes.[521] Another study released two years ago cites the correlation between dairy products and ovarian cancer.[522]"

"We're not trying to put the ranchers out of business," said a VSH writer about SB 2010. "We're trying to put them *in* business. What they're asking for is welfare. Government support of animal source food makes no more sense than would support for marijuana or cocaine. Doubtless, individuals should have access to meat if they want it, but there is no reason the government should pay their butcher's bill."

Distance runner, Patrick Moore, writing against SB 2010 noted, "When Captain Cook arrived in Hawaii, the natives were slender. Only after eating the haole diet did the majority of Hawaiians become fat...how many people die in Hawaii each year from eating too much meat?..please allow these bills to die."

Neal Pinckney, Ph.D., was told in 1992 that his coronary arteries were blocked and that he needed an operation. Instead, he switched to a vegan diet, dropped his cholesterol from 286 mg/dL to 136 mg/dL and now bikes 12 miles a day without anginal pain. He now conducts free classes at Kaiser hospital to teach other cardiac patients how to follow his own path. In testimony against SB 2876, Dr. Pinckney said, "Bailouts have proven to be costly blunders, angering voters and causing legislators to lose their seats in subsequent elections. If the fair market conditions on Oahu cannot support a profitable slaughterhouse operation, it may be reasonable to conclude that this enterprise is not a sound business proposition."

Responding to hardship arguments favoring the dairy bills, another VSH writer said, "Horticulturalists don't get government handouts. Nevertheless, they lead regular lives because the carrots, kale, and spinach don't have disastrous calvings at midnight, or moan at 4:00 a.m. because their udders are full, or run up veterinary bills, or leave behind mountains of manure. The dairy farmer's life is a hard one but no one forced him into it. Nothing that he and his bovine accomplices produce is a work of sacrifice indispensable to human health, and if he can't stand the heat, he should get out of the kitchen."

Cynthia Smith, lecturer in history at Leeward Community College, cited the historical record of animal agriculture and the fall of ancient civilizations brought upon by overgrazing and desertification.

"Many individuals have ethical objections to the use of their taxes for the killing and eating of animals," said another opponent of SB 2010. "As a parallel it should be noted that Right-to-Life activists (who often dine on steak, thus raising the question of how much life they really think has a right) have, through the Hyde Amendment, effectively shut off federal funding for abortion.[523] Yet while Right-to-Lifers have persuasive arguments, there are legitimate arguments on the Freedom-of-Choice side. Many of life's ethical questions simply have no answers, but I feel that in the question of meat-eating, there is a clear answer: there are no logical arguments for its continuation. However, with a less morally ambiguous position I am not demanding prohibition but merely an end to subsidies."

Representatives and Senators thanked us for our input, one of them writing: "Thanks for taking the time to gather a petition of persons concerned with developing slaughterhouses on both Molokai and Oahu. Another said: "You raise some very good points which will be deeply considered as we discuss further these allocations of taxpayer's monies."

Finally, one legislator said: "As a vegetarian myself, your letter strikes a responsive chord. However, I think that the bills in question will rise or fall on whether there is money available rather than on the health merits of eating meat." Paraphrased this reads: "If you give us money, we'll spend it."

We learned a few things. Influencing legislation is exhausting and frustrating work. It helps to have a computer with a modem, assuming that your state government has a legislative update service like ours, FYI (808) 587-4800, (19200 baud N,8,1). There's also an audio version that works with a touch-tone phone at 800-486-4644 (or 586-7000 in Hawaii). There's no guarantee the information will be correct; ACCESS still listed SB 2010 as "pending House Finance Committee," even after it passed.

It's hard to get people to go down to the capitol and testify against bills. It's fairly cost effective to mail out $.19 postcards to a mailing list asking that recipients call, write, or FAX testimony at critical points in the legislative process, such as committee hearings. Some of them will be annoyed that you asked, and it's almost impossible to know how many actually did it or how effective their comments were. Since many do not know who their Senators and Representatives we furnished a list of all committee members with their districts, phone, and FAX numbers. Legislative assistants take the phone messages, but it's difficult to know how often the messages are passed along. Return phone calls by legislators will be promised but seldom occur. Bills are supposed to retain their original content and identity, but this occurs roughly in the same way an amoeba retains its shape.

One cannot expect help from the newspapers which accept extensive meat advertising. At least three short articles questioning the bills were rejected by the two Honolulu dailies in spite of advance work by VSH member Eliot Rosen, M.S.W., who has extensive experience in public relations.

Our simplest strategy turned out to be the petition suggested by Georgiana Yap, R.N. We made up 200 petitions with room for 18 names and addresses, put stamps, dumbbell closures, and a return address on each one and distributed them to health food stores and volunteers with instructions to mail back each one as soon as it was filled. The cooperation was startling; the cost of xeroxing and mailing copies of the 380 collected names to all 26 members of FIN and WAM was only $250.

The assumption behind our campaign was simple. Animal source food can't compete on the free market against naturally healthy vegetables, fruits, and other plant foods. People will eat *something* with or without agricultural supports and what they eat is determined by cost, habit, taste, and understanding of nutritional health. If the cost of meat goes up, they tend to eat more vegetables. But given the profit margin resulting from taxpayer support, the meat industry mounts well-financed propaganda campaigns that drown out vegetarian attempts to educate the taxpayers to the dangers of disastrously unecological, unethical, and unhealthy food.

ADDENDUM

While Governor Waihee approved the Molokai slaughterhouse appropriation, the incoming Governor, Ben Cayetano, reviewed the budget bill and recommended that the appropriation "be lapsed." The matter then went back to the legislature. As of April 2, 1996 the House Finance Committee (FIN) had no plans to resuscitate it so it remained to be seen whether Donna Ikeda and Rosalind Baker, Chair and Vice-Chair of the Ways and Means Committee (WAM) and authors of the original bill would attempt to re-insert it into the 1996 budget bill.

XVII. CONCLUSION

"Vivisection is the killing of animals to find cures for the diseases caused by eating animals. "

-Victoria Moran

In reviewing the preceding chapters, it becomes apparent that what started out as an exposition of vegetarianism became a diatribe against government policy. Not much was said about the transition to vegetarianism, but for that, there are many fine books and cookbooks readily available.

The American Vegan Society has a comprehensive book and video tape list including the original articles from which this book was taken plus three extras:

The American Vegan Society (AVS)
P.O. Box H
Malaga, NJ 08328
(609) 694-2887

The Vegetarian Society of Honolulu (VSH) has a large book list and the VSH newsletter carries recipes as well as a calendar of local vegetarian events.

VEGETARIAN SOCIETY
OF HONOLULU
P.O. Box 25233
Honolulu, HI 96825
(808) 395-1499

There are a number of ethical considerations that were not covered at all. There is no rational defense for the continued use of animal food and certainly no excuse for the government using tax monies to subsidize it. Government support of the meat biz is like a huge ammo dump with no anti-aircraft guns in place; one well-placed rocket and it goes up in smoke. By contrast, consider other animal rights concerns such as vivisection. It's probably indefensible too, in the long view, but attacking it first is like dive-bombing a solitary hand grenade, hidden in a concrete bunker, manned by amiable scientists all poised to trigger a battery of SAMs. Pick off the ammo dump first, then the grenade, the bunker and the ack-ack wither away and the scientists wander off to other areas of investigation.

The ethical problem can also be put into game theory since questions of ethical behavior invariably boil down to value judgements.

Briefly there are two Options:

1.) It really doesn't matter whether we kill and eat animals.

2.) It is wrong to kill and eat animals.

If one bets on Option 2.) but it turns out that 1.) is correct (by some as yet undefined ethical calculus), then no real harm has been done. One merely gives up fatty food and improves one's chances for health.

If, on the other hand Option 2.) is correct but the bet was on 1.), then an irreparable moral error has occurred. If the animals were in charge of cosmic justice, the graphs in Chapter VII would be the court records.

Perhaps the AVS Sanscrit motto "Ahimsa" sums it all up: "Do no harm." It's a moral concept that requires constant awareness of action, but it is a feasible and practical substitute for our usual baroque hodgepodge of inconsistent moral laws; eventually it becomes second nature.

REFERENCES

1.Leveille GA, Zabik ME, and Morgan KJ. *Nutrients in Foods*. The Nutrition Guild. Cambridge, 1983. pp I-11,14. ISBN 0-938550-00-4.

2.Murray RK, Granner DK, Mayes PA, and Rodwell VW.*Harper's Biochemistry*. pp 576, 578.Appleton and Lange. Norwalk, CT 1990. ISBN 0-8385-3640-9.

3.Scientific American. *Human Nutrition*. W.H Freeman. San Francisco, 1978. p 149. ISBN 0-7167-0183-9.

4.*ibid*. p 151.

5.Scientific American. *Evolution*. 1978;239(3):54. ISSN 0036-8733.

6.Martin DW, Mayes PA, Rodwell VW, and Granner DK. *Harper's Review of Biochemistry*. p 673. Lange Medical Publications. Los Altos, CA 1985. ISBN 0-87041-038-5.

7.See note 3. *Human Nutrition*. p 158.

8.See note 2. *Harper's 1990*. p 563.

9.Goodwin and Mercer. *Introduction to Plant Biochemistry*. p 118. Pergamon Press. Oxford, 1983. ISBN 0-08-024921-3.

10.*ibid*. p 92.

11.Van Nostrand Reinhold Co. *Van Nostrand's Scientific Encyclopedia*. New York, 1968. p 441.

12.See note 2. *Harper's 1990*. p 548.

13.American Society of Hospital Pharmacists. *American Hospital Formulary Service*. pp 2036-7. Bethesda, 1990. ISBN 0-930530-96-9.

14.Graham S, Marshall J, Haughey B, et al. *Nutritional epidemiology of cancer of the esophagus*. Am J Epidemiol. 1990;131(3):454-67. ISSN 0002-9262.

15.Bendich A, Langseth L. *Safety of vitamin A*. Am J Clin Nutr. 1989;49(2):358-71. ISSN 0002-9165.

16.Loomis, W.F. *Four Billion Years*. Sinauer Associates. Sunderland, Mass. 1988. p 35. ISBN 0-87893-476-6.

17.See note 2. *Harper's 1990*. p 551.

18.Lindner M. *Nutritional Biochemistry and Metabolism*. Elsevier Science Publishing Co. New York, 1985. pp 70-71.ISBN 0-444-01241-9.

19.Loomis W. *Rickets*. Scientific American. *Human Nutrition*. p 193. W.H. Freeman. San Francisco, 1978. ISBN 0-7167-0183-9.

20.Cantarow AC, and Schepartz BS. *Biochemistry*. W.B. Saunders. Philadelphia 1957. p 152. LOCCC 57-11267.

21.Jacobs C, and Dwyer T. *Vegetarian children: appropriate and inappropriate diets*. First International Congress on Vegetarian Nutrition. Am J Clin Nutr.1988;48(3):811.

22.Encyclopedia Britannica, Inc. *Encyclopedia Britannica*. Chicago, 1974. Vol. X, p 470. ISBN 0-85229-290-2.

23.Smith M, and Elvove E. *The Action of Irradiated Ergosterol in the Rabbit*. Public Health Reports. 1929;44(21):1248.

24.Kingma J, Roy P. *Ultrastuctural Study of Hypervitaminosis D Induced Arterial Calcification in Wistar Rats*. Artery 1988;16(1):51-61.

25.Jacobus C, Holick M, et al. *Hypervitaminosis D Associated with Drinking Milk*. NEJM. 1992;326(18):1173-77.

26.see note 2. *Harper's 1990*. p 557.

27.Ellis, F.R. and Montegriffo, V.M.E. *Veganism, Clinical Findings and Investigations*. Am J Clin Nutr. 1970;23(3):250.

28.Herbert VL. *Vitamin B12:Plant Sources, Requirements,and Assay.* First International Congress on Vegetarian Nutrition. Am J Clin Nutr. 1988;48(3):857. ISSN 0002-9165.

29.Salisbury F, Ross C. *Plant Physiology.* Wadsworth Publishing Co. Belmont 1985. p 269. ISBN 0-534-04482-4.

30.Simopoulos A. *Omega-3 fatty acids in health and disease and in growth and development.* Am J Clin Nutr 1991;54:446. ISSN 0002 9165.

31.Random House. Random House Encyclopedia. New York, 1977. p 406. ISBN 0-394-40730-X

32.See note 11. Van Nostrand. p 113.

33.See note 2. *Harper's 1990.* pp 25-27.

34.See note 6. *Harper's 1985.* p 276.

35.*The Holy Bible: New International Version.* Zondervan Bible Publishers.Grand Rapids 1978. LOCCC 78-69799.

36.Fleagle J. *Primate Adaptation and Evolution.* Academic Press, Inc. San Diego 1988. ISBN 0-12-260340-0.

37.Lee and DeVore. *Man the Hunter.* Aldine Publishing Co. New York. pp.218-227.

38.See note 22. *Encyclopedia Brittanica.* Vol. 14, pp 1014-1031.

39.Chivers, Wood, and Bilsborough. *Food Acquisition and Processing in Primates.* Plenum Press. New York 1982. ISBN 0-306-41701-4.

40.See note 37. Lee. p.345.

41.Hawkes, Hill, and O'Connell. *Why Hunters Gather: Optimal Foraging and the Ache' of Eastern Paraguay.* American Ethological Society 1982. 0094-0496/82/020379-20. p.386.

42.See note 37. Lee. p.48.

43. Harris, David R. and Hillman, Gordon C. *Foraging and Farming, the Evolution of Plant Exploitation.* Unwin Hyman. Boston 1989. p.126. ISBN 0-04-445025-7.

44. See note 3. *Human Nutrition* p. 44.

45. See note 41. Hawkes. p.394.

46. United States Department of Agriculture. *Composition of Foods.* Agriculture Handbook No.8. Washington, 1963.

47. United States Department of Agriculture. *Agricultural Statistics.* US Government Printing Office. Washington: 1988. p.395.

48. Lewin R. *Disease Clue to Dawn of Agriculture.* Science. 1981;211:41.

49. Food and Agriculture Organization of The United Nations. *FAO Production Yearbook 1986.* Rome, 1987.

50. See note 2. *Harper's 1990.* pp 218-21.

51. See note 18. Lindner. p 36.

52. N-Squared Computing. *Nutritionist III, v4.5.* Salem OR, 1988.

53. See note 1. Leveille. p I-17.

54. See note 2. *Harper's 1990.* p 219.

55. See note 22. *Encyclopedia Britannica.* Vol. 13, p 524c.

56. Wohl and Goodhart. *Modern Nutrition in Health and Disease.* Lea and Febiger. Philadelphia 1968. p 191.

57. See note 31. Random House. p 1562.

58. See note 29. Salisbury. p 124.

59. Borland International. *Quattro Pro for Windows* v5.0. (A Graphic Spreadsheet). Scotts Valley, CA 1993.

176

60.See note 49. *FAO Production Yearbook.*

61.Committee on Health Statistics. *SEAMIC Health Statistics.* Southeast Asia Medical Information Center. International Medical Foundation of Japan 1988.

62.Miller W, Lindeman A, Wallace J, Niederpruem M. *Diet composition, energy intake, and exercise in relation to body fat in men and women.* Am J Clin Nutr. Sept 1990;52(3):426-30.

63.Gurney M, and Gorstein J. *The Global Prevalence of Obesity-An Initial Overview of Available Data.* World Health Statistics Quarterly.1988;41(3/4):251-254.

64.See note 22. *Encyclopedia Britannica.* Vol.13 p 530a.

65.Mensink RP, Katan MB. *Effect of dietary trans fatty acids on high-density and low-density lipoprotein cholesterol levels in healthy subjects.* New England Journal of Medicine. Aug 16 1990:323(7):439-45.

66.See note 18. Lindner. p 47.

67.Galdiero F, Folgore A, et al. *Effect of modification of HEp 2 cell membrane lipidic phase on susceptibility to infection from herpes simplex virus.* Infection. 1990;18(6):372-5. ISSN 0300-8126.

68.See note 22. *Encyclopedia Britannica.* Vol. 13, p 523b.

69.*Oxford English Dictionary.*Vol VI p 236. Oxford University Press. Oxford 1989. ISBN 0-19-861186-2.

70.See note 56. Wohl and Goodhart. p 43.

71.See note 46. USDA No. 8.

72.Alexander JC. *Heated and Oxidized Fats.* Dietary Fat and Cancer. pp 185-209. Alan R. Liss, Inc. New York 1986. ISBN 0-8451-5072-3.

73.Carney W, and Herzog H. *Microbial Transformation of Steroids.* Academic Press. New York 1967. Library of Congress 68-18661. p.48

74.See note 2. *Harper's 1990.* p 249.

75.Robbins SL, Kumar V, and Cotran RS. *Pathologic Basis of Disease.* p 464. W.B. Saunders Co. Philadelphia 1989. ISBN 0-7216-2302-6.

76.de Duve C. *A Guided Tour of the Living Cell.* p. 72. Scientific American Books, Inc. 1984. ISBN 0-7167-6002-9. .

77.Myant NB. *The Biology of Cholesterol and Related Steroids.* p 611. William Heinemann Medical Books Ltd. London 1981.

78.Goodwin and Mercer. *Introduction to Plant Biochemistry.* p 415. Pergamon Press. Oxford, 1983. ISBN 0-08-024921-3.

79.Weihrauch JL. Nutritionist, United States Department of Agriculture.*Personal communication.* May 3 1990. "In our publications we report cholesterol to the nearest milligram.Most plant products contain cholesterol in amounts less than one milligram per 100 grams. At this time we have no plans to report cholesterol values in foods of plant origin...cholesterol in plant foods is insignificant when compared to the amounts in foods of animal origin."

80.Weihrauch JL, and Gardner JM. *Sterol content of foods of plant origin.* J Am Diet Assoc. July 1978;73(1):39-46.

81.Osagie AU. *Phytosterols in Some Tropical Tubers.* J Agric Food Chem. 1977;25(5):1222-23.

82.Whitaker BD, and Lusby WR. *Steryl lipid content and composition in bell pepper fruit at three stages of ripening.* J Am Soc for Horticultural Science. July 1989;114(4):648-651.

83.Oka Y, Kiriyama S, and Yoshida A. *Sterol composition of spices and cholesterol in vegetable foods.* J Japanese Soc Food and Nutr. 1974;27(7):347-355 (Abstract).

84.Oka Y, Kiriyama S, and Yoshida A. *Sterol composition of vegetables.* J Japanese Soc Food and Nutr. 1973;26(2):121-128 (Abstract).

85.See note 22.*Encyclopedia Britannica.* Vol. 14, p 193e. Vol. 17, p 680d.

86.Lee John R. *Natural Progesterone: The Multiple Roles of a Remarkable Hormone.* BLL Publishing. Sebastapol, CA 1993. ISBN 0-9643737-1-8.

87.Burslem J, Schonfeld G, Howald MA, and Weidman SW. *Plasma apoprotein and lipoprotein levels in vegetarians.* Metabolism. 1978;27:711-719.

88.See note 77. Myant. p 734.

89.*ibid.* p 733.

90.See note 3. *Human Nutrition.* p 249.

91.Connor WE, Connor SL. *Dietary treatment of familial hypercholesterolemia.* Arteriosclerosis. 1989;9 (1 Suppl):I91-105. ISSN 0276-5047.

92.Mokuno H, Yamada N, Sugimoto T, et al. *Cholesterol-free diet with a high ratio of polyunsaturated to saturated fatty acids in heterozygous familial hypercholesterolemia: significant lowering effect on plasma cholesterol.* Horm Metab Res. 1990;22(4):246-51. ISSN 0018-5043.

93.Langley G. *Vegan Nutrition, a Survey of Research.* The Vegan Society. Oxford, 1988. ISBN 0-907337-15-5.

94.Ornish DM, Brown SE, Scherwitz LW, et al. *Can lifestyle changes reverse coronary heart disease?* Lancet 1990;336:129-133.

95.Blankenhorn DH et al. *Beneficial effects of combined colestipol-niacin therapy on coronary atherosclerosis and coronary venous bypass grafts.* JAMA 1987;257:3233.

96.Connor WE, and Connor S. *The Key Role of Nutritional Factors in the Prevention of Coronary Heart Disease.* p 57. Preventive Medicine. 1972;1:49-83.

97.Serway R, and Faughn J. *College Physics.* p 236.
Saunders College Publishing. Philadelphia,
1989. ISBN 0-03-022952-9.

98.Ganong WF. *Review of Medical Physiology.*
Appleton & Lange. Norwalk 1991. p 284.
ISBN 08385-8418-7.

99.Carlson E, Kipps M, Lockie A, and Thomson J.
*A comparative evaluation of vegan, vegetarian, and
omnivore diets.* J Plant Foods. 1985;6:89-100.

100.Castelli W. *Epidemiology of coronary heart
disease: the Framingham study.*
Am J Med 1984; 76(2A):4.

101.Science Service, Inc. *Science News*
1989;135 Jan 28. ISSN 0036-8423.

102.Brown, M.S., and Goldstein, J.L.
*How LDL Receptors Influence Cholesterol
and Atherosclerosis.* Scientific American.
Nov 1984; 251:5 p 66.

103.Voit C. *Über die entwicklung die lehre von
der quelle der muselkraft und einiger theile
der ernährung seit 25 jahren.(Development
of the source of muscular power during 25
years).* Zeitschr. f. Biol.1870;6:389.

104.See note 22. *Encyclopedia Brittanica.*
Vol. X, p 482.

105.Chittendon RH. *Physiological Economy in
Nutrition With Special Reference to the
Minimal Proteid Requirements of the Healthy
Man. An Experimental Study.* Frederick Stokes
Co. New York, 1904

106.Messina V. *Protein: Exploding the Myths.*
Guide to Healthy Eating. Physicians Committee
for Responsible Medicine. Sept-Oct 1990.

107.Sherman HC.*Protein requirements of maintenance
in man and the nutritive efficiency of bread
protein.* J Biol Chem. 1920;41:97.

108.Hegsted DM, Tsongas AG, Abbott DB, and Stare
FJ. *Protein Requirements of Adults.* J Lab Med.
1946;31:261.

109.See note 3. *Human Nutrition.* p 165.

110.See note 56. Wohl and Goodhart. p 588.

111.See note 1. Leveille. p I-10.

112.See note 22. *Encyclopedia Britannica.*
Vol VII. p 207.

113.See note 20. Cantarow. p 331.

114.See note 6. *Harper's 1985.* p 283.

115.See note 1. Leveille. p 178.

116.See note 49. FAO 1987.

117.See note 52. *Nutritionist III.*

118.Slonaker JR. *The Effect of a Strictly Vegetable
Diet on the Spontaneous Activity, the Rate of
Growth, and the Longevity of the Albino Rat.
Stanford University.* Stanford, Calif. 1912.

119.Wu H, and Chen TT. *Growth and reproduction of
rats on vegetarian diets.* Chin J Physiol.
1929;3:157.

120.Rose WC. *Amino Acid Requirements in Man.*
Federation Proceedings. 1949;8:546-52.

121.Luckey TD, Mende TJ, and Pleasants J.
*The Physical and Chemical Characterization of
Rat's Milk.* Journal of Nutrition.
1954;154:345-59.

122.See note 56. Wohl and Goodhart. p 109.

123.Arnould: *L'Utilisation des Proteines Pour la
Croissance.* University of Louvain.
Doctoral Dissertation.Louvain, Belgium 1961.

124.See note 2. *Harper's 1990.* p551.

125.See note 56. Wohl and Goodhart. p 747.

126.Adrian J, and Peyrot F. *Possible use of the
cassava leaf (manihot utillissima) in human
nutrition.* Plant Foods for Human Nutrition.

Jan 1971;2(2):61-65.

127.See note 22. *Encyclopedia Britannica.*
Vol.3 p1166-7.

128.Bowes A deP, and Church CF. *Food Values of
Portions Commonly Used.* J.B. Lippincott Co.
Philadelphia,1966. p 18.

129.See note 76. de Duve. p 253.

130.Kaufman SA. *Scientific American.* Scientific
American, Inc. New York. ISSN 0036-8733.
Aug 1991 p 79.

131.See note 98. Ganong. p 487.

132.See note 2. *Harper's 1990.* p 533.

133.Dayhoff MO, and Eck RV. *Atlas of Protein
Sequence and Structure.* National Biomedical
Research Foundation. Silver Spring, MD.
1968. Library of Congress No. 65-29342.

134.Hyde RM, and Patnode RA. *Immunology.* John Wiley
& Sons. New York, 1987. p 28. ISBN 0-471-82925-0.

135.See note 133. Dayhoff. p 301.

136.See note 134. Hyde and Patnode. p 25.

137.Guyton AC. *Textbook of Medical Physiology.*
WB Saunders.Philadelphia, 1971. p 769.
ISBN 0-7216-4392-2.

138.*ibid.* p 771.

139.Genetics Computer Group. *Sequence Analysis
Software Package v6.0.* Madison, 1989.

140.See note 76 deDuve. pp 251-59.

141.Halpern GM. *Alimentary Allergy.* Journal of
Asthma. 1983;20(4):258.

142.Lindahl O, Lindwall L, Spångberg A, Öckerman P.
*Vegan regimen with reduced medication in the
treatment of bronchial asthma.*J Asthma.
1985;22(1):45-55. ISSN 0277-0903.

143.Kjeldsen-Kragh J, Haugen M, Førre Ø, *et al.*
Controlled trial of fasting and one-year
vegetarian diet in rheumatoid arthritis.
Lancet 1991;338:899-902

144.See note 134. Hyde and Patnode. p 64.

145.Atassi MZ. *Immunochemistry of Proteins.* Plenum
Press. New York, 1977. p 391.
ISBN 0-306-36221-X (v.1).

146.U.S. Dept of Health and Human Services. *Health,*
United States, 1990. Public Health Service.
Centers for Disease Control. National Center for
Health Statistics. Hyattsville, 1990. Table 5.

147.*ibid.* Tables 1 and 24.

148.World Health Organization. *World Health*
Statistics Annual. WHO Geneva 1989.
ISBN 92-4-067890-5.

149.See note 49. *FAO.*

150.Dawson-Saunders B and Trapp RG. *Basic and*
Clinical Biostatistics. Appleton and Lange.
Norwalk, 1990.ISBN 0-8385-6200-0. p 93.

151.*ibid.* p 93.

152.Williams A. *Increased blood cell agglutination*
following ingestion of fat, a factor
contributing to cardiac ischemia,
Coronary insufficiency, and anginal pain.
Angiology. 1957;8:29.

153.Hutt MSR, and Burkitt DP. *The Geography of Non-*
*Infectious Disease.*Oxford University Press.
Oxford 1986. pp 67-68.

154.See note 152. Williams.

155.Levy RI, Rifkind BM, Dennis BH, Ernst N.
Nutrition, Lipids, and Coronary Heart
*Disease.*Raven Press. New York 1979.(Stamler J.
Population Studies).

156.Kurian GT. *The Book of World Rankings.* p 299
"Death Rate From Heart Disease." Facts on File
Inc.119 West 57th St.New York 1979.

157.Wynder EL. *The Dietary Environment and Cancer.*
J Amer Dietetic Assoc.1977;71:385-92.

158.*ibid.* Wynder. p 28.

159.Adlercreutz H, Hämäläinen E, Gorbach SL et al.
*Diet and plasma androgens in postmenopausal
vegetarian and omnivorous women and
postmenopausal women with breast cancer.*
Am J Clin Nutr. 1989;49:433-42.

160.Carroll K. *Experimental Evidence of Dietary
Factors and Hormone Dependent Cancers.*
Cancer Research.1975;35:3374.

161.Willett W, Hunter D, et al.*Dietary Fat and Fiber
in Relation to Risk of Breast Cancer: an Eight
Year Follow-up.*JAMA 1992; 268 (15):2037-44.

162.See note 160. Carroll.

163.Kradjian R. *Save Yourself from Breast Cancer.*
Berkley Books, 1994. ISBN 0-425-14390.

164.Holm L, Nordevang E, Hjalmar M, *et al.*
*Treatment Failure and dietary habits in women
with breast cancer.* J Natl Cancer Inst.
1993;85(1):32-6. ISSN 0027-8874.

165.Rose DP.*The Biochemical Epidemiology of
Prostatic Carcinoma.* Dietary Fat and Cancer.
Alan R. Liss, Inc. New York 1986.
ISBN 0-8451-5072-3

166.See note 153. Hutt and Burkitt. p 111.

167.Malter M, Schriever G, and Eilber U.
*Natural Killer Cells, Vitamins, and Other
Blood Components of Vegetarian and Omnivorous
Men.* Nutr Cancer.1989;12:271-278.

168.See note 159. Kurian 1979. p 297.

169.U.S. Dept of Commerce. *Statistical Abstract of
the United States.* Bureau of the Census.
U.S. Government Printing Office 1989.

Washington, DC 20402. LOCCC 4-18089.

170.Cunningham AS. *Lymphomas and Animal-Protein Consumption.*Lancet.1976;Nov.27:1184-86. ISSN 0023-7507.

171.See note 75. Robbins. p 998.

172.Karjalainen J, Martin J, Knip M. *et al. A bovine albumin peptide as a possible trigger of insulin-dependent diabetes mellitus.*N Eng J Med.1992;327(5):302-7.

173.Scott, FW. *Cow milk and insulin-dependent diabetes mellitus:is there a relationship?* Am J Clin Nutr.1990;51:489-91.

174.See note 156. Kurian 1979. p 298.

175.Diabetes Epidemiology Research International Group. *Geographic Patterns of Childhood Insulin-Dependent Diabetes Mellitus.* Diabetes. 1988;37:1115.

176.Swank R. *Changes in Blood Produced by a Fat Meal and by Intravenous Heparin.* Am J Physiol. 1951;164(3):798-811.

177.Fukuzaki H, Okamoto R, Matsuo T.*Studies on pathophysiological effects of postalimentary lipemia in patients with ischemic   heart disease.* Jpn Circ J. 1975;39(3):317-24.

178.Davis JC, Finn R, Hipkin LJ, St. Hill CA. *Do Plasma Glycoproteins Induce Lymphocyte Hyporesponsiveness and Insulin Resistance?* The Lancet. 1978; Dec 23 & 30:1343-1345. ISSN 0023-7507.

179.Shanmugasundarum KR, Visvanathan A, et al. *Effect of high-fat diet on cholesterol distribution in plasma lipoproteins, cholesterol esterifying activity in leukocytes, and erythrocyte membrane components studied: importance of body weight.* Am J Clin Nutr. 1988;44:805-15. ISSN 0002-9165.

180.Margen S, Chu JY, Kaufmann NA, and Calloway DH. *Studies in Calcium metabolism. I: The calciuretic effect of dietary protein.* Am J Clin Nutr. 1974; 27:584-589.

181.Anand CR, and Linksweiler HM. *Effect of Protein Intake on Calcium Balance of Young Men Given 500 mg Calcium Daily.* Journal of Nutrition. 1974;104:695-699.

182.Zemel MB, Schuette SA, Hegsted M, and Linkswiler HM. *Role of the sulfur-containing amino acids in protein-induced hypercalciuria in men.* J Nutr. 1981;111(3):545-52.

183.See note 52. *Nutritionist III, v4.5.*

184.See note 2. *Harper's 1990.* p 269.

185.*ibid.*, p 309.

186.See note 182. Zemel. pp 545-52.

187.See note 22. *Encyclopedia Britannica.* Vol. 7, p 41.

188.Cummings, Kelsey, Nevitt, and O'Dowd. *Epidemiology of Osteoporosis and Osteoporotic Fractures.* Johns Hopkins University of Hygiene and Public Health. Epidemiologic Reviews. 1985;7:178.

189.*ibid.* and note 49.*FAO.*

190.See note 148. WHO.

191.See note 75. Robbins. pp 163-237.

192.*ibid.* Robbins. p 1024.

193.Baron EJ, and Finegold SM. *Diagnostic Microbiology.* p 657 C.V. Mosby. St.Louis 1990. ISBN 0-8016-0344-7.

194.Sato M, Takayama K, Wakasa M, and Koshikawa S. *Estimation of Circulating Immune Complexes Following Oral Challenge With Cow's Milk in Patients with IgA Nephropathy.* Nepron. 1987;47:43-48.

195.See note 22. *Encyclopedia Britannica.* Vol. VIII. p 960.

196.See note 193.Baron. p 93.

197.See note 148. WHO.

198.World Book, Inc. *The World Book Encyclopedia.*
Chicago 1990. ISBN 0-7166-0091-9. Vol 1, p 851.

199.Kopple J, Shinaberger J, et al. *Protein
Nutrition in Uremia: A review.* Am J Clin Nutr.
1968;21(5):512.

200.Barsotti G, Morelli E, et al. *A special
supplemented 'vegan' diet for nephrotic
patients.* Am J Nephrol. 1991;11(5):380-5.
ISSN 0250-8095.

201.See note 49. *FAO.*

202.See note 148. *WHO.*

203.Nsouli T, Nsouli S, Linde R, et al. *Role of food
allergy in serous otitis media.* Annals
of Allergy. ISSN 0003-4738. 1994;73:215-219.

204.Science Service, Inc. *Science News.*
1989;135:60. ISSN 0036-8423.

205.Brown ML. *The National Economic Burden of
Cancer: An Update.* Journal of the
National Cancer Institute.1990;82(23):1812.

206.Silverberg E, Boring C, Squires TS.
Cancer Statistics, 1990. Ca-A Cancer Journal
for Clinicians.American Cancer Society.
1990;40(1):9-26. ISSN 0007-9235.

207.Arthritis Foundation. *Basic Facts: Answers to
Your Questions.* Atlanta 1988.

208.U.S. Department of Health and Human Services
*The National Kidney and Urological Diseases
Advisory Board 1990 Long-Range Plan Window of the
21st Century.* NIH Publication Number 90-583.
March 1990.

209.*Diabetes Statistics 1994.* U.S. Dept. of Health
and Human Services. Public Health Service. NIH
Publication #94-3822.

210.Riggs B, Melton L. *Osteoporosis and age-related
fracture syndromes.* Ciba Foundation
Symposium 1988;134:129-42.

211.Freund JE. *Statistics, a First Course.* Prentice-Hall. New Jersey, 1981. ISBN 845958-4. p 364.

212.U.S. Dept. of Public Health and Human Services. Warner Books. 1989. ISBN 0-446-39061-5.

213.American Lung Assn. *Lung Disease Data 1993.* *(Paper #04456 p 26).* N.Y. 1993.

214.Jacobson M. *Grappling with Alcohol Abuse: When Will We Take a Stand?* in: Nutrition Action. Center for Science in the Public Interest. 1981, October:6-7 CSPI.

215.Hoiberg A, and McNally MS. *Profiling overweight patients in the U.S. Navy: health conditions and costs.* Milit. Med. 1991;156(2):76-82.ISSN 0026-4075.

216.Cramer DW, Harlow BL, *et al. Galactose consumption and metabolism in relation to the risk of ovarian cancer.* Lancet 1989;2(8654):66-71. ISSN 0023-7507.

217.See note 203. Nsouli.

218.Bell JC, Palmer SR, and Payne JM. *The Zoonoses: Infections transmitted from animals to man.* Edward Arnold. London,1988. ISBN 0-7131-4561-7.

219. Mackie TT, Hunter GW, and Worth CB. *A Manual of Tropical Medicine.* W.B. Saunders Company. Philadelphia, 1954. LCCCN 54-5314.

220.Schroeder SA, Krupp MA, Tierney LM, and McPhee SJ. *Current Medical Diagnosis & Treatment 1990.* Appleton Lange. Norwalk, 1990. ISBN 0-8385-1428-6. p 1016.

221.*ibid.*Schroeder. p 1022.

222.*Salmonella Contamination in a Commercial Poultry Processing Operation.* Poultry Science. 1974;53:814-21.

223.See note 220. Schroeder. p 353.

224.Hawaii State Department of Health, *Epidemiology Branch Communicable Disease Report.* PO Box 3378 Honolulu, HI 96801. June/July 1991.

225.*ibid.* p 5.

226.See note 146. *Health, United States,1990.*

227.See note 193. Baron. Appendix A.

228.Streets RB. *The Diagnosis of Plant Diseases.*
p 2.13. University of Arizona Press. Tucson, 1982.
ISBN 0-8165-0350-8.

229.See note 224. *Hawaii Epidemiology.* Feb/Mar 1991.

230.Matossian MK. *Poisons of the Past: Molds,
Epidemics, and History.* Yale University Press, 1989.

231.See note 220. Schroeder. p 944.

232.See note 224. *Hawaii Epidemiology.* Aug 1990.

233.Luttrell, Clifton B. *The High Cost of Farm
Welfare.* Cato Institute. Washington, 1989.
ISBN 0-932790-70-4. p 15.

234.Bovard J. *Farm Bill Follies of 1990.* p 4. Policy
Analysis. Cato Institute. Washington, July 12, 1990.

235.See note 22. *Encycyclopedia Brittanica.*
Vol. 1:318d.

236.*ibid.* Encyc Vol. 1:318d.

237.United States Department of Agriculture. *History
of Budgetary Expenditures of the Commodity
Credit Corporation: Fiscal Year 1990-1991 Actual.*
ASCS/BUD/CPB Book 3.

238.Code of Federal Regulation Parts 1200-1499.
*Agricultural and Trade Act Amendments. 7 CFR part
718,719,1413 and 1414.* Agricultural
Stabilization and Conservation Service and Commodity
Credit Corporation of the USDA. Federal Register.
National Archives and Records Administration 1993.

239.United States Department of Agriculture.
Agricultural Stabilization and Conservation
Service. *Production Adjustment/Price Support
Programs.* Bl no. 3, Dec. 1992. p 10.

240. United States Department of Agriculture. Economic Research Service. *Provisions of the Food, Agriculture, Conservation, and Trade Act of 1990*. Agriculture Information Bulletin Number 624. Washington, 1991. p vii.

241. ASCS Commodity Fact Sheet. *Feed Grains: Summary of Support Program and Related Information*. United States Department of Agriculture. June 1991.

242. U.S Department of Agriculture, Office of Budget & Program Analysis, 3/7/90.

243. United States Department of Agriculture. *Agricultural Statistics, 1989*. United States Government Printing Office. Washington, 1989. Table 623.

244. Note 237. *USDA Budgetary Expenditures*. Budget Division. Book 3, p2.

245. Bovard, James. *The Farm Fiasco*. Institute for Contemporary Studies. San Francisco, 1989. ISBN 1-55815-001-3.

246. Consumer Reports. *Udder Insanity*. p 330 Consumers Union of U.S. Inc. Yonkers 1992. May 1992. ISSN 0010-7174.

247. McMenamin M, and McNamara W. *Milking the Public: Political Scandals of the Dairy Lobby from L.B.J. to Jimmy Carter*. Nelson-Hall. Chicago, 1980. ISBN 0-88229-552-7.

248. See note 233. Luttrell. p 102.

249. See note 245. Bovard. p 76.

250. See note 52. *Nutritionist III, v7.0*.

251. Borland International. *Quattro Pro for Windows*. Scotts Valley, CA 1989.

252. Cullison A. *Feeds and Feeding*. Reston Publishing Co., Inc. Reston, 1982. p 24. ISBN 0-8359-1905-6.

253. *1992 CRB Commodity Year Book*. Commodity Research Bureau. Knight-Ridder Financial Publishing. New York, 1992. ISBN 0-910418-28-4.

254.Department of the Treasury. Bureau of Alcohol, Tobacco, and Firearms. *Statistical Release*. Report 76, 6/23/93 and Report ATF R A:1 5130-2, 6/11/93.

255.*MVAs and Alcohol*. Emergency Medicine News. J.B. Lippincott Co. Hagerstown. April, 1995. p 13. ISSN 1054-0725.

256.Personal communication 12/7/92. See also: Hur R. *Food Reform: Our Desperate Need*. Heidelberg Publishers. Austin, 1975. ISBN 0-913206-05-9.

257.See note 252. Cullison.

258.United States Department of Agriculture. Economic Research Service. *Provisions of the Food, Agriculture, Conservation, and Trade Act of 1990*. p vii. Agriculture Information Bulletin Number 624. Washington, 1991

259.See note 243. *Agricultural Statistics, 1989*. Table 623 p 449.

260.Ensminger M. *Animal Science*. Interstate Publishers. Danville,1991.p 23. ISBN 0-8134-2887-4

261.Jacobson MF. *The complete eater's digest and nutrition scoreboard*. Anchor Press. New York, 1985.p 119. ISBN 0-385-18245-7.

262.Durning AB, Brough HB. *Taking Stock: Animal Farming and the Environment*. p 15. Worldwatch Paper #103. Worldwatch Institute, 1991.(From USDA data). ISBN 1-878071-04-1.

263.See note 243. *Agricultural Statistics, 1989*. Table 572.

264.See note 46. USDA #8.

265.See note 3. *Human Nutrition*. p 35.

266.See note 243. *Agricultural Statistics, 1989*. Tables 566 and 567.

267.Find Your Feet-USA. *Sustainable Agriculture, the Environment, and Leaf Concentrate*. 2720 Hutchinson Rd. Murfreesboro, TN 37130, 1989.

268.Spedding CRW. *The Biology of Agricultural Systems*. Academic Press. London, 1975. ISBN 0-12-656550-3. p 107.

269.Manchester AC. *The Public Role in the Dairy Economy: Why Governments Intervene in the Milk Business*. Westview Press. p 287. Boulder 1983. ISBN 0-86531-590-6.

270.Robbins J. *Diet for a New America*. Stillpoint Publishing.Walpole, 1987. p 367. ISBN 0-913299-54-5.

271.See note 245. Bovard. p 62.

272.Yanagida J, Azzam A, Linsenmeyer D. *Two Alternative Methods of Removing Price Supports: Implications to the U.S. Corn and Livestock Industries*. Journal of Policy Modeling. 1987;9(2):331-320. Nebraska Agricultural Experiment Station.

273.See note 234. *Budgetary Expenditures*.

274.Schultze CL. *The Distribution of Farm Subsidies: Who Gets the Benefits?* The Brookings Institution. Washington 1971. ISBN 0-8157-7753-1.

275.Friedman M. *Free to Choose*. Harcourt, Brace, Jovanovich. p 293. New York, 1979. ISBN 0-15-133481-1.

276.Pasour EC. *Agriculture and the State*. Holmes & Meier. New York, 1990. p 171. ISBN 0-8419-1272-6.

277.United States Department of Agriculture *Nutritive Value of Foods*. Home and Garden Bulletin Number 72. U.S. Government Printing Office. Washington, DC 20401, 1981.

278.See note 46. USDA #8.

279.See note 1. Leveille.

280.See note 128. Bowes and Church.

281.N-Squared Computing. *Nutritionist II, v2.0* Silverton OR, 1984.

282.Farrell, Carl. *Carl's Wizard.*(BASIC sorting program for Nutritionist II). Honolulu, 1987.

283.See note 22. *Encyclopedia Britannica.* Vol. 13, p.527.

284.See note 98. Ganong pp 218-222.

285.See note 204. *Science News* 1994;146:359.

286.See note 281. *Nutritionist IV. v2.0.* Salem OR, 1992.

287.Hertzler, Anna and Anderson, Helen *Food Guides in the United States.* J. Am. Diet. Ass'n. 1974;64:19-28.

288.Haughton, Gussow, and Dodds. *An Historical Study of the Underlying Assumptions for United States Food Guides from 1917 Through the Basic Four Food Group Guide.* Society for Nutrition Education. Vol. 19 No.4 July/August 1987.

289.Hill, Mary and Cleveland, Linda.*Food Guides-Their Development and Use.* Nutrition Program News U.S Department of Agriculture. Washington D.C. July-October 1970.

290.Hausman, Patricia.*Jack Sprats Legacy. The Science and Politics of Fat & Cholesterol.* Center for Science in the Public Interest. New York,1981

291.Obert, Craig. *Community Nutrition.* John Wiley & Sons. New York, 1978.ISBN 0-471-65236-9.

292.Christian, Janet L. and Greger, Janet L. *Nutrition for Living.* Benjamin Cummings, Inc. Menlo Park 1988.ISBN 0-8053-2006-7.

293.Hanson, Wyse, and Sorenson. *Nutritional Quality Index of Foods.* AVI Publishing Co. Westport, 1979. ISBN 0-87055-320-8.

294.Akers, Keith. *A Vegetarian Sourcebook.* G.P Putnam. New York, 1983. ISBN 0-399-12802-6.

295.McDougall, John A. and McDougall, Mary A. *The McDougall Plan.* pp.322-328. New Century 1983. ISBN 0-8329-0289-6.

296.See note 108. Hegsted p 41.

297.Sims L, and Light L. *Directions for nutrition education research-the Penn State conferences.* p 16. Pennsylvania State University, 1981.

298.Clinton S. *The Vegetarian Perspective: An Examination of Nutrition Education and the American Diet.* Vegetarian Education Network. PO Box 3347. West Chester, PA 19381.

299.Imperato P. *Acceptable Risks.* Viking Penguin. New York 1985.ISBN 0-670-10205-9.

300.See note 290. Hausman.

301.See note 246. Consumer Reports. *A pyramid topples at the USDA.* October 1991. pp 663-666.

302.See note 297. Sims and Light. p 18.

303.Stare F. *Adventures in Nutrition.* Christopher Publishing House. Hanover, 1991. p 126. ISBN 0-8158-0470-9.

304.See note 287. *Food Guides in the United States.*

305.See note 303. Stare. p 23.

306.*ibid.* Stare. p 153.

307.*ibid.* Stare. p 91.

308.Diane Morris Ph.D. R.D. (President, Mainstream Nutrition) Review of *Adventures in Nutrition* in: *Medicine, Exercise, Nutrition, and Health.* p 58. Blackwell Scientific Publications. Cambridge, 1992. Vol. 1 #1 Jan/Feb 1992. ISSN 1057-9354.

309.Hess J. *Harvard's Sugar-Pushing Nutritionist.* Saturday Review.Aug 1978. p 10. Saturday Review Magazine Corp. New York, 1978.

310.See note 303. Stare. p 126.

311.Hofman L. *The Great American Nutrition Hassle.* Mayfield Publishing Co. Palo Alto 1978. ISBN 0-87484-446-0 p 379.

312.Jacobson M. *The Complete Eater's Guide and Nutrition Scoreboard.* p 168. Anchor Press. Garden City, 1985. App.III. ISBN 0-385-18245-7.

313.See note 311. Hofman. p 333.

314.See note 246. Consumer Reports. *Pushing Drugs to Doctors.* Feb 1992.

315.See note 200. Barsotti.

316.See note 143. Kjeldsen-Kragh.

317.See note 142. Lindahl.

318.*Position Paper on the vegetarian approach to eating.* Journal of the American Dietetic Association. 1980;77:61-69. p 66.

319.The Vegetarian Resource Group. *Vegetarian Journal.* Baltimore 1991;X(1):3. ISSN 0885-7636.

320.*Journal of the American Dietetic Association.* 1991;91(10):1299.American Dietetic Association. ISSN 0002-8223.

321. Am J Clin Nutr. *First International Congress on Vegetarian Nutrition.* 1988;48(3):707-927. ISSN 0002-9165.

322.Ensminger M. *Animal Science.* Interstate Publishers. Danville,1991. p 25. ISBN 0-8134-2887-4.

323.Diet-Ethics. *Issues in Vegetarian Dietetics.* 3835 Route 414. Burdett, Ny 14818. 1990;Vol IV(1):1.

324.See note 22. Encyclopedia Britannica. Vol.1, p 103.

325.Starch INRA Hooper. *World Advertising Expenditures: A Survey of World advertising Expenditures in 1985.* pp 5-10. Mamaroneck NY, 1986.

326.Kinnucan H, Thompson S, and Chang H. *Commodity Advertising and Promotion.* Iowa State University Press. Ames, 1992. ISBN 0-8138-1297-6. p 4.

327.Microsoft Corporation. *Microsoft Small Business Consultant and Stat Pack.* (Licensed from the Regents of the University of California). Redmond WA, 1988.

328.See note 326.Kinnucan. p xiv.

329.See note 326. Kinnucan. p 344.

330.Morrison RM. *Generic Advertising of Farm Products*. United States Department of Agriculture. Economic Research Service. Agricultural Service Bulletin Number 481. p 3. Washington, 1985.

331.See note 326. Kinnucan. p 24.

332.See note 326. Kinnucan. p xiv.

333.Consumer Protection Division. *Letter to Charles Stahler-Baltimore Vegetarians*. Maryland Attorney General. Aug 22, 1988.

334.See note 46. USDA #8. Item #367.

335.*ibid*. item #737.

336.Urban Medicine. *Living with Osteoporosis*. Medical Publishing Enterprises. Fair Lawn NJ. May 1992;7(2). No ISSN.

337.Senate Select Committee on Nutrition and Human Needs. *Dietary Goals for the United States*. U.S. Government Printing Office. Washington, 1977.

338.See note 290. Hausman.

339.*Health and Nutrition Claims in Food Labeling*. U.S. Senate, Committee on Governmental Affairs. One Hundred First Congress. U.S.Government Printing Office. Washington, 1991.

340.See note 326. Kinnucan. p xv.

341.*Advertising Age Yearbook*. p 36. Crain Books. Chicago, 1984. ISBN 0-87251-093-X.

342.Jacobson MF, and Fritschner S. *The Completely Revised and Upgraded Fast-Food Guide*. p 20. Center for Science in the Public Interest. Workman Publishing. New York, 1991.

343.*GAO/RCED-92-15 Generic Promotion of Produce*. p 2. Resources,Community, and Economic Division. United States General Accounting Office. Washington, 1991.

344.*ibid*. p 4.

345.Ross Roundtable on Medical Issues. *Nutrition Education for physicians-Problems and Opportunities.*p 14. Ross Laboratories. Columbus 1980. LCCC No. 80-52247.

346.Fischer P, Schwartz M, et al. *Brand Name Logo Recognition by Children Aged 3 to 6 Years.* Journal of the American Medical Association. 1991;266(22):3145-3148. ISSN 0098-7484.

347.DiFranzi J, Richards J, et al. *RJR Nabico's Cartoon Camel Promotes Camel Cigarettes to Children. ibid.* pp 3149-3153.

348.Advertising is a tax deductible business expense. Corporate tax rates are 35%, above income of $18 million/year. Tobacco income is $50 billion/year, according to The Tobacco Institute ((202)-457-4800), so savings (S) from income (I) tax deductions on advertising (A~$2,500 million) are:
(S)=.35(I)-.35(I-A)=.35(A)=$870 million.
1994 Instructions for Forms 1120 and 1120A. U.S. Department of the Treasury, OMB and IRS.

349.See note 213. *Lung Disease Data 1993.*

350.See note 243. *Agricultural Statistics, 1989.*

351.See note 262. Durning.

352.Banzhaf J. *Ads for Dangerous Products May be Banned/Regulated:Cigarette Ads Enjoy Little First Amendment Protection.* ASH Smoking and Health Review. May/June 1992 Vol XXII (3):2. 2013 H. St. NW Washington, DC 20006.

353.McAuliffe RE. *Advertising, Competition, and Public Policy: Theories and New Evidence.* D.C Heath & Co. Lexington, 1987. ISBN 0-669-12391-9. p 3.

354.White L. *Merchants of Death: The American Tobacco Industry.* William Morrow and Company. New York, 1988. ISBN 0-688-06706-9. p 120.

355.See note 22 *Encyclopedia Britannica.* Vol.1, p 104c.

356.*ibid.* Vol.9, p 269.

357.See note 275. Friedman p 306.

358.See note 22. *Encyclopedia Britannica.*
Vol.1, p 106.

359.Business Week. *What Happened to Advertising?*
McGraw-Hill.Sept 23, 1991.p 66. ISSN 0007-71351.

360.See note 353. McCauliffe.

361.See note 326. Kinnucan. p 65.

362.O'Toole J. *The Trouble With Advertising.* p 6.
Times Books. New York, 1985. ISBN 0-8129-1265-9. .

363.Adbusters Media Foundation. *Adbusters Quarterly.*
1243 West 7th Ave. Vancouver BC, V6H 1B7.

364.U.S. Dept. of Health, Education, and Welfare.
*Alcohol and Health: from the Secretary of Health
Education and Welfare.* June 1974. p 42.

365.Kurian, George Thomas. *The New Book of World
Rankings.* p 214. Facts on File Inc. New York,
1991. ISBN 0-8160-1931-2.

366.*ibid.* pp 149, 180, and 181.

367.See note 49. *FAO.*

368.Macintyre S. *The effects of family position and
status on health.* Soc Sci Med. 1992;35(4):453-64.
ISSN 0277-9536.

369.See note 2. *Harper's 1990.* p 467.

370.Spector W. *Handbook of Biological Data: Values
in Mammalian Reproduction.* W.B. Saunders Co.
London 1961.p 128. LOCCC 56-13410.

371.Altman P, Dittmer D. *Biology Data Book. Second
Edition Vol. I.* p 137 Federation of American
Societies for Experimental Biology. Bethesda 1972.
LOCCC 72-87738.

372.LeVay S. *The Sexual Brain.* MIT Press. Cambridge
1993. ISBN 0-262-12178-6.

373.Bakerman S. *ABC's of Interpretive Laboratory Data*. Interpretive Laboratory Data, Inc. Greenville, NC 1984. ISBN 0-945577-00-1.

374.Schiavi R, Owen D, Theilgaard A, White D. *Sex chromosome anomalies, hormones, and aggressivity*. Archives of general psychiatry.1994;41(1):93-99. ISSN: 0003-990X.

375.Christiansen K, Knussmann R. *Androgen levels and components of aggressive behavior in men*. Horm Behav. 1987;21(2):170-80. ISSN 0018-506X.

376.U.S. Dept of Commerce. *Statistical Abstract of the United States*. p 199. Bureau of the Census. U.S. Government Printing Office, 1993. Washington, DC 20402. LOCC No. 4-18089.

377.See note 162. Adlercreutz.

378.Howie B, Shultz T. *Dietary and hormonal interrelationships among vegetarian Seventh-Day Adventists and nonvegetarian men*. Am J Clin Nutr. 1985;42(1):127-34. ISSN 0002-9165.

379.Bennett F, and Ingram D. *Diet and female sex hormone concentrations: an intervention study for the type of fat consumed*. Am J Clin Nutr. 1990;52:80812.

380.Rose D, Goldman G, et al. *High-fiber diet Reduces serum estrogen concentrations in premenopausal women*. Am J Clin Nutr. 1991;54:520-5. ISSN 0002-9165.

381.Bennett F, and Ingram D. *Diet and female sex hormone concentrations: and intervention study for the type of fat consumed*. Am J Clin Nutr. 1990;52:808-12. ISSN 0002 9165.

382.Mousavi Y, Adlercreutz H. *Genistein is an effective stimulator of sex hormone-binding globulin production in hepatocarcinoma human liver cancer cells and suppresses proliferation of these cells in culture*. Steroids. 1993;58(7):301-4. ISSN 0039-128X.

383.See note 2. *Harper's 1990*. p 256.

384.See note 98. Ganong. p 387.

385.See note 372. LeVay. p 18.

386.See note 35. *The Holy Bible.*

387.See note 49. *FAO.*

388.See note 365. Kurian 1991. p 31.

389.See note 156. Kurian 1979 pp 92-3.

390.See note 22. *Encyclopedia Britannica.*
Vol.19, p 1023.

391.Rhodes R. *Man-made Death: A Neglected Mortality.*
JAMA 1988;260(5):686-7.

392.See note 365. Kurian 1991. p 20.

393.See note 98. Ganong. p 421.

394.Rennie J. *Malignant Mimicry: False estrogens may
cause cancer and lower sperm counts.* Scientific
American. Sept 1993 p 34-38. ISSN 0036-8733.

395.American Association for the Advancement of
Science. *Contraceptive Methods Go Back to   Basics.*
Science. Dec 1994; 266:1480. ISSN 0036-8075.

396.Raloff J. *The Gender Benders.* Science News.
1994;145:24-27. ISSN 0036-8423.

397.See note 394. Rennie. p 38.

398.Crews D. *Animal Sexuality.* Scientific American
1994; January:108-114. ISSN 0036-8733.

399.Raloff J. *That Feminine Touch: Are men suffering
from prenatal exposures to "hormonal" toxicants?*
Science News. 1994;145:56-58. ISSN 0036-8423.

400.*ibid.* Science News. 1992;142:10. ISSN 0036-8423.

401.Virag R, Bouilly P, Frydman D. *Is impotence an
arterial disorder? A study of arterial risk factors
in 440 impotent men.* Lancet 1985;1(8422):181-4.
ISSN 0023-7507.

402.Rosen M, Greenfield A, et al. *Cigarette smoking: an independent risk factor for atherosclerosis in the hypogastric-cavernous arterial bed of men with arteriogenic impotence.* J Urol Apr 1991;145(4):759-63. ISSN 0022-5347.

403.Condra M, Morales A, Owen J, et al. *Prevalence and significance of tobacco smoking in impotence.* Urology. Jun 1986;27(6):495-8. ISSN 0090-4295.

404.Monastersky R. *Impotence: More than a middle-age metaphor.* Science News. 1994;145:21. ISSN 0036-8423.

405.Jarow J, Kirkland J, Koritnik D, Cefalu W. *Effect of obesity and fertility status on sex steroid levels in men.* Urology. 1993;42(2):171-4. ISSN 0090-4295.

406.See note 98. Ganong. p 395.

407.Frisch R. *Fatness, menarche, and female fertility.* Perspect Biol Med. 1985;28(4):611-33. ISSN 0031-5982.

408.Kiddy D, Hamilton-Fairley D, et al. *Improvement in endocrine and ovarian function during dietary treatment of obese women with polycystic ovary syndrome.* Clin Endocrinol (Oxf). 1992;36(1):105-11. ISSN 0300-0664.

409.Koloszar S, Godo G, Sas M. *A koros testsuly szerepe a functionalis noi infertilitas kialakulasaban. [Role of pathological body weight in the development of functional female infertility]* Orv Hetil. 1985;126(17):1017-9. ISSN 0030-6002. (Hungarian) English Abstract.

410.Dwyer JT. *Health aspects of vegetarian diets.* Am J Clin Nutr. 1988;48(3 Suppl):712-38.ISSN 0002-9165.

411.Kumar A, Mittal S, Buckshee K, Farooq A. *Reproductive functions in obese women.* Prog Food Nutr Sci (ENGLAND). 1993;17(2):89-98. ISSN 0306-0632.

412.Kusakari M, Takahashi K, Yoshino K, Kitao M. *Relationship between the delayed-reaction type of LH-RH test and obesity in sterile women with ovulatory disturbances: a preliminary report.* Int J Fertil. 1990;35(1):14-6, 21-2. ISSN 0020-725X.

413.Jaffe R, Abramowicz J, et al. *Sonographic monitoring of ovarian volume during LHRH analogue therapy in women with polycystic ovarian syndrome.* J Ultrasound Med. 1988;7(4):203-6. ISSN 0278-4297.

414.Green B, Daling J, Weiss N, Liff J, Koepsell T. *Exercise as a risk factor for infertility with ovulatory dysfunction.* Am J Public Health. 1986;76(12):1432-6. ISSN 0090-0036.

415.Pirke K, Schweiger U, et al. *Dieting influences the menstrual cycle: vegetarian versus nonvegetarian diet.* Fertil Steril.1986;46(6):1083-8. ISSN 0015-0282.

416.Pedersen A, Bartholomew M, et al. *Menstrual differences due to vegetarian and nonvegetarian diets.* Am J Clin Nutr.1991;53(4):879-85. ISSN 0002-9165.

417.Dugowson C, Drinkwater B, Clark J. *Nontraumatic femur fracture in an oligomenorrheic athlete.* Med Sci Sports Exerc. 1991;23(12):1323-5. ISSN 0195-9131.

418.Highet R. *Athletic amenorrhoea. An update on aetiology, complications and management.* Sports Med. 1989;7(2):82-108. ISSN 0112-1642.

419.Drinkwater B, Nilson K, Ott S, Chesnut C. *Bone mineral density after resumption of menses in amenorrheic athletes.* JAMA. 1986;256(3):380-2. ISSN 0098-7484.

420.Simkin A, Ayalon J, and Leichter I. *Increased trabecular bone density due to bone loading exercises on post-menopausal osteoporotic women.* Calcif Tissue Int. 1987;40:59-63.

421.See note 86. Lee. *Natural progesterone.*

422.Loucks A. *Does exercise training affect reproductive hormones in women?* Clin Sports Med. 1986;5(3):535-57. ISSN 0278-5919.

423.Murray C. *Losing Ground: American Social Policy, 1950-1980.* pp 53-68. Basic Books, 1984. ISBN 0-465-04232-5.

424.Davis D, Schwartz J. *Trends in cancer mortality: US white males and females, 1968-83.* National Research Council, Washington, DC. Lancet 1988;1(8586):633-6, ISSN 0023-7507.

425.Bailar J, Smith E. *Progress against cancer?* N Engl J Med 1986;314(19):1226-32. ISSN 0028-4793.

426.Office of the Actuary. Health Care Financing Administration.

427.McKeown, Thomas.*The Modern Rise of Populations.* pp 152-163. Academic Press (Harcourt Brace).New York, 1976.

428.McKinlay J, and McKinlay S. *The Questionable Contribution of Medical Measures to the Decline of Mortality in the United States in the Twentieth Century.* Health and Society. Milbank Memorial Fund. Summer 1977.

429.See note 146. *Health United States 1990.* Tables 15, 105,111, 113.

430.See note 49. *FAO.*

431.Hamowy R. *Dealing with Drugs: Consequences of Government Control.* Pacific Research Institute for Public Policy. San Francisco, 1990. ISBN 0-936488-32-8.

432.Szasz T. *The Theology of Medicine.* Syracuse University Press, 1988. ISBN 0-8156-0225-1. 29-48.

433.Horgan J. Scientific American. July 1993 p 26.

434.See note 94. Ornish.

435.Kirklin J, and Barratt-Boyes B. *Cardiac surgery: morphology, diagnostic criteria, natural history,techniques, results, and indications.* pp 109, 302, 313. Churchill Livingstone Inc. New York 1993. ISBN 0-443-08845-4.

436.Acinapura A, Jacobowitz I, et.al. *Internal mammary artery bypass: thirteen years of experience. Influence of angina and survival in 5125 patients.* J Cardiovasc Surg (ITALY). 1992;33(5):5549.ISSN 00219509.

437.Ellis F. *Angina and vegan diet.* American Heart Journal. 1977;93(6):803-4.

438.Connor WE, and Connor S. *The Key Role of Nutritional Factors in the Prevention of Coronary Heart Disease.* Preventive Medicine. 1972;1:49-83.

439.Blankenhorn DH, et al. *Beneficial effects of combined colestipol-niacin therapy on coronary atherosclerosis and coronary venous bypass* grafts. JAMA 1987;257:3233.

440.HPMG Professional Services Fee Schedule, 1991.

441.Hoffman M. *The World Almanac and Book of Facts 1992.* p 951. Pharos Books, New York 1992. ISBN 0-88687-642-7.

442.*ibid.* Hoffman. p 140.

443.*ibid.* Hoffman. p 139.

444.Meiners R, and Miller R. *Gridlock in Government: How to Break the Stagnation of America.* Free Congress Foundation. ISBN 0-942522-20-6. p 58.

445.Leading National Advertisers, IMPACT. Reported in USA Today.

446.See note 441. Hoffman. p 319.

447.Consumer Reports. *Pushing Drugs to Doctors.* Consumers Union. Yonkers, 1992. Feb 1992. pp 87-94. ISSN 0010-7174.

448.See note 441. Hoffman. p 685.

449.*ibid.* Hoffman. p 319.

450.*ibid.* Hoffman. p 319.

451.*Part 101-Food Labeling.* Federal Register 1993;58(158). U.S. Government Printing Office. Washington D.C.

452.See note 363. Adbusters.

453.See note 262. Durning. p 39.

454. Data assembled by *Free Our Public Lands*, PO Box 5784, Tucson AZ 85703, (from USDA and USDI publications).

455. American Lung Association. *Lung Disease Data 1993 (paper # 0456 p 26)*. New York, 1993.

456. See note 214. *Grappling with Alcohol Abuse*.

457. Sugarman C. *From Adversary To Appointee At Agriculture*. Washington Post 10/4/93.

458. See note 245. Bovard.

459. Data derived by Common Cause, from Federal Election Commission reports, and appearing in the *Common Cause Newsletter*, Oct. 1993.

460. Painter J, Bristow L, Todd J. *AMA's Analysis of the Clinton Plan*. American Medical Association. September 1993 (Brochure).

461. Leutwyler K. *The Price of Prevention*. Scientific American. April 1995 pp 124-129.

462. Ferrara P. *More Than a Theory: Medical; Savings Accounts at Work*. Cato Institute, 1000 Massachussetts Ave. Washington, D.C. 20001. Mar 1995; Policy Analysis No. 220.

463. Fingarette H. *Heavy Drinking: The Myth of Alcoholism as a Disease*. University of California Press. Berkeley 1988.

464. Madsen W, Berger D, Bremy F. *Alcoholism a Myth?* The Skeptical Inquirer. 1990;14(4):440-42. Committee for the Scientific Investigation of Claims of the Paranormal. ISSN 0194-6730.

465. Peele S. *The Diseasing of America: Addiction Treatment Out of Control*. D.C. Heath and Co. Lexington, 1989. ISBN 0-669-20015-8.

466. See note 22. *Encyclopedia Britannica*. Vol. 6, p 411.

467. *Doctors counterattack with countersuits*. Medical World News, 1977 Mar 21, p 66.

468.Dowling P, Alfonsi G, et. al. *An education program to reduce unnecessary laboratory tests by residents.* Acad Med 1989;64(7):410-2. ISSN 1040-2446.

469.Mayewski L, Dhru J. *A health care treatment.* Best's Review, 1993;94(2):36-44. ISSN: 0161-7745.

470.Hackney D. *Skull Radiography in the Evaluation of Acute Head Trauma: A Survey of Current Practice.* Radiology 1991;181:711-714.

471.Helms C. *Fundamentals of Skeletal Radiology: Unnecessary Examinations.* pp 1-8 W.B. Saunders. Philadelphia, 1989. .ISBN 0-7216-2346-8.

472.See note 468. Dowling.

473.Mayer M. *Unnecessary laboratory tests in diagnosis and treatment.* Harefuah (Israel) 1991;120(2):66-9.ISSN 0017-7768.

474.Valenzuela T, Criss E, Facter K, Spaite D, Meislin H. *Medical versus regulatory necessity: regulation of ambulance service in Arizona.* J Emerg Med 1989;7(3):253-6. ISSN 0736-4679.

475.Brown E, Sindelar J. *The emergent problem of ambulance misuse.* Ann Emerg Med. 1993;22(4):646-50. ISSN 0196-0644.

476.Illich I. *Medical nemesis: the expropriation of health.* Pantheon Books. New York, 1976.

477.Mandel C. *Solving the workers' compensation problem through coalitions.* Risk Management. 1993;40(4):77-82. ISSN 0035-5593.

478.See note 469 Mayewski.

479.Bass C. *Non-cardiac chest pain.* Practitioner. 1989;233(1464):352, 355-7. ISSN 0032-6518.

480.Luke L, Cusack S, Smith H, Robertson C, Little K. *Non-traumatic chest pain in young adults: a medical audit.* Arch Emerg Med (ENGLAND). 1990;7(3):183-8. ISSN 0264-4924.

481.Gardner J. *Grendel.* Ballantine Books, New York 1972. ISBN 345-02876-7-095. p 104.

482.See note 441. Hoffman. pps 40 and 950.

483.Fein R. *Health Care Reform*. Scientific American. Nov 1992:46-53.

484.Bennett J, and DiLorenzo T. *Official Lies: How Washington Misleads Us*. Groom Books. Alexandria, 1992. ISBN 0-9632701-0-9.

485.Ho K, Mikkelson B, et al. *Alaskan Arctic Eskimo: responses to a customary high fat diet*. Am J Clin Nutr. 1972;25:738.

486.Simopoulos A. *Omega-3 fatty acids in health and disease and in growth and development*. Am J Clin Nutr 1991;54:446. ISSN 0002 9165. p 439.

487.Sinclair A, and Gibson R. *Essential Fatty Acids and Eicosanoids: Invited papers from the Third International Congress*. p 25. American Oil Chemists Society. Champaign, 1992. ISBN 0-935315-43-8.

488.Thomas L, and Holub B. *Modification of Human Platelet Phospholipids and Agonist-Stimulated Phosphoinositide Phosphorylation by Omega-3 Fatty Acids*. In note 496. Sinclair, p 305.

489.Yasugi T, Tochihara T, Fujioka T, et al. *Eicosopentanoic Acid, Docosahexanoic Acid and Cerebral Hemorrhage: EPA and DHA Loading Study in Spontaneously Hypertensive Rats*. In note 496. Sinclair. p339.

490.See note 2. *Harper's 1990*. pp 219-20.

491.Note 487. Sinclair. p 25.

492.See note 30. *Simopoulis*. p 446.

493.Exler J, and Weihrauch JL. *Provisional Table on the Content of Omega-3 Fatty Acids and Other Fat Components in Selected Foods*. United States Department of Agriculture. Human Nutrition Information Service. HNIS/PT-103 1988.

494.See note 487. Sinclair. p 318.

495.See note 30. Simopoulis. p 438.

496.Siguel E, Lerman R. *Trans-fatty acid patterns in patients with angiographically documented coronary artery disease.* Am J Cardiol. 1993;71(11):916-20. ISSN 0002-9149.

497.Spector A, and Moore S. *Role of Cerebromicrovascular Endothelium and Astrocytes in Supplying Docosahexanoic Acid to the Brain.* In note 487. Sinclair. p 100.

498.See note 141. Halpern.

499.American Academy of Pediatrics Committee on Nutrition. *The use of whole cow's milk in infancy.* Pediatrics. 1992;89(6 Pt 1):1105-9. ISSN 0031-4005.

500.See note 487. Sinclair. p 367.

501.Carlson S, Werkman S, Peeples J, et al. *Growth and Development of Very Low-Birthweight Infants in Relation to n-3 and n-6 Essential Fatty Acid Status.* In Note 487, Sinclair, p 194.

502.See note 487. Sinclair. p 279.

503.Honolulu Advertiser. April 13, 1995. Reporting study published in the New England Journal of medicine. Primary citation not yet available.

504.TenBruggencate J. *Morgan: Stampede to bad-mouth feedlot unjustified.* Honolulu Star-Bulletin. March 31, 1991 p A16. Gannett Pacific Corporation.

505.Honolulu Star Bulletin 2/23/94.

506.Lum C. *Animal Industry Division.* Department of Agriculture. State of Hawaii. Annual Report 1993. p 12.PO Box 22159, Honolulu, HI 96823.

507.Famighetti R. *The World Almanac and Book of Facts 1994.* Funk and Wagnalls Corporation. Mahwah NJ 1993. ISBN 0-88687-745-8. p 364.

508.Hawaii Agricultural Statistics Service. *Statistics of Hawaiian Agriculture 1991.* December 1992. p87. PO Box 22159. Honolulu, HI 96823-2159.

509.*ibid.* p 105.

510.Gottlieb A. *Testimony before the Senate Agriculture Committee of the State of Hawaii, Tuesday, February 11, 1992, 1:00 PM.*

511.Hawaii Department of Agriculture. *Agricultural Park Status Report. November, 1992.*

512.See note 508.*Statistics of Hawaiian Agriculture 1991.* p 6.

513.TenBruggencate J. *Cattle Industry in upheaval in Isles.* Sunday Star-Bulletin and Advertiser. Gannett Pacific Corporation. March 24 1991 p A3.

514.See note 141. Halpern.

515.See note 508. p 6. Schwind P. *Planning and Development Office.*

516.See note 30. Simopoulos. p 446.

517.See note 493. Exler and Weihrauch.

518.See note 487. Sinclair. p 25.

519.Kefford N. *Testimony for SB 2876: Making an Appropriation for a Slaughterhouse on the Island of Oahu.* Presented 3/7/94.

520.Garrod P, and Plasch B. *"What's to come of all the land released from sugar and pineapple?"* The Price of Paradise II. pp 139-4. Edited by Randall Roth. Mutual Publishing. Honolulu 1993. ISBN 1-56647-040-0.

521.See note 172. Karjalainen.

522.See note 216. Cramer. *Galactose consumption.*

523.Gold R, and Daley D. *Public Funding of Contraceptive, Sterilization, and Abortion Services, Fiscal Year 1990.* Family Planning Perspectives. 1991;23(5):209.

INDEX

If you enjoyed *The Scientific Basis of Vegetarianism* you'll want to read Ruth Heidrich's *A Race for Life,* the story of a battle against breast cancer waged with determination, triathlon competition, and a strict vegetarian diet. There's also *The Race for Life Cookbook* with over 100 cheap, healthy, easy, and fat free recipes and *The Race for Life VHS Video* featuring Ruth on camera.

Please rush me:

A Race for Life @ $14.95   #____ $_____

The Race for Life Cookbook @ $14.95   #____ $_____

A Race for Life VHS Video @ $19.95   #____ $_____

The Scientific Basis of
Vegetarianism @ 15.95   #____ $_____

Shipping: (bookrate) @ $2.00 $_____
              Priority Mail @ $3.00 $_____

Total $_____

(Check or money order please)

Please print your mailing label:

Name_____

Street_____

City_____State____Zip_____

****

HHP

Hawaii Health Publishers
1415 Victoria St.
Suite 1106
Honolulu, HI 96822-3663